PENGUIN TWENTIETH-

SELECTED ESSAYS A

Albert Camus was born in Algeria in 1913. His childhood was poor although not unhappy. He studied philosophy at the University of Algiers and became a journalist as well as organizing the *Théâtre de l'équipe*, a young avant-garde dramatic group. His early essays were collected in *L'Envers et l'endroit (The Wrong Side and the Right Side)* and *Noces (Nuptials)*. He went to Paris where he worked on the newspaper *Paris Soir* before returning to Algeria. His play *Caligula* appeared in 1939. His first two important books *L'Etranger (The Outsider)* and the long essays *Le Mythe de Sisyphe (The Myth of Sisyphus)* were published when he returned to Paris. After the occupation of France by the Germans in 1941, Camus became one of the intellectual leaders of the Resistance movement. He edited and contributed to the underground newspaper *Combat*, which he had helped to found. After the war he devoted himself to writing and established an international reputation with such books as *La Peste (The Plague)* (1947), *Les Justes (The Just)* and *La Chute (The Fall)* (1956). During the late 1950s, Camus renewed his active interest in the theatre, writing and directing stage adaptations of William Faulkner's *Requiem for a Nun* and Dostoyevsky's *The Possessed*. He was awarded the Nobel Prize for Literature in 1957. He was killed in a road accident in 1960.

Sartre paid tribute to him in his obituary notice: 'Camus could never cease to be one of the principal forces in our cultural domain, nor to represent, in his own way, the history of France and of this century.'

ALBERT CAMUS

SELECTED ESSAYS AND NOTEBOOKS

EDITED AND TRANSLATED BY
PHILIP THODY

PENGUIN BOOKS

PENGUIN BOOKS

Published by the Penguin Group
Penguin Books Ltd, 80 Strand, London WC2R ORL, England
Penguin Group (USA), Inc., 375 Hudson Street, New York, New York 10014, USA
Penguin Group (Canada), 90 Eglinton Avenue East, Suite 700, Toronto, Ontario, Canada M4P 2Y3
(a division of Pearson Penguin Canada Inc.)
Penguin Ireland, 25 St Stephen's Green, Dublin 2, Ireland
(a division of Penguin Books Ltd)
Penguin Group (Australia), 250 Camberwell Road, Camberwell, Victoria 3124, Australia
(a division of Pearson Australia Group Pty Ltd)
Penguin Books India Pvt Ltd, 11 Community Centre, Panchsheel Park,
New Delhi – 110 017, India
Penguin Group (NZ), 67 Apollo Drive, Rosedale, North Shore 0632, New Zealand
(a division of Pearson New Zealand Ltd)
Penguin Books (South Africa) (Pty) Ltd, 24 Sturdee Avenue, Rosebank, Johannesburg 2196, South Africa

Penguin Books Ltd, Registered Offices: 80 Strand, London WC2R ORL, England

www.penguin.com

Carnets 1935–42 first published in Great Britain by Hamish Hamilton Ltd 1963
Copyright © 1962 by Librairie Gallimard
Translation copyright © 1963 by Hamish Hamilton Ltd and Alfred A. Knopf Inc.
Carnets 1942–1951 first published in Great Britain by Hamish Hamilton Ltd 1966
Copyright © 1964 by Éditions Gallimard
Translation copyright © 1966 by Hamish Hamilton Ltd
Lyrical and Critical first published in Great Britain by Hamish Hamilton Ltd 1967
Copyright © 1950, 1951, 1954, 1956, 1958, 1959, 1963 by Éditions Gallimard
Translation copyright © 1967 by Hamish Hamilton Ltd and Alfred A. Knopf Inc.

This selection from *Carnets* and *Lyrical and Critical* first published in Peregrine Books 1970
Reprinted in Penguin Books 1979
5
Introduction, Notes and selection copyright © Philip Thorly, 1970
All rights reserved

Printed in Great Britain by
Clays Ltd, St Ives plc

Set in Linotype Pilgrim

Except in the United States of America,
this book is sold subject to the condition
that it shall not, by way of trade or otherwise,
be lent, re-sold, hired out, or otherwise circulated
without the publisher's prior consent in any form of
binding or cover other than that in which it is
published and without a similar condition
including this condition being imposed
on the subsequent purchaser

www.greenpenguin.co.uk

Penguin Books is committed to a sustainable future
for our business, our readers and our planet.
The book in your hands is made from paper
certified by the Forest Stewardship Council.

CONTENTS

Introduction

PART ONE
LYRICAL ESSAYS

1. BETWIXT AND BETWEEN (*L'Envers et l'endroit*, 1937)	15
Preface (1958)	17
Irony	29
Between Yes and No	38
Iron in the Soul	47
Love of Life	57
Betwixt and Between	62
2. NUPTIALS (*Noces*, 1939)	67
Nuptials at Tipasa	69
The Wind at Djemila	75
Summer in Algiers	81
The Desert	92
3. SUMMER (*L'Été*, 1954)	103
The Minotaur or the Halt at Oran	105
The Almond-trees	125
Prometheus in the Underworld	128
Short Guide to Towns without a Past	132
Helen's Exile	136
The Enigma	141
Return to Tipasa	147
The Sea Close By	155

PART TWO
CRITICAL ESSAYS

La Nausée [*Nausea*] by Jean-Paul Sartre	167
Le Mur [*The Wall*] by Jean-Paul Sartre	170
Encounters with André Gide	173
Herman Melville	178
On Faulkner	183

Intelligence and the Scaffold 185
Lecture Given in Athens on
 the Future of Tragedy 192

PART THREE

CAMUS ON *THE OUTSIDER* AND *THE PLAGUE*

Preface to the American university edition
 of *The Outsider* 207
The reception of *The Outsider*.
 From the entries in *Notebook IV* for 1942 209
The composition of *The Outsider*.
 From the entries in *Notebooks I, II*, and *IV* between
 1937 and 1940 213
Letter to Roland Barthes on *The Plague* 220
The composition of *The Plague*.
 From the entries in *Notebooks II, III*, and *IV* between
 1938 and 1944 223

PART FOUR

SKETCHES FOR A SELF-PORTRAIT

From *Notebook I*, May 1935–September 1937 235
From *Notebook II*, September 1937–April 1939 242
From *Notebook III*, April 1939–February 1942 250
From *Notebook IV*, January 1942–July 1945 261
From *Notebook V*, September 1945–April 1948 275
From *Notebook VI*, April 1948–March 1951 285

NOTES

Notes to Part One 295
Notes to Part Two 301
Notes to Part Three 303
Notes to Part Four 308

INTRODUCTION

ALBERT CAMUS was born in Mondovi, Algeria, on 7 November 1913. His father, Lucien Camus, was an agricultural labourer, descended from one of the French families which emigrated to Algeria when Alsace was ceded to Prussia after the French defeat of 1870. His mother, Catherine Sintès, was of Spanish descent.

In 1914 his father volunteered for military service, and was killed in action at the first battle of the Marne. Camus's mother then returned to Algiers, where she shared a small flat with her own widowed mother in the working-class district of Belcourt, She earned money to bring up her two sons – Camus's elder brother, Lucien, was born in 1909 – by working as a charwoman.

In 1923 Camus won a scholarship which enabled him to go to the Lycée in Algiers, later to be renamed Lycée Albert Camus. He was helped to win his scholarship by Louis Germain, a teacher at the École Communale which he attended from 1918 to 1923; and he never failed to send this teacher, on publication day, a copy of each of his books. In 1958 he dedicated to Louis Germain the two speeches which he gave in Stockholm on being awarded the Nobel Prize for Literature in 1957.

Camus was an athletic young man, fond of football and swimming, and between 1928 and 1930 he kept goal for the Racing-Universitaire d'Alger. In 1930, however, he fell ill with tuberculosis, and was to suffer recurrent attacks of this illness throughout his life. He nevertheless continued his studies, and read philosophy at the University of Algiers. In 1934 he joined the Communist Party, but left it shortly afterwards, probably as a result of the change in the party line which led the Algerian communists, in 1935, to modify their campaign in favour of the Arabs. His first marriage, to Simon Hié, took place in 1934, and was dissolved a year later.

In 1936 Camus collaborated with two of his friends in writing a play entitled *Révolte dans les Asturies*. In the same year he began to write the essays later published under the title of *Betwixt and Between* (*L'Envers et l'endroit*), while at the same time earning his living by doing a variety of jobs: working as a clerk at the Préfecture, selling spare parts for cars, taking measurements for the Meteorological Institute in Algiers. In 1936 he also completed a short thesis on the relationship between Plotinus and Saint Augustine, and continued his association with the theatre by working with the touring company belonging to Radio Algiers. In the following year he produced a number of plays at the Théâtre de l'Équipe – the new name of the Théâtre du Travail, an amateur company which he himself had founded – and also visited Italy.

Normally a student of Camus's ability would have taken the Agrégation de Philosophie, a competitive examination qualifying him to teach in a *lycée*. However, for health reasons, he was not eligible, and after turning down the opportunity of teaching at a secondary school in Sidi-bel-Abbès, he became a journalist on the left-wing newspaper, *Alger Républicain*. His main work lay in book reviewing, but he also wrote a variety of other articles, and learned to set up and compose type as well as to read proofs. In 1937 *Betwixt and Between* was published, and he had begun to write *Nuptials* (*Noces*), first published in 1939.

At the outbreak of the Second World War Camus was rejected as medically unfit, and continued to work as a journalist. He became editor of an evening paper, *Le Soir Républicain*, but had so many quarrels with the military censorship imposed on all newspapers that he was unable to obtain any kind of work in Algiers itself when this newspaper was forced to close down early in 1940. One of his friends, Pascal Pia, found him a job in Paris as a type-setter on *Paris-Soir*, and Camus remained in Paris – where he was not particularly happy – until the German invasion of France in May 1940.

Camus himself dated his decision to join the Resistance Movement from 19 December 1941, the day on which the German authorities executed a workman called Gabriel Péri. He joined the network known as 'Combat', which formed part of the *Mouvement Libération-Nord*. His main work consisted of preparing the clandestine newspaper *Combat*, of which he officially became editor in August 1944. In 1942 his novel *The Outsider* (*L'Étranger*) made him well known in literary circles, and the publication in the following year of *The Myth of Sisyphus* (*Le Mythe de Sisyphe*) confirmed his reputation.

In 1940 Camus married Francine Faure, who remained in her native Oran throughout the German occupation of France. The allied landings in North Africa on 8 December 1942 prevented Camus from seeing his wife until the Liberation, and the importance of the theme of separation in *The Plague* (*La Peste*) may perhaps be explained by this fact. In 1945 his twin children, Catherine and Jean, were born in Paris, and Camus lived and worked there until his death. In 1943 he had accepted a post as reader with the publishing firm of Gallimard, and remained with them for the rest of his life. He never, he said, wanted to be forced to write books in order to earn money.

Camus's great fame in post-war France stemmed partly from his reputation as a writer, partly from the performance of his plays, and partly from his work as a journalist. *Cross-Purpose* (*Le Malentendu*) was performed in 1944, and *Caligula*, written in its first version as early as 1938, in 1945. His editorials in *Combat* expressed many of the hopes and ideals of the Resistance Movement and of post-war France, while the publication in *Combat* in November 1946 of a series of articles entitled *Neither Victims nor Executioners* (*Ni victimes ni bourreaux*) showed that he was becoming increasingly concerned with the problem of totalitarianism in general, whether Communist or Fascist. His best known novel, *The Plague*, published in France in June 1947, is in many ways a politically committed work as well as a statement of the more general problem of moral evil.

In 1948 and 1949 two more of Camus's plays were produced, *State of Siege* (*L'État de Siège*) in October 1948, and *The Just* (*Les Justes*) in December 1949. Late in 1951 his major essay in political philosophy, *The Rebel* (*L'Homme révolté*), presented an analysis and criticism of the tradition of metaphysical and political revolt from the Greeks to the present day, but with particular reference to the French and Russian revolutions. Largely because of its strong attack on Marxism the book was regarded by many as constituting a farewell on Camus's part to his own left-wing past, and led to a public quarrel with Jean-Paul Sartre in August 1952. In the same year Camus resigned from Unesco in order to protest against the entry into that organization of Franco's Spain, and in June 1953 he protested with equal energy against the Russian repression of the riots in East Berlin. In 1956 he was to voice similar protests against the Russian invasion of Hungary.

Apart from the essays collected in *Summer* (*L'Été*) in 1954, Camus published no further major literary work until 1956. Then, his short novel *The Fall* (*La Chute*) presented his most complex fictional character, Jean-Baptiste Clamence, in whom many critics saw a self-portrait of Camus himself, and from whose apparently total despair of man's natural goodness other readers inferred an imminent conversion to Christianity. In the same year Camus's adaptation of William Faulkner's *Requiem for a Nun* scored great success, and the publication in 1957 of a volume of short stories entitled *Exile and the Kingdom* (*L'Exil et le Royaume*) showed an increased awareness on Camus's part of individual problems and a movement away from the political and philosophical preoccupations of *The Rebel*. In October 1957 he became the youngest French writer ever to receive the Nobel Prize for Literature.

From the outbreak of the Algerian war in 1954 Camus refrained from any statement which might appear to indicate that he favoured one side rather than the other. On 23 January 1956, however, he launched an appeal for a truce in the fighting, and he repeated this in the preface to his volume of *Algerian Chronicles* (*Chroniques-Algériennes*) in 1958. As a European Algerian and one whose mother and brother still lived in Algiers, he was unable to ally himself with those members of the French left wing who identified themselves completely with the Arab insurgents. But as a man of the left, who had protested throughout the 1930s

Introduction

and again in 1945 against the French treatment of the Algerian Arabs, he was equally reluctant to lend his support to the extremist advocates of *Algérie Française*.

In January 1959 Camus scored what was perhaps his greatest success in the theatre with his adaptation of Dostoyevsky's *The Possessed*. In the same year he spent long periods of time working on a novel with the tentative title of *Le Premier Homme* (*The First Man*), but had not finished it when he was killed in a car accident on 4 January 1960.

The essays and other texts published in this volume are not primarily concerned with Camus's philosophical or political ideas. They are intended to give a portrait of Camus the writer and literary critic, as well as of Camus the individual. Those grouped together in Part I were all published in volume form in Camus's life-time, *Betwixt and Between* in 1937, *Nuptials* in 1939, *Summer* in 1954. *Betwixt and Between* was his first published work, and remained – as he himself remarked in his 1958 preface – virtually unobtainable for many years. It is also his most openly autobiographical work, for there is little doubt that the grandmother described in 'Irony' was Camus's own maternal grandmother, Marie Sintès. The description of the mother in the same essay also coincides exactly with what is known of Catherine Camus. *Nuptials* is also something of a self-portrait, especially of the young Camus's basic paganism, and it is only with 'The Enigma', written in 1950 and collected in *Summer* in 1954, that Camus's idea of himself as an 'objective' or 'impersonal' writer makes its appearance.

The texts in Part II were not collected in book form until the two volumes of Camus's *Œuvres Complètes* appeared in the Pléiade edition in 1963 and 1965. Like the essays in Part I, they are taken from different stages in Camus's life – the reviews of Sartre's books came out in *Alger Républicain* in the later 1930s, the lecture on tragedy was given in Athens in 1955 – and they have been chosen from the large number of texts available in order to illustrate the nature and variety of Camus's aesthetic interests.

Introduction

Part III consists almost exclusively of texts that did not even appear in book form during Camus's life-time. The preface to *The Outsider* was specifically written for an American schools' edition in 1955, but was not presented to the general French literary public until much later. The letter to Roland Barthes on *The Plague* appeared in the literary review *Club* in 1955, while the different extracts from the translation of Camus's *Notebooks* (*Carnets*) have been selected for this Penguin edition. I am very grateful to Madame Camus for having authorized this edition of Camus's *Selected Essays and Notebooks*, and especially for having allowed me to choose those passages from the *Notebooks* that seemed to me to throw most light on the composition of his two major novels and on his attitude towards them.

The fourth and last section again consists of my own selection from the two volumes of the *Notebooks*, published in France in 1962 and 1964. My aim here has been to group together in chronological order those passages which I felt were most revelatory of Camus's ideas, of his attitude towards nature, his reaction to certain events of his time, and of the aims which he set himself as a writer.

PHILIP THODY

PART ONE
LYRICAL ESSAYS

PART ONE
LYRICAL ESSAYS

I
BETWIXT AND BETWEEN
1937

To Jean Grenier

PREFACE
(1958)

THE essays collected in this volume were written in 1935 and 1936 (I was twenty-two at the time) and published a year later, in Algiers, in a very limited edition. For a long time now, this edition has been unobtainable and I have always refused to allow *Betwixt and Between* to be reprinted.

There are no mysterious reasons for my obstinacy. I reject nothing of what these essays express, but their form has always seemed clumsy to me. The prejudices which I cannot help myself maintaining on the subject of art (I shall explain what I mean later on) have for a long time prevented me from considering their republication. This hesitation, it would appear, reveals great vanity, and implies that I find my other works uniformly perfect. Need I say that this is in no way the case? I am simply more aware of the clumsiness of *Betwixt and Between* than in my other works, where I know it can be found. I can explain this awareness only by confessing that the clumsiness of these essays is linked to the subject closest to my heart, which to some extent it reveals. Since, therefore, I claim no literary value for this little book, I can indeed confess that it has, for me, considerable value as testimony. I say for me, since it is in my presence that it bears witness, and from me that it demands a fidelity whose depth and difficulties I alone can see. I should like to try to explain why.

Brice Parain often maintains that this little book contains my best work. Parain is wrong. I am not saying this, knowing how honest he is, because of that impatience which every artist feels when people are impertinent enough to prefer what he has been to what he is. No, he is wrong because, at twenty-two, unless one is a genius, one scarcely knows how to write. But I can understand what Parain, a learned enemy of art and a philosopher versed in compassion, is trying to say. He means, and he is right, that there is more genuine love in these clumsy pages than in all the others which have followed them.

Each artist thus keeps in his heart of hearts a single stream which, so long as he is alive, feeds what he is and what he says. When that stream runs dry, you see his work gradually shrivel up and start to crack. These are the wastelands of art which the invisible current has ceased to feed. The artist, his hair thin and dry, covered over with thatch, is ripe for silence or for salons, which amount to the same thing. I myself know that my stream is in *Betwixt and Between*, in this world of poverty and sunlight in which I lived for so long, and whose memory still saves me from the two opposite dangers which threaten every artist, resentment and self-satisfaction.

Poverty, first of all, was never a misfortune for me: it was radiant with sunlight. Even my revolts were lit up by the sun. These revolts were almost always, I think I can say this in all honesty, revolts on everyone's behalf, aimed at lifting up everybody's life into the light. Quite possibly my heart was not naturally disposed to this kind of love. But circumstances helped me. To correct my natural indifference, I was placed half-way between poverty and the sun. Poverty prevented me from thinking that all is well under the sun and in history; the sun taught me that history is not everything. Change life, yes, but not the world which I worshipped as my God. It is thus, no doubt, that I embarked upon my present difficult career, stepping innocently on to a tightrope along which I now move painfully forward, unsure of ever reaching the end. In other words, I became an artist, if it is true to say that there is no art without refusal or consent.

In any case, the radiance and warmth which shone over my childhood freed me from all resentment. I lived with very little money, but also in a kind of rapture. I felt infinite strength within me: all I had to do was find a use for it. It was not poverty that stood in the way of that strength: in Africa the sun and the sea cost nothing. The obstacle lay rather in prejudices or stupidity. These gave me every opportunity to develop a 'Castilian pride' which has done me much harm, which my friend and teacher Jean Grenier is right to make fun of, and which I tried in vain to correct, until I realized that our natures must follow their destiny as well. It then became better to accept my own pride and try to make use of it, rather than give myself, as Chamfort would say, principles stronger than my character. But, after some self-questioning, I can state that among my many weaknesses I have never found the most widespread of our faults – envy, that veritable cancer in societies and doctrines.

I take no credit for this fortunate immunity. I owe it to my family, first of all, who lacked almost everything and who envied practically nothing. Merely by its silence, its reserve, its natural and sober pride, this family, which did not even know how to read, taught me my most valuable lessons, which I still remember. And then I myself was too much taken up with my feelings to think about anything else. Even nowadays, when I see the life of a very rich person in Paris, I often feel sorry for him, as well as quite uninterested in being like him. There are many injustices in the world, but there is one that is never mentioned, that of climate. For a long time, without realizing it, I profited from that particular injustice. I can already hear our fierce philanthropists, if they are reading me, levelling their accusations: I want to pass off the workers as rich and the bourgeoisie as poor, so as to prolong the happy serfdom of the former and the power of the latter. No, that is not true. On the contrary, when poverty accompanies a life where men can neither hope nor see the sky – the kind of life which, on reaching manhood, I found in the ghastly suburbs of our towns – then this is the final and most revolting injustice of all. Everything in fact must be done so that these men may escape the double damnation of poverty and ugliness. Though I was born poor, in a working-class area, I did not know what real misery was like until I saw our cold suburbs. Even extreme Arab poverty cannot be compared to it, since the weather is so different. But I believe that anyone who has seen the industrial areas of our towns feels for ever tainted and responsible for their existence.

What I have said nevertheless remains true. I sometimes meet people who live in the midst of fortunes that I cannot even imagine. I still have to make an effort to realize that others can feel envious of these fortunes. For a week, a long time ago, I did live abundantly off the goods of this world: we slept without a roof, on a beach, I lived off fruit and spent half my days in an empty sea. It was then that I learned a truth that has always led me to greet the signs of comfort, or of a well-appointed house, with irony, impatience or sometimes with fury. Although I now live without thought for the morrow, and thus as one of the privileged, I do not know how to own things. I never feel that what I have, and which is always given to me without my asking, is mine to keep. Less through generosity, I feel, than by another kind of parsimony: I cling like a miser to that liberty which immediately disappears with the arrival of excess wealth. For me the highest luxury has always included a certain bareness. I love the bare interior of houses in Spain or North Africa. The place where I prefer to live and work (and, something more rare, where I would not mind dying) is a hotel bedroom. I have never felt capable of indulging in what they call home life (which is so often the opposite of an inner life); bourgeois happiness bores and terrifies me. There is in any case nothing glorious about this inability; it has made no small contribution to my worse qualities. I envy nothing, as is my right, but I do not always consider other people's desires; this makes me unimaginative, that is to say unkind. It is true that I have invented a maxim for my own personal usage: 'We must put our principles into great things, mercy is enough for small ones.' Alas! We invent maxims for ourselves in order to plug the gaps in our natures. In my case, a better name for the mercy I speak of is indifference. Its effects, as one can imagine, are less miraculous.

But all I want to underline is that poverty does not necessarily involve envy. Even later on, when a serious illness temporarily deprived me of that natural vigour which for me transfigured everything, in spite of the invisible infirmities and new weaknesses which this illness brought me, I knew fear and discouragement but never bitterness. This illness certainly did add new fetters, and these were the hardest to bear, to those which were already mine. But in the last resort, it encouraged that freedom of the heart, that slight detachment from human concerns, which has always saved me from resentment. And, since living in Paris, I have known that this privilege is a royal one. But I have enjoyed it without restrictions or remorse, and at any rate up to the present it has illuminated the whole of my life. As an artist, for example, I began by admiring other writers, which in a sense is heaven on earth. (As we know, the custom in France nowadays, by contrast, is to begin and even to conclude one's literary career by choosing an artist to make fun of.) Similarly, my human passions have never been directed against other people. The people whom I have loved have always been better and greater than I. Poverty, as I knew it, thus taught me not resentment but, on the contrary, a certain fidelity and a silent obstinacy. If I have ever forgotten this, it is my own fault, or that of my own failings, not that of the world in which I was born.

It is also the memory of these years which has prevented me from ever being satisfied in the exercise of my calling. Here I would like to discuss as simply as possible what writers normally never mention. I shall not even speak of the satisfaction which is apparently to be found before a perfectly written book or page. I do not know whether many artists experience this. As far as I am concerned, I do not think that I have ever found delight in re-reading a finished page. I will even admit, and am prepared to be believed, that I have always been surprised by the success of some of my books. Of course one gets used to it, and rather despicably. Nevertheless, even today I feel myself an apprentice by the side of living writers whom I value at their real merit, and of whom one of the greatest is the man to whom these essays were dedicated as long as twenty years ago.[1] The writer does of course have satisfactions for which he lives and which can fill him with delight. But I personally experience these at the moment of conception, the instant when the subject reveals itself, when the form of the work stands out before our suddenly heightened sensitivity, those delicious moments when imagination and intelligence are as one. These moments go as they are born. What

[1]. Jean Grenier.

remains is the actual composition – that is to say a long period of toil.

On another plane an artist also has the delights of vanity. The writer's profession, especially in French society, is largely one of vanity. I say this moreover without scorn, and scarcely with regret. I am like the others in this respect; who can claim that he is free from this ridiculous infirmity? After all, in a society devoted to envy and derision a day always comes when, covered with scorn, our writers pay a high price for these petty joys. But the fact is that in twenty years of literary life my profession has brought me very few such joys, fewer and fewer with the passage of time.

It is surely the memory of the truths glimpsed in *Betwixt and Between* which has always prevented me from feeling at ease in the public exercise of my calling, and led me to so many refusals which have not always brought me friends. It is indeed true that when we pass over compliments and homages we make the person paying us the compliment feel that we look down on him, when we are only doubting ourselves. By the same token, if I had shown this mixture of harshness and indulgence that is sometimes found in the literary world, if I had exaggerated my haughty bearing, like so many others, I should have received more sympathy. I should, in fact, have been playing the game. But what is the point, the game does not amuse me! The ambition of Lucien de Rubempré or of Julien Sorel often disconcerts me by its naïvety and by its modesty. That of Nietzsche, Tolstoy or Melville overwhelms me, precisely because of their failure. In my heart of hearts I feel humble only in the presence of the poorest lives or of the greatest adventures of the mind. What lies between the two is a society which I find laughable.

Often, on those theatrical 'first nights', which is the only time when I ever meet what is insolently termed 'le Tout-Paris', I have the impression that the audience is going to vanish, that this world, as it stands before me, does not exist. It is the others who seem real to me, the great figures shouting on the stage. If I am to stay, I need to remember that each of these spectators also has a rendezvous with himself; that he knows this, and doubtless will be keeping it a few moments from now. Immediately I see him again as one of my brothers: loneliness joins together those whom society separates. How, knowing this, can we flatter this society, beg for these paltry privileges, agree to congratulate every author of every book, ostentatiously thank the favourable critic, why should we try to seduce our opponents, and, above all, how ought we to greet all those admiring compliments which French society (in the author's presence at any rate, for once he has left ...) uses as extensively as Pernod or the sentimental magazines? All this is beyond me, it is true. Perhaps the fault lies mainly with churlish pride whose powers and range I know so well. But if this were all, if my vanity were the only factor involved, it seems to me that I would enjoy compliments, superficially at least, instead of always being embarrassed by them. No, I am most conscious of the vanity which I share with many members of my profession when I hear certain rather justified criticisms. When I am being complimented, it is not pride which gives me that stupid and clumsy air which I know I have, but (at the same time as that deep indifference which dwells in me like a natural infirmity) a strange feeling which comes over me: 'You're missing the point. ...' Yes, they are missing the point, and that is why a reputation, which is what people call it, is sometimes so hard to bear that we find a malicious pleasure in doing everything necessary to lose it. When, on the contrary, I re-read *Betwixt and Between* for this edition so many years after writing it, I knew instinctively with certain pages, in spite of their clumsiness, that this is right, that this is what really matters: that old woman, a silent mother, poverty, the light on the olive trees of Italy, the populated loneliness of love, everything that in my own eyes bears witness to the truth.

Since the time when these pages were written, I have grown older and lived through many things. I have learned about myself, knowing my limits and almost all my weaknesses. I have learnt less about people, since I am interested more in their destiny than in their reactions, and destinies barely differ one from another. I have at least learnt that other people do exist and that selfishness, if it cannot disappear, must try to be clear-sighted.

Enjoying oneself alone is impossible. I know this, in spite of the great gifts which I possess in this direction. If solitude exists, and I don't know if it does, we would certainly have the right, on occasions, to dream of it as of a paradise. Sometimes, like everybody else, I have such dreams. But two tranquil angels have always kept me from this paradise: one shows the friend's, the other the enemy's face. Yes, I know all this, and I have also or almost learnt the price of love. But I know no more about life itself than what is awkwardly said in *Betwixt and Between*.

'There is no love of life without despair of life,' I wrote, rather pompously, in these pages. I did not know at the time how right I was; I had not yet known the years of real despair. These years have come, and have managed to destroy everything in me, except, in fact, this uncontrolled appetite for life. I still suffer from this simultaneously fruitful and destructive passion which bursts through even in the darkest pages of *Betwixt and Between*. People say that we really live for only a few hours of our life. This is true in one sense, false in another. For the famished ardour that can be felt in these essays has never left me, and in the last analysis it is life at its best and at its worst. I have doubtless tried to correct the worst effects to which this ardour has given rise. Like everyone I have tried, as best I could, to improve my nature by morality. This, alas, is what has cost me most dear. With energy, which is something I possess, we sometimes manage to act morally, but never to be moral. The man of passion who longs for goodness yields to injustice at the very moment when he speaks of justice. Man sometimes seems to me to be a walking injustice: I am thinking of myself. If I now have the impression that I was wrong, or that I lied in what I sometimes wrote, it is because I do not know how to make my injustice honestly known. I have doubtless never said that I was a just man. I have merely happened to say that we should try to be just, and also that such an ambition involved great toil and misery. But is this distinction so important? And can the man who does not even manage to make justice prevail in his own life preach its virtues to other people? If only we could live according to honour, that virtue of the unjust! But our society finds this word obscene;

'aristocrat' is a literary and philosophical insult. I am not an aristocrat, my reply is contained in this book : here are my people, my masters, my race; here is what, through them, links me with everyone. And yet I do need honour, because I am not big enough to be able to do without it!

What does it matter? I merely wanted to show that, if I have travelled a long way since this book, I have not made much progress. Often, when I thought I was moving forward, I was losing ground. But, in the end, my mistakes, together with the gaps in my knowledge and my fidelities, have always brought me back to this ancient path that I began to open with *Betwixt and Between*, whose traces are visible in everything that I have achieved since then, and along which, on certain mornings in Algiers, for example, I still walk with the same slight intoxication.

Why then, if this is the case, should I have so long refused to produce this feeble testimony? First of all because, I must repeat, I have artistic scruples as other men have moral and religious ones. Prohibitions, the idea that 'such things are not done', which is something fairly foreign to me in so far as I am a child of free nature, are present in me so far as I am a slave, and an admiring one, to a severe artistic tradition. This mistrust may also be aimed at my profound anarchy, and thus remain useful. I know my disorder, the violence of certain instincts, the graceless abandon into which I can cast myself. To be constructed the work of art must first of all use these dark forces of the soul. But not without canalizing them, surrounding them with dikes, so that their tide also rises. Perhaps my dikes are still too high today. Hence, sometimes, this stiffness. . . . It is simply that on the day when a balance is established between what I am and what I say, perhaps on that day, and I scarcely dare write it, I shall be able to compose the work of which I dream. What I have tried to say here is that in one way or another it will be like *Betwixt and Between*, and that it will speak of a certain form of love. The second reason why I have kept these youthful essays for myself will now be clear: clumsiness and disorder reveal too much of the secrets closest to our hearts; we also betray them through too careful a disguise. It is better to wait until we are skilful enough to give them a form that does not stifle their voice, until we know how to mingle nature and art together in fairly equal doses; in short, to be. For being is the ability to do everything at the same time. In art everything comes at once or not at all. One day Stendhal cried out: 'But my soul is a fire which suffers if it does not blaze.' Those who are like him in this respect should create only in this blazing fire. At the height of the flame the cry leaps straight upwards and creates the words which re-echo it in their turn. I am talking here about what all of us, artists unsure of being artists, but certain that we are nothing else, wait for day after day, so that in the end we may agree to live.

Why then, since I am concerned with what is probably a vain expectation, should I now agree to republishing these essays? First of all because a number of readers have been able to find a convincing argument.[2] And then a time always comes in an artist's life when he must take his bearings, draw closer to his own centre, and then try to stay there. Such is the case today, and I need say no more about it. If, in spite of so many efforts to build up a language and bring myths to life, I never manage to rewrite *Betwixt and Between*, I shall have never achieved anything. I feel it in my bones. But there is nothing to prevent me from dreaming that I shall succeed, from imagining that I shall still place in the centre of this work the admirable silence of a mother and the effort of a man to rediscover a justice or a love which matches this silence. Behold, in life's dream, the man who finds his truths and loses them, in the land of death, in order to return through wars, cries, the madness of justice and love, in short through pain, to that quiet country where death itself is a happy silence. Here still.... Yes, nothing prevents me from dreaming of this in the very hour of exile, since at least I know with sure and certain knowledge that a man's work is nothing but this slow trek to rediscover through the detours of art those two or three great and simple images in whose presence his heart first opened. This is why, perhaps, after working and producing

2. A simple one. 'This book already exists, but in a small number of copies sold by booksellers at a very high price. Why should wealthy readers be the only ones with the right to read it?' Why indeed?

for twenty years, I still live with the idea that my work has not even begun. From the very moment that the republication of these essays made me go back to the first pages that I wrote, it is principally this that I have wanted to say.

IRONY

Two years ago I knew an old woman. She was suffering from an illness that had almost killed her. The whole of her right side had been paralysed. She only had half of herself in this world while the other half was already foreign to her. This bustling, chattering old lady had been made to sit still and keep quiet. Illiterate, rather insensitive, alone day after day, her whole life was reduced to God. She believed in him. The proof is that she had a rosary, a lead statue of Christ, and a stucco statue of Saint Joseph carrying the infant Jesus. She herself doubted whether her illness was incurable, but she said it was to make other people pay attention to her. For everything else she relied on the God she loved so poorly.

On that particular day someone did pay attention to her. A young man. (He thought that there was a truth and also knew that this woman was going to die, but did not worry about solving this contradiction.) He had become genuinely interested in this old woman's boredom. This was something she had really noticed. And this interest was a godsend for the invalid. She was eager to talk about her troubles: she was at the end of her tether, and you have to make way for the rising generation. Did she get bored? Of course she did. She had been put in her corner, like a dog. It would be better to have done with it once and for all. Since she would much sooner die than be a burden to anyone.

Her voice had taken on a quarrelsome note, like someone haggling over a bargain. Still, the young man understood her. Nevertheless, he was of the opinion that being a burden on other people was better than dying. But that proved only one thing: that he had doubtless never been a burden on anybody. And of course he told the old lady – since he had seen the rosary: 'You still have God.' It was true. But even here she had her troubles. If she happened to spend rather a long time in prayer, if her eyes strayed and followed a pattern in the wallpaper, her daughter would say: 'There she is, praying again!' 'What business is that of yours?' the invalid would say. 'It's none of my business, but it ends up by getting on my nerves.' And the old woman would fall silent, casting a long, reproachful look at her daughter.

The young man listened to all this with an immense and unfamiliar pain that hurt his chest. And the old woman went on: 'She'll see when she's old. She'll need it as well.'

You felt that this old woman had been freed of everything except God, wholly abandoned to this final evil, virtuous through necessity, too easily convinced that what still remained for her was the only thing worth loving, finally and irrevocably plunged into the wretchedness of man in God. But if hope in life is once reborn, then God is powerless against human interests.

They had sat down at table. The young man had been invited to dinner. The old lady wasn't eating, because food is difficult to digest in the evening. She had stayed in her corner, just behind the young man who had been listening to her. And because he felt that he was being watched he couldn't eat very much. Nevertheless, the dinner proceeded. They decided to extend the party by going to the cinema. As it happened, there was a funny film on that week. The young man had blithely accepted, without thinking about the person who continued to exist behind him.

The guests had risen from table to go and wash their hands before leaving. There was obviously no question of the old lady coming as well. Even if she hadn't been half paralysed, she was too ignorant to be able to understand the film. She said she didn't like the cinema. The truth was that she couldn't understand it. In any case, she was in her corner vacantly absorbed in the beads of her rosary. That was where she put all her confidence. The three objects that she still kept by her represented the material point where God began. Beyond and behind the rosary, the statue of Christ or of Saint Joseph, there opened up a vast, deep blackness in which she placed all her hope.

Everyone was ready. They went up to the old lady to kiss her and wish her a good night. She had already realized what was happening and was clutching her rosary tightly in her hand. But it was quite apparent that this showed as much despair as zeal.

Irony

Everyone else had kissed her. Only the young man was left. He had given her an affectionate handshake and was already turning away. But she saw that the one person who had taken an interest in her was leaving. She didn't want to be alone. She could already feel the horror of loneliness, the long sleepless hours, the frustrating intimacy with God. She was afraid, could now rely only on man, and, clinging to the one person who had shown any interest in her, held on to his hand, squeezing it, clumsily thanking him in order to justify this insistence. The young man felt embarrassed. The others were already turning round to tell him to hurry up. The film began at nine and it was better to arrive early so as not to have to queue up.

He felt confronted by the most atrocious suffering he had ever known: that of a sick old woman left at home by people going to a cinema. He wanted to leave, escape, withdraw his hand, forget it. He felt a moment of intense hatred for the old woman, and almost slapped her hard across the face.

Finally he did manage to get away, while the invalid, half rising from her arm-chair, watched with horror as the last certainty in which she could have found rest faded away. There was now nothing to protect her. And, defenceless before the idea of death, she did not know exactly what terrified her, but felt that she did not want to be alone. God was of no use to her. All He did was cut her off from people and make her lonely. She did not want to be without people. So she began to cry.

The others were already outside in the street. The young man could not get rid of his feelings of remorse. He looked up at the lighted window, a great dead eye in the silent house. The eye closed. The old woman's daughter told the young man: 'She always turns the light off when she's by herself. She likes to sit in the dark.'

*

The old man brought his eyebrows triumphantly together, waggling a sententious forefinger. 'When I was a young man,' he said, 'my father used to give me five francs a week out of my wages as pocket money to last me till the following Saturday. Well, I still managed to save. First of all, when I went to see my fiancée, I walked four miles through the open country to get there and four miles to get back. Just you listen to me now, young men just don't know how to amuse themselves nowadays.' There were three young men sitting at a round table with this one old man. He was describing his petty little adventures: valued acts of crass stupidity, onsets of fatigue that he celebrated as victories. He never paused in his story, and, in a hurry to tell everything before his audience left him, retained only those aspects of his past that he thought likely to impress them. Making people listen to him was his only vice: he refused to notice the irony of the glances and the sudden mockery that greeted him. The young men saw him as the usual old man for whom everything was marvellous in his day, while he saw himself as the respected elder whose experience carries weight. The young don't know that experience is a defeat and that we must lose everything to win a little knowledge. He had suffered. He never mentioned it. It's better to seem happy. And if he was wrong in this pretence he would have been even more mistaken to try and make people sympathize with him. What do the sufferings of an old man matter when life absorbs you completely? He talked on and on, wandering blissfully through the grey monotony of his own mutterings. But it couldn't last. He needed to be listened to, and the young men had stopped paying attention. He wasn't even funny any longer; he was old. And young men are fond of billiards and cards, which take their minds off the idiocy of everyday work.

Soon he was alone in spite of his efforts and the lies he told to enliven his story. With no attempt to spare his feeling the young men had left. Once again he was alone. To be no longer listened to: that's the terrible thing about being old. He was condemned to silence and loneliness. He was being told that he would soon be dead. And an old man who is going to die is useless, he is even an insidious embarrassment. Let him go. He ought to go. Or, if he doesn't, to shut up: it's the least he can do. And he suffers because as soon as he stops talking he realizes that he is old. Yet he did get up and go, smiling to everyone around him. But the faces he saw were either indifferent, or convulsed by a gaiety that he

Irony 33

had no right to share. A man was laughing: 'She's old, I don't deny it, but you sometimes make the best stews in old pots.' Another, already more seriously: 'Well, we're not rich but we eat well. Look at my grandson now, he eats more than his father. His father needs a pound of bread, he needs two! And you can pile on the sausage and camembert. And sometimes when he's finished he says: "*Han, Han!*" and keeps on eating.' The old man moved away. And with his slow step, the short step of the ass turning the wheel, he walked through the crowds of men on the long pavements. He felt ill and did not want to go home. Normally, he was quite happy to go back to the table and the oil lamp, the plates where his fingers moved quite mechanically to their place. He still liked to eat his supper without talking, the old woman on the other side of the table, chewing over each mouthful, gazing into vacancy with an empty mind. This evening he would arrive home later. His supper would have been served and gone cold, his wife would be in bed, not worrying about him since she knew that he often came home unexpectedly late. She would say 'He's in the moon again,' and that said everything.

Now he was walking along with his gently insistent step. He was old and alone. When life is reaching its end, old age wells up in bouts of nausea. Everything comes down to not being listened to. He walks along, turns at the corner of the street, stumbles, and almost falls. I have seen him. It's ridiculous, but what can you do about it? After all, he prefers being in the street, being there rather than at home where for hours on end fever hides the old woman from him and shuts him alone in his room. Then, sometimes, the door slowly opens and gapes ajar for a moment. A man comes in. He is wearing a light-coloured suit. He sits down facing the old man and the minutes pass while he says nothing. He doesn't move, just like the door which stood ajar a moment ago. From time to time he strokes his hair and sighs gently. When he has watched the old man for a long time with the same heavy sadness in his eyes, he leaves, silently. The latch clicks to behind him and the old man stays there, horrified, with an acid and painful fear in his stomach. In the street, on the other hand, however few people he may meet, he is never alone. His fever sings. He walks a little faster: tomorrow everything will be different, tomorrow. Suddenly he realizes that tomorrow will be the same, and, after tomorrow, all the other days. And he is crushed down by this irreparable discovery. It's ideas like this that kill you. Men kill themselves because they cannot stand them – or, if they are young, they turn them into epigrams.

Old, mad, drunk, nobody knows. His will be a worthy end, tear-stained and admirable. He will make a good end, that is to say he will suffer. That will be a consolation for him. And besides, where can he go? He will always be old now. Men build on their future old age. They try to give this old age, besieged by hopelessness, an idleness which leaves them with no defence. They want to become foremen so as to be able to retire to a small house in the country. But once they are deep in years, they realize perfectly well that this is a mistake. They need other men for protection. And as far as he was concerned, he needed to be listened to if he was to believe in his life. Now the streets were darker and emptier. There were still voices going by. In the strange calm of the evening they were becoming more solemn. Behind the hills encircling the town there were still glimmers of daylight. From somewhere out of sight smoke rose, imposingly, behind the wooded hilltops. It rose slowly in the sky, in tiers, like the branches of a pine-tree. The old man closed his eyes. As life carried away the rumblings of the town, and the heavens smiled their foolish, indifferent smile, he was alone, forsaken, naked, already dead.

Need I describe the other side of this fine coin? Doubtless, in a dark and dirty room, the old woman was laying the table. When dinner was ready she sat down, looked at the clock, waited a little longer, and then began to eat a hearty meal. She thought to herself: 'He is in the moon.' That said everything.

*

There were five of them living in the same apartment: the grandmother, her younger son, her elder daughter and the daughter's two children. The son was almost dumb; the daughter, an invalid, thought with difficulty, and of the two children one was already working for an insurance company while the other was continuing his studies. At seventy, the grandmother still ruled over all these people. Above her bed you could still see a portrait taken of her five years previously, sitting bolt upright in a black dress that was held together at the neck by a medallion, not a wrinkle on her face. With enormous clear cold eyes, she had that regal posture which she relinquished only with increasing age and still sometimes tried to recover when she went out.

It was these clear eyes that held a memory for her grandson which still made him blush. The old woman would wait until there were visitors and would then ask, looking at him severely, 'Whom do you like best? Your mother or your grandmother?' She enjoyed it more when her daughter herself was there. For in every case the child would always reply 'My grandmother', with a great upsurge of love in his heart for his ever silent mother. Then, when the visitors were surprised at this preference, the mother would say: 'It's because she was the one who brought him up.'

It was also because the old woman thought that love is something you can demand. The knowledge that she herself had been a good mother gave her a kind of rigidity and intolerance. She had never deceived her husband and had borne him nine children. After his death, she had energetically brought up her young family herself. After leaving their little farm on the outskirts, they had ended up in an old and poor part of the town where they had now been living for a long time.

And this woman was certainly not lacking in qualities. But for her grandsons, who were at the age of making absolute judgements, she was nothing but a fraud. Thus one of their uncles had told them a significant story: he had gone to pay a visit to his mother-in-law, and had seen her sitting idly at the window. But she had come to the door with a duster in her hand and had apologized for carrying on working by saying that she had so little free time left after doing her housework. And it must be confessed that this was typical. She had the greatest ease in fainting after a family discussion. She also suffered from painful vomiting caused by a liver complaint. But she never showed the slightest modesty when she was ill. Far from shutting herself away, she would vomit noisily into the kitchen rubbish bin. And when she came back into the room, pale, her eyes running with tears from the efforts she had been making, she would tell anyone who begged her to go to bed that she had to get the next meal ready and play her part in running the house : : 'I do everything here.' Or again : 'I don't know what you'd do without me.'

The children grew used to ignoring her vomitings, her 'attacks' as she called them, as well as her complaints. One day she went to bed and demanded the doctor. They sent for him to humour her. On the first day he diagnosed a slight stomach upset, on the second a cancer of the liver, on the third a serious attack of jaundice. But the younger of the two children insisted on seeing all this as yet another performance, a more sophisticated act, and felt no concern. This woman had bullied him too much for his initial reaction to be pessimistic. And there is a kind of desperate courage in being lucid and refusing to love. But people who play at being ill can succeed : the grandmother carried simulation to the point of death. On her last day, her children around her, she began freeing herself of the fermentations in her intestines. She turned and spoke with simplicity to her grandson: 'You see,' she said, 'I'm farting like a little pig.' She died an hour later.

As for her grandson, he now realized that he had not understood a thing that was happening. He could not free himself of the idea that he had just witnessed the last and most monstrous of this woman's performances. And if he asked himself whether he felt any sorrow, he could find none at all. Only on the day of the funeral, because of the general outburst of tears, did he weep, but was afraid of being insincere and telling lies in the presence of death. It was on a fine winter's day, shot through with sunlight. In the pale blue sky, you could sense the cold all spangled with yellow. The cemetery overlooked the town, and you could see the fine transparent sun setting in the bay quivering with light, like a moist lip.

None of this fits together? How very true! A woman you

Irony

abandon to go to the cinema, an old man to whom you have stopped listening, a death which redeems nothing, and then, on the other hand, the whole radiance of the world. What difference does it make if you accept everything? What you have here are three destinies which are different and yet alike. Death for us all, but his own death to each. After all, the sun still warms our bones for us.

BETWEEN YES AND NO

IF it is true that the only paradises are those that we have lost, I can find a name for this tender and inhuman feeling which inhabits me today. An emigrant is returning to his country. And I am remembering. The irony and tension fade away and I am back at home. I don't want to chew over my happiness. It is much simpler and much easier than that. For what has remained untouched in those hours which I am bringing back from the depths of forgetfulness is the memory of a pure emotion, a moment suspended in eternity. Only this memory is true in me and I always discover it too late. We love the gentleness of certain gestures, the way a tree fits into a landscape. And we have only one detail to recreate all this love, but this is enough: the smell of a room that has been shut up for too long, the particular sound of a footstep on the road. This is also true for me. And if I then loved and gave myself, I finally became myself since only love can restore us to ourselves.

Slow, peaceful and grave, these hours return, just as strong, just as moving – because it is evening, because it is a sad hour, and because the dull sky holds a kind of vague desire. Each rediscovered gesture reveals me to myself. Someone once said to me: 'It's so difficult to live.' And I remember the tone of voice. On another occasion, someone murmured: 'The worst mistake still lies in making people suffer.' When everything is over, the thirst for life has gone. Is that what they call happiness? As we walk alongside these memories, we clothe everything in the same quiet garb, and death looks like a backcloth whose colours have lost their glow. We turn back upon ourselves. We feel our distress and love ourselves better for it. Yes, that is perhaps what happiness is, the self-pitying awareness of our unhappiness.

That is certainly true of this evening. In this Moorish café, at the far end of the Arab town, I recall not a moment of past happiness but a feeling of strangeness. It is already night. On the walls canary yellow lions pursue green-clad sheikhs among five-branched palm trees. In the corner of the café an acetylene lamp gives a flickering light. The real light comes from the fire at the bottom of a small oven adorned with yellow and green enamel. The flames light up the middle of the room, and I can feel them reflected on my face. I am facing the doorway and the bay. Crouching in one corner, the café owner seems to be looking at my glass, which stands there empty with a mint leaf at the bottom. There is no one in the main room, noises rise from the town below, while farther off in the bay lights shine. I hear the Arab breathe heavily, and his eyes glow in the dusk. Is that the sound of the sea far off? The world sighs towards me in a long rhythm, and brings me the peace and indifference of immortal things. Tall red shadows make the lions on the walls sway with a wave-like motion. The air grows cool. The lighthouses begin to turn: green, red, white. And still the world sighs its long sigh. A kind of secret song is born from this indifference. And I am home again. I think of a child living in a poor district. That district, that house! There were only two floors, and the staircases were unlit. Even now, long years later, he could go back there on the darkest night. He knows that he would climb the staircase without stumbling once. He bears this house in his very body. His legs retain the exact height of the steps; his hand, the instinctive, never-conquered horror of the banister. Because of the cockroaches.

On summer evenings the working men go out on to the balcony. In his flat there was only one tiny window. So they brought down the chairs and put them in front of the house, and enjoyed the evening air. There was the street, the ice-vendor next door, the cafés opposite, and the noise of children running from door to door. But above all, through the wide fig-trees, there was the sky. There is a solitude in poverty, but a solitude which gives everything back its value. At a certain level of wealth the heavens themselves and the star-filled night seem natural goods. But at the bottom of the ladder the sky recovers its full meaning: a priceless grace. Summer evenings, mysteries with crackling stars! Behind the child lay a stinking corridor and his little chair, splitting across the bottom, sank slightly beneath his weight. But he had only to raise his eyes to drink straight from the pure sky. Sometimes a large tram would rattle swiftly past. And a drunk would stand singing at a street corner, without disturbing the silence.

The child's mother never spoke either. Sometimes people would ask her: 'What are you thinking about?' And she would reply: 'Nothing.' And that was the truth. Everything was already there, so she thought about nothing. Her life, her interests, her children were simply there, with a presence too natural to be felt. She was an invalid, had difficulty in thinking. She had a harsh and domineering mother who sacrificed everything to a touchy animal pride and who had long ruled over her daughter's feeble mind. Emancipated by her marriage, the daughter obediently came home when her husband died. He died a soldier's death, as they say. In a place of honour you can see in a golden frame his military medal and *croix de guerre*. The hospital also sent the widow the small shell splinter found in his body. The widow has kept it. Her grief has long since disappeared. She has forgotten her husband, but still speaks of her children's father. To bring up these children, she goes out to work and gives her wages to her mother, who brings up the children with a whip. When she hits them too hard, her daughter tells her: 'Don't hit them on the head.' Because they are her children, she is very fond of them. She loves them with a hidden and impartial love. Sometimes, as on those evenings which he now remembers, she would come back from her exhausting work (as a charwoman) and find the house empty. The old woman out shopping, the children still at school. Then she huddles in a chair, gazing in front of her, wanders off in the dizzy pursuit of a crack along the floor. Around her night thickens and then her silence is a grief without repair. If the child comes in at this moment, he sees the thin shape with its bony shoulders and stops: he is afraid. He is beginning to feel a lot of things. He is scarcely aware of his own existence, but this animal silence makes him cry with pain. He feels sorry for his mother, but is this loving her? She has never hugged or kissed him for she wouldn't know how. Then he will stand a long time watching her. Feeling separate from her, he becomes conscious of her suffering. She can't hear him, for she is deaf. In a few moments the old woman will come back, life will start up again: the round light cast by the paraffin lamp, the oilcloth on the table, the shouts, the swear-words. But in the meantime this silence marks a pause, an immensely long moment. Because he is vaguely aware of this, the child thinks that the upsurge of feeling in him is love for his mother. And this must be so, because after all she is his mother.

She is thinking of nothing. Outside, the light, the noises; here, silence in the night. The child will grow, will learn. They are bringing him up and will ask him to be grateful, as if they were sparing him pain. His mother will always have these silences. He will grow in pain. Being a man is what counts. His grandmother will die, then his mother, then himself.

His mother has given a sudden start. Something has frightened her. He looks stupid standing there gazing at her. He ought to go and do his homework. The child has done his homework. Today he is in a sordid café. He is now a man. Isn't this what counts? That can't be so, since doing homework and accepting manhood only leads to being old.

Still crouching in his corner, the Arab is clasping his hands round his feet. From the terraces there rises the scent of roasting coffee mingled with the excited chatter of young voices. A tug adds its grave and tender note. The world is ending here as it does each day, and all its measureless torments give rise to nothing but this promise of peace. The indifference of this strange mother! The only thing which can serve as a measure for it is the immense solitude of the world. One evening they had called her son – he was already quite old – to his mother's side. A fright had brought on a serious mental shock. She was in the habit of going on to the balcony at the end of the day. She would take a chair and lean her mouth against the cold and salty iron of the balcony rail. Then she would watch the people going past. Behind her the night gradually thickened. In front of her the shops were suddenly lighting up. The street was filling up with people and lights. She would gaze emptily at it until she forgot where she was. On this particular evening a man had loomed up behind her, dragged her backwards, knocked her about, and run away on hearing a noise. She had seen nothing, and had fainted. She was in bed when her son arrived. He decided, on the doctor's advice, to spend the night with her. He stretched out on the bed, by her side, lying on the top of the blankets. It was summer. The fear left by the recent drama hung in the air of the overheated room. Footsteps were rustling and doors creaking. In the heavy air there floated the smell of the vinegar used to cool the invalid's brow. She, in the meantime, moved restlessly about, whimpering, sometimes giving a sudden start. She then pulled him out of brief snatches of sleep from which he emerged drenched in sweat, prepared to act – and into which he fell back, heavily, after glancing at his watch on which the night-light threw three dancing shadows. It was only later that he realized how much they had been alone that night. Alone against everybody. The 'others' were asleep, while they both breathed the same fever. In this old house everything then seemed hollow. The midnight trams drained away with them all the hope which comes to us from men, all the certainties given to us by town noises. The house was still humming with their passage, and little by little everything died away. All that remained was a great garden of silence peopled from time to time with the terrified groans of the sick woman. He had never felt so cut off from everything. The world had melted away, taking with it the illusion that life begins again each morning. Nothing was left, neither studies, ambitions, preferences in a restaurant or favourite colours. Nothing but the sickness and death in which he felt himself plunged. ... And yet, at the very moment when the world was crumbling, he was alive. And he had finally even gone to sleep. Yet not without taking with him the tender and despairing image of two people's loneliness together. Later, much later, he was to remember this mingled scent of sweat and vinegar, this moment when he had felt the ties which attached him to his mother. As if she were the immense pity of his heart, spread out around him, made flesh, and dili-

Between Yes and No

gently playing, with neither posture nor pretence, the part of a poor old woman whose fate moves men to tears.

Now the ashes in the grate are beginning to choke the fire. And still the same sight from the earth. The pearled song of an Arab drum can be heard in the air, overladen with a woman's laughter. Lights come closer in the bay – fishing vessels, no doubt, returning to harbour. The triangle of sky that I can see from where I am sitting has been stripped of its daylight clouds. Overflowing with stars, it quivers in a pure breeze and the padded wings of night beat slowly around me. How far will this night in which I cease to belong to myself go? There is a dangerous virtue in the word simplicity. And on this night I can understand a man wanting to die because things cease to matter when he sees through life completely. A man suffers and endures misfortune after misfortune. He bears them, settles down to his fate. People think well of him. And then, one evening, that's it: he meets a friend of whom he has been very fond. The latter speaks to him absent-mindedly. On returning home the man kills himself. People then talk about private sorrows and secret dramas. No. And if a reason really must be found, he killed himself because a friend spoke to him absent-mindedly. Thus every time that it seemed to me as if I had grasped the deep meaning of the world, it is its simplicity that has always overwhelmed me. My mother, that evening, and her strange indifference. On another occasion I was living in a villa in the suburbs, along with a dog, a pair of cats and their kittens, all black. The mother cat could not feed them. One by one, all the kittens died. They filled their room with filth. And every evening, when I arrived home, I would find one stiff on the floor, its gums laid bare. One evening I found the last one, half eaten by the mother. It already stank. The smell of death mingled with the stench of urine. Then, with my hands in the filth, and the stench of rotting flesh reeking in my nostrils, I sat down in the midst of all this misery and gazed for hour after hour at the demented flame shining in the cat's green eyes as she crouched motionless in the corner! Yes. And it is just like that this evening. When we are stripped down to a certain point, nothing leads anywhere any more, hope and despair are equally groundless, and the whole of life can be summed up in an image. But why stop there? Simple, everything is simple, from the lights alternating in the lighthouses, one green, one red, one white, to the cool of the night and the smell of the town and poverty which reaches me from below. If this evening it is the image of a certain childhood which comes back to me, how can I refrain from welcoming the lesson of love and poverty which it offers? Since this hour is like a pause between yes and no, I leave hope in life or disgust with it for another time. Yes, catch only the transparency and simplicity of paradises lost: in an image. And thus it was that not long ago, in a house in an old part of the town, a son went to see his mother. They sat down facing each other, in silence. But their eyes met:

'Well then, mother.'

'Well then, here we are.'

'Are you bored? Don't I talk much?'

'Oh, you've never talked much.'

And, though her lips do not move, her face lights up in a beautiful smile. It's true, he has never talked very much to her. But did he ever really need to? When you keep quiet, the situation becomes clear. He is her son, she is his mother. She can say to him: 'You know.'

She is sitting at the foot of the divan, her feet together, her hands together in her lap. He, on his chair, scarcely looks at her and smokes ceaselessly. A silence.

'You ought not to smoke so much.'

'It's true.'

The whole smell of the district rises in through the window. The accordion from the neighbouring café, the traffic hurrying in the evening, the smell of the skewers of grilled meat that are eaten between small springy rolls of bread, a child crying in the road. The mother rises and picks up her knitting. Her fingers are clumsy, twisted with arthritis. She works only slowly, taking up the same stitch three or four times or undoing a whole row with a dull ripping sound.

'It's a little cardigan. I shall wear it with a white collar. With that and my black coat, I shall be dressed for the season.'

She has risen to switch on the light.

'It gets dark early nowadays.'

It was true. Summer was over and autumn had not yet begun. Swifts were still calling in the gentle sky.

'You'll come back soon?'

'But I've not left yet. Why do you talk about that?'

'No, it was just to say something.'

A tram passes. A car.

'Is it true that I look like my father?'

'His spitting image. Of course, you didn't know him. You were six months old when he died. But if you had a little moustache!'

It was without conviction that he mentioned his father. No memory, no emotion. Doubtless someone quite ordinary. Besides, he had been very keen to go. At the battle of the Marne his head split open. Blind and dying for a week: his name on his village war memorial.

'Basically,' she says, 'it's better that way. He would have come back blind or mad. So, poor chap . . .'

'It's true.'

And what then is it that keeps him in this room, except the certainty that it's always the best thing to do, the feeling that the whole *absurd* simplicity of the world has come to seek refuge here?

'You'll come back?' she says. 'I know that you have work to do. Just from time to time. . .'

But where am I now? And how can I separate this empty café from that room in my past? I can no longer tell whether I am living or remembering. The lighthouse beams are there. And the Arab standing in front of me is telling me that he is going to close. I have to leave. I no longer wish to go down so dangerous a slope. It is true that, as I take a last look at the bay and its lights, what rises towards me is not the hope of better days but a serene and primitive indifference to everything and to myself. But I must break this curve which is too easy and too soft. And I need my lucidity. Yes, everything is simple. It is men who complicate things. Don't let them tell us any stories. Don't let them say of the man sentenced to death: 'He is going to pay his debt to society,' but: 'They're going to cut his head off.' It looks like nothing at all. But it does make a little difference. And then, there are people who prefer to look their fate in the eye.

IRON IN THE SOUL

I ARRIVED in Prague at six in the evening. I immediately took my suitcases to the left luggage office. I still had two hours in which to look for a hotel. And I was full of a strange feeling of liberty because I no longer had my two suitcases hanging on my arms. I came out of the station, walked by some gardens, and found myself suddenly thrown into the middle of the Avenue Wenceslas, swarming with people at that time in the evening. Around me were a million people who had been alive all this time and whose existence had never impinged upon mine. They were alive. I was thousands of kilometres away from a familiar country. I could not understand their language. They all walked quickly. And as they overtook me, they all cut themselves off from me. I felt lost.

I had little money. Enough to live for six days. But after that, friends were coming to meet me. Nevertheless, I also began to feel anxious about that. So I set out to look for a cheap hotel. I was in the new part of the town, and all those that I could see were bursting with lights, laughter and women. I walked faster. Something in my rapid pace already seemed like flight. However, towards eight in the evening, exhausted, I reached the old town. There I was attracted by a modest-looking hotel with a small doorway. I go in. I fill in the form, take my key. I have room number thirty-four on the third floor. I open the door and find myself in a most luxurious room. I look to see how much it costs: twice as expensive as I thought. The problem of money becomes really acute. I can now live only poorly in this great city. My anxiety, still rather vague a few moments ago, fixes itself on this one point. I feel uneasy. I feel hungry and empty. Nevertheless, a moment of lucidity: I have always been credited, rightly or wrongly, with the greatest indifference concerning money. Why then should I be worried about the expense? But already my mind is working. I must have something to eat, start walking again and look for a cheap restaurant. I must not spend more than ten crowns on each of my meals. Of all the restaurants that I can see the least expensive is also the least attractive. I walk up and down in front of it. The people inside begin to notice my antics: I have to go in. It is a rather murky cellar, painted with pretentious frescoes. A fairly mixed clientele. In one corner, a few prostitutes are smoking and talking seriously to one another. A number of men for the most part colourless and of intermediate age sit eating at the tables. The waiter, a colossus in a greasy dinner jacket, leans his enormous expressionless head in my direction. I quickly make a random choice of a dish from what, for me, is the incomprehensible menu. But it would appear that this needs to be explained. And the waiter asks me a question in Czech. I reply with the small amount of German that I know. He does not know German. He summons one of the prostitutes who comes forward in the classic pose, left hand on hip, cigarette in the right hand, simpering smile. She sits down at my table and asks me questions in a German which I judge as bad as my own. Everything becomes clear. The waiter wanted to sing me the praises of the *plat du jour*. Game for anything, I take the *plat du jour*. The prostitute talks to me but I can't understand her now. Naturally, I say yes in my most sincere tone of voice. But I am not here. Everything annoys me, I waver, I don't feel hungry. And still this twinge of pain in me and the tightness in my stomach. I buy the girl a glass of beer because I know how to behave. The *plat du jour* having arrived, I start to eat: a mixture of porridge and meat, made disgusting by an unbelievable quantity of cummin. But I think about something else, of nothing at all rather, staring at the fat, laughing mouth of the woman in front of me. Does she think I am inviting her favours? She is already close to me, starts to make advances. An automatic gesture from me holds her back. (She was ugly. I have often thought that if she had been pretty I would have avoided everything that happened later.) I was afraid of being sick, there and then, in the middle of all these people ready to laugh, but still more afraid of being alone in my hotel room, without money or enthusiasm, reduced to myself and to my poverty-stricken thoughts. Even today I still wonder with embarrassment at the weary and cowardly creature that then emerged from me. I left. I walked in the old town, but could not stand my own presence any longer and ran all the way to my hotel, went to bed, and waited for sleep, which came almost at once.

Every country where I am not bored is a country that teaches me nothing. That was the kind of remark which I used to try to cheer myself up. But need I describe the days that followed? I went back to my restaurant. Morning and evening, I endured the atrocious, nauseating cummin-flavoured food. I consequently walked around all day with a constant desire to vomit. But I resisted, knowing that one must take in nourishment. Besides, what did this matter compared with what I should have to endure if I tried out a new restaurant? There, at least, I was 'recognized'. People gave me a smile even if they didn't speak to me. On the other hand, anguish was gaining ground. I paid too much attention to that sharp twinge of pain in my head. I decided to organize my days, to cover them with points of reference. I stayed in bed as late as possible and consequently my days were shortened. I washed, shaved and methodically explored the town. I lost myself in the sumptuous baroque churches, trying to rediscover a homeland in them, but emerging emptier and in deeper despair after this disappointing encounter with myself. I wandered along the Vltava and saw the water swirling and foaming at its dams. I spent endless hours in the immense silent and empty district of the Hradchin. At sunset in the shadow of its cathedral and palaces my lonely step echoed along the streets. As I noticed this, panic seized hold of me again. I dined early and went to bed at half-past eight. The sun tore me from myself. I visited churches, palaces and museums, I tried to calm my anguish in every kind of work of art. A classic dodge: I sought to melt down my rebellion into melancholy. But in vain. As soon as I came out, I was a foreigner again. Once, however, in a baroque cloister at the far end of the town, the gentleness of the hour, the softly tinkling bells, the clusters of pigeons flying from the old tower, together with something like a scent of herbs and nothingness, gave birth in me to a silence full of tears that almost delivered me. And, back in my hotel room that evening, I wrote out the following passage at one sitting, and now reproduce it unchanged, since its very pomposity reminds me of how complex my feelings were:

And what other profit can we seek to draw from travel? Here I am stripped bare, in a town where the notices are written in strange, incomprehensible hieroglyphics, where I have no friends to talk to, in short where I have no distractions. I am fully aware that nothing can rescue me from this room filled with the noises of a foreign town, and carry me away to the more delicate light of a fireside or a beloved place. Shall I call, cry out? All I shall see will be unknown faces. Everything, churches, gold and incense, casts me back into a daily life where my anguish gives everything its value. And now the curtain of habits, the comfortable loom of words and gestures in which the heart sinks down to slumber, slowly opens and lays bare the ashen visage of anxiety. Man is face to face with himself: I defy him to be happy.... And yet this is how travel enlightens him. A great gulf widens between him and things. The world's music finds its way more easily into this less solid heart. As he is finally stripped bare, the slightest solitary tree becomes the most tender and fragile of images. What travel gives us is a landscape which we can feel and love, composed of works of art and women's smiles, of races of men at home in their land, and of monuments that tell the story of the centuries. And then, at close of day, I find this hotel room where once again I have this deep hollow feeling, as if my soul were hungry.

But need I confess that all this was just a way of sending myself to sleep? And I can now say that what I retain of Prague is the smell of cucumbers soaked in vinegar, which are sold at every street corner to eat between your fingers, and whose bitter, piquant flavour would awake and feed my anguish as soon as I had crossed the threshold of my hotel. That, and also perhaps a certain tune played on an accordion. Beneath my windows, a blind, one-armed man, sitting on his instrument, kept it in place with one buttock while opening and shutting it with his one good hand. It was always the same childish and tender tune which woke me every morning and set me down brusquely in the unadorned reality where I was floundering.

I can also remember that on the banks of the Vltava I would suddenly stop, and seized by this smell or that melody, carried almost beyond myself, would murmur: 'What does it mean? What does it mean?' But I had doubtless not yet gone over the edge. On the fourth day, in the morning, I was getting ready to go out. I wanted to find a particular Jewish cemetery that I had not been able to find the previous day. Someone knocked at the door of the next room. After a moment's silence, they knocked again. A long knock this time, but apparently in vain. A heavy step went down the stairs. Without paying attention to what I was doing, my mind empty, I wasted a few moments reading the instructions for a shaving cream that I had in any case been using for a month. The day was heavy. From the sunless sky a coppery light fell on the spires and domes of old Prague. The newsboys were shouting as they did every morning when selling the *Narodni Politika*. I tore myself with difficulty from the torpor that was overcoming me. But just as I was going out, I passed the waiter who looked after my particular floor, armed with a bunch of keys. I stopped. He knocked again, for a long time. He tried to open the door. No success. It must have been bolted on the inside. More knocks. The room sounded hollow, with so lugubrious a note that, depressed as I was, I left without asking my questions. But in the streets of Prague, I was pursued by a painful foreboding. How shall I ever forget the waiter's stupid face, the funny way his polished shoes curled upwards, and the button that was missing from his jacket? I did finally have lunch, but with a growing feeling of disgust. Towards two in the afternoon I went back to my hotel.

In the hall the servants were whispering. I rapidly climbed the stairs in order to come face to face more quickly with what I was expecting. It was what I thought. The door of the room was half open, so that all that could be seen was a high wall painted blue. But the dull light that I mentioned above threw two shadows on this screen: the dead man lying on the bed and a policeman guarding the body. These two shadows were at right-angles to each other. This light overwhelmed me. It was authentic, a real living light, of an afternoon of life, a light which makes you notice that you are alive. He was dead. Alone in his room. I knew that this was not suicide. I dashed back into my room and threw myself on to the bed. A man no different from many others, short and fat, if I was to believe the shadow. He had doubtless been dead for some time. And life had gone on in the hotel, until the waiter had had the idea of calling him. He had arrived in this hotel without suspecting anything and he had died alone. And I, during that time, had been reading the advertisement for my shaving cream. I spent the whole afternoon in a state that I should not like to describe. I lay stretched out on my bed, thinking of nothing, with a strange heaviness in my heart. I cut my finger nails. I counted the cracks in the floorboards. 'If I can count up to a thousand...' At fifty or sixty I collapsed. I couldn't go on. I could understand nothing of the noises outside. Once however, in the corridor, a stifled voice, a woman's voice, said in German: 'He was so good.' Then I thought desperately of my own town on the shores of the Mediterranean, of the summer evenings that I love so much, so gentle in the green light and full of young and beautiful women. For days now I had not uttered a single word and my heart was bursting with the cries and protests I had stifled. I should have wept like a child if anyone had opened his arms to me. Towards the end of the afternoon, broken with weariness, I was staring madly at my door handle, a popular accordion tune endlessly running through my empty head. At that moment I had gone as far as I could. I was without a country, a town, a room or a name, and on the verge either of a victory and an inspiration in which I would finally know, or of a madness and humiliation in which I would disappear. There was a knock at my door and my friends came in. I was saved even if I was cheated of the outcome. I even think that I said: 'I'm happy to see you again.' But I am sure that I confessed nothing further and that in their eyes I was still the man they knew when they left.

*

I left Prague a short time later. And, certainly, I did take an interest in what I saw there later: I could note down such and such an hour in the little Gothic cemetery of Bautzen, with the brilliant red of its geraniums and the blue morning sky. I could speak of the long, pitiless and graceless plains of Silesia. I went through them at daybreak. A heavy flight of birds was passing in the thick misty morning above the sticky earth. I also like tender and grave Moravia, with its distant, pure horizons, its roads bordered with sour plum trees. But I still felt dizzy, like a man who has spent too long gazing into a bottomless pit. I arrived in Vienna, left it after a week, and was still held captive within myself.

Nevertheless, in the train taking me from Vienna to Venice I was waiting for something. I was like a convalescent who has been fed on soups and who is thinking about what it will be like to eat his first crust of bread. A light was coming to birth. I now know what it was: I was ready for happiness. I shall speak only of the six days that I lived on a hill near Vicenza. I am still there, or, rather, I still find myself there again, as the scent of rosemary brings everything flooding back to me.

I enter Italy. A land that fits my soul, whose features I recognize one by one as I draw near. The first houses with scaly tiles, the first vines flat against a wall made blue by sulphur dressings, the first clothes hung out in the courtyards, the disorder, the men's untidy, casual dress. And the first cypress (so slight and yet so straight), the first olive-tree, the dusty fig-tree. Shadow-filled squares of small Italian towns, midday hours when pigeons seek rest, slowness and sloth, in these the soul exhausts its rebellions. Passion travels gradually into tears. And then, here in Vicenza. Here the days revolve upon themselves, from the daybreak stuffed with cockcrows to this unequalled evening, sweetish and tender, silky behind the cypress-trees, its hours punctuated by the long measure of the crickets' cry. This inner silence which accompanies me is born of the slow stride which leads from one day to the next. What more can I long for than this room opening out on to the plain, with its antique furniture and its crocheted lace? I have the whole sky on my face, and feel that I could follow these slow, turning days for ever, spinning motionlessly with them. I breathe in the only happiness I can attain – an attentive and friendly awareness. I spend the whole day walking about: from the hill, I go down to Vicenza or else farther into the country. Every person I meet, every scent on this street is a pretext for my measureless love. Young women looking after a children's holiday camp, the trumpet of the ice-cream sellers (their cart is a gondola on wheels, pushed by two handles), the displays of fruit, red melons with black pips, translucent and sticky grapes – all are props for the person who can no longer be alone.[3] But the tender and bitter piping of the grasshoppers, the perfume of water and stars that you meet in the September nights, the scented paths among the lentisks and rose-bushes, all are signs of love for the person forced to be alone.[3] Thus the days pass. After the dazzling glare of the sun-filled days, evening comes, in the splendid décor offered by the gold of the setting sun and the black of the cypress-trees. I then walk along the road, towards the crickets that can be heard so far away. As I advance, they begin one by one to sing more softly, and then fall silent. I walk slowly forward, weighed down by so much ardent beauty. Behind me, one by one, the crickets swell their voices and sing: a mystery in this sky from which indifference and beauty now descend. And in a last gleam of light I can read on the fronting of a villa: 'In magnificentia naturae, resurgit spiritus.' This is where I must stop. Already the first star shines, then three lights gleam on the hill opposite, unharbingered the sudden night has fallen, a breeze murmurs in the bushes behind me, the day has fled, leaving me its gentleness.

I of course had not changed. It was simply that I was no longer alone. In Prague I could not breathe between the walls. Here I was face to face with the world, and, freed from myself, peopled the universe with forms in my own likeness. For I have not yet spoken of the sun. In the same way that I took a long time to realize my attachment and love for the world of poverty in which I spent my childhood, it is only now that I can see the lesson of the sun and of the countries which witnessed my birth. Shortly before midday I went out and walked towards a spot that I knew and which looked out over the immense plain of Vicenza. The sun had almost reached its zenith, the sky was of an intense and airy blue. All the light descending from it poured down the slope

3. That is to say everybody.

of the hills, clothing the cypresses and olive-trees, the white houses and the red roofs, in the warmest of robes, before vanishing in the plain which lay steaming in the sun. And each time I had the same feeling of being laid bare. In me there was the horizontal shadow of the little fat man. And what I could touch with my finger in these plains whirling with sunlight and dust, in these close-cropped hills all crusty with burnt grass, was a form, bared down from attractions to essentials, of that taste for nothingness which I carried within me. This country restored me to my heart of hearts and placed me face to face with my secret anguish. But it was and yet was not the anguish of Prague. How can I explain this? Certainly, looking at this Italian plain, peopled with trees, sun and smiles, I seized more firmly than elsewhere this odour of death and inhumanity which had been pursuing me for a month. Yes, this fullness without tears, this joyless peace which dwelt in me, consisted solely of a very clear awareness of what I did not like, of renunciation and lack of interest. In the same way as the man who is about to die, and knows it, takes no interest in what will happen to his wife, except in novels. He fulfils man's destiny, which is to be an egoist, that is to say someone who despairs. For me this country held no promise of immortality. What was the point in being alive again in my soul, without eyes to see Vicenza, without hands to touch the grapes of Vicenza, without flesh to feel the night's caress on the road between Monte Berico and the villa Valmarana?

Yes, all this was true. But, at the same time, the sun filled me with something that I cannot really express. At this extreme point of extreme awareness everything came together, and my life stood before me like a solid block to be accepted or rejected. I needed greatness. I found it in the confrontation between my deep despair and the secret indifference of one of the most beautiful landscapes in the world. I drew from it the strength to be at one and the same time both courageous and aware. So difficult and paradoxical a thing was enough for me. But I may perhaps have exaggerated something of what I then felt so sincerely. Besides, I often think about Prague and about the mortal days that I lived there. I have found my town again. Sometimes, however, the sour smell of cucumbers and vinegar returns to awake my anxiety. I then have to think of Vicenza. Both are dear to me, and I cannot separate my love for light and life from the secret attachment I bear for the experience of despair that I have tried to describe. It will be clear that I do not want to choose between them myself. In the suburbs of Algiers, there is a little cemetery with black iron gates. If you go to the far end, you look out over the valley with the bay in the distance. You can spend a long time dreaming as you gaze at this offering which sighs with the sea. But when you retrace your steps, you find a flagstone that bears the words 'Eternal regrets', above an abandoned grave. Fortunately there are idealists to set things right.

LOVE OF LIFE

AT night in Palma life ebbs slowly back towards the district where cafés provide music, behind the market. The streets are dark and silent until you reach the latticed doors and find light and music filtering through. I spent almost a whole night in one of these cafés. It was a small very low room, rectangular, painted green and hung with pink garlands. The wooden ceiling was covered with tiny red light bulbs. Miraculously fitted into this minute space were an orchestra, a bar with multi-coloured bottles, and the customers, squashed so tight that they could hardly breathe. Only men. In the middle, two square yards of free space. Glasses and bottles streamed from it as the waiter carried them to all four corners of the room. Not a single person here was conscious. They were all bellowing. A kind of naval officer was belching alcohol-laden compliments into my face. At my table an ageless dwarf was telling me his life-story. But I was too tense to listen to him. The orchestra kept on playing, but all you could gather of the tunes was the rhythm, beaten out by every foot in the place. Sometimes the door would open. In the midst of shouts a new arrival would be fitted in between two chairs.[4]

Suddenly the cymbals clashed, and a woman leaped swiftly into the minute circle in the middle of the cabaret. 'Twenty-one,' the officer told me. I was stupefied. The face of a young girl, but carved out of a mountain of flesh. She was perhaps six feet tall. With all her fat, she must have weighed three hundred pounds. Hands on hips, wearing a sweater of yellow net through whose meshes swelled a chessboard of white flesh, she was smiling; and each corner of her mouth sent a series of small waves of flesh right to her ear. The excitement in the room knew no bounds. You felt that this girl was known, loved, expected. She was still

---

4. There is a certain ease of enjoyment that defines true civilization. And the Spanish people is one of the few in Europe that is civilized.

smiling. She looked round at the customers and, still silent and smiling, wriggled her belly forward. The customers screamed, then demanded a song that everyone seemed to know. It was an Andalusian song, nasalized, and accompanied by a strong three-beat rhythm on the muffled drums. She sang, and at each drum beat mimed the act of love with her whole body. In this monotonous and passionate movement, real waves of flesh stemmed from her hips and moved upwards until they died away on her shoulders. The room was overwhelmed. But, with the refrain, the girl, pivoting round, seizing her breasts with both hands, opening her red, moist mouth, took up the tune, in chorus with the room, until everyone stood upright in the tumult.

As she stood in the centre, feet apart, sticky with sweat, hair hanging loose, she lifted up her immense torso, which burst out of its yellow sweater. Like an unclean goddess rising from the waves, forehead villainous low, hollow-eyed, she lived only by a slight quiver at the knee, like that of a horse after the race. In the midst of the foot-stamping joy around her she was like an ignoble and exalting image of life, with despair in her empty eyes and thick sweat on her belly ...

Without cafés and newspapers it would be difficult to travel. A paper printed in our language, a place where in the evenings we try to rub shoulders with other men, enable us to mime in familiar gestures the man we were at home, and who, seen from a distance, is so like a stranger. For what gives value to travel is fear. It breaks down a kind of inner décor in us. We can't cheat any more – hide ourselves away behind the hours in the office or at the plant (these hours against which we protest so strongly and which protect us so surely against the suffering of being alone). Thus I have always wanted to write novels in which my heroes would say: 'What would I do without my office hours?', or again: 'My wife has died, but fortunately I have all these parcels to get ready for tomorrow.' Travel takes this refuge from us. Far from our own people, our own language, wrenched away from all support, deprived of our masks (we don't know the fare on the tram and everything is like that), we are completely on the surface of ourselves. But also, because we feel our soul is sick,

Love of Life

we restore its miraculous value to every being and every object. A woman who dances without a thought in her head, a bottle on a table, glimpsed behind a curtain, each image becomes a symbol. The whole of life seems to be reflected in it, in so far as it sums up our own life at the time. When we are aware of every gift, the contradictory intoxications we can enjoy (including that of lucidity) are indescribable. And never perhaps has any country, except the Mediterranean, taken me so far from myself and yet so near.

This is doubtless the source of what I felt in this café at Palma. But at noon, on the other hand, what struck me in the empty district round the cathedral, among the old palaces with their cool courtyards, in the streets with their scented shadows, was the idea of a certain 'slowness'. No one in the streets. In the miradors motionless old women. And, walking along by the side of the houses, stopping in courtyards full of green plants and round, grey pillars, I melted into this smell of silence, I slipped my chains, became nothing more than the sound of my footsteps or this flight of birds whose shadow I could see on the still sunlit part of the walls. I would also spend long hours in the little Gothic cloister of San Francisco. Its delicate and precious colonnade was shining with this fine golden yellow colour found on old Spanish monuments. In the courtyard were rose-laurels, false pepper-plants, a wrought-iron well from which hung a long spoon of rusted metal. Passers-by drank from it. I sometimes still remember the clear sound it made as it dropped back on the stone of the well. Yet it was not the sweetness of life that this cloister taught me. In the sharp sound of their wingbeats as the pigeons flew away, the silence that suddenly came and crouched in the middle of the garden, in the lonely squeaking of the chain on its well, I rediscovered a new and yet familiar savour. I was lucid and smiling as I watched this unique play of appearances. And I felt that a single gesture was enough to splinter this crystal in which the world's face was smiling. Something would slacken, the flight of pigeons would die and each of them slowly fall, on its outstretched wings. Only my motionless silence lent plausibility to what looked so like an illusion. I joined in the game. I accepted appearances without being taken in by them. A fine, golden sun was gently warming the yellow stones of the cloister. A woman was drawing water from the well. In an hour, a minute, a second, now perhaps, everything could collapse. And yet this miracle continued. The world lived on, modest, ironic and discreet (like certain gentle and reserved forms taken by women's friendship). A balance continued, coloured however by all the apprehension of its own end.

There lay all my love of life: a silent passion for what would perhaps escape me, a bitterness beneath a flame. Each day I would leave this cloister like a man who has been lifted from himself, inscribed for a brief moment in the continuance of the world. And I know why I then thought of the expressionless eyes of the Doric Apollos or of the stiff and motionless characters in Giotto's painting.[5] For it was then that I really understood what countries like this could offer me. I am surprised that men can find certainties and rules for life on the shores of the Mediterranean, that they can satisfy their reason there and justify optimism and social responsibility. For what in fact struck me was not a world made to the measure of man, but one that closed in upon him. No, if the language of these countries harmonized with what sounded deeply within me, it was not because it answered my questions but because it made them superfluous. It was not prayers of thanksgiving that rose to my lips, but this *Nada* whose birth is possible only at the sight of landscapes crushed by the sun. There is no love of life without despair of life.

At Ibiza I went every day to sit in the cafés that are dotted around the port. Towards five in the evening, the local youths walk side by side up and down the length of the jetty. That is where marriages and the whole of life are arranged. One cannot help thinking that there is a certain greatness in thus beginning one's life with the world as witness. I would sit down, still dizzy from that day's sun, my head full of white churches and crumbling walls, of dry fields and hairy olive-trees. I would drink a

[5]. It is with the appearance of smiles, and expression in the eyes, that the decadence of Greek sculpture and the dispersion of Italian art begin. As if beauty ended where the mind begins.

Love of Life

sweetish syrup. I looked at the curve of the hills in front of me. They sloped gently down to the sea. The evening was turning green. On the largest of the hills the last breeze was turning the sails of a windmill. And, by a natural miracle, everyone lowered his voice. So there was nothing but the sky and the singing words rising towards it, as if heard from a great distance. In the brief moment of dusk there reigned something fleeting and melancholy which could be felt not only by one man but also by a whole people. As for me, I longed to love as people long to cry. I felt that every hour I slept would henceforth be an hour stolen from life ... that is to say, from the hours of undefined desire. I was tense and motionless, as I had been in those vibrant hours in the cabaret at Palma and the cloister at San Francisco, powerless against this great upsurge that sought to put the world between my hands.

I know that I am wrong, that we cannot give ourselves completely. Otherwise, we could not create. But there are no limits to loving, and what does it matter to me if I clasp things badly if I can embrace everything? There are women at Genoa whose smile I loved for a whole morning. I shall never see them again and, doubtless, nothing is simpler. But words will never quench the flame of my regret. By the little well in the cloister of San Francisco, I watched the pigeons flying past and forgot my thirst. But a moment always came when my thirst was reborn.

BETWIXT AND BETWEEN

SHE was a lonely and peculiar woman. She maintained a close relationship with the Spirits, identified herself with their quarrels, and refused to see certain members of her family who had a bad reputation in the world where she sought refuge.

One day she received a small legacy from her sister. These five thousand francs, coming at the end of her life, turned out to be something of an encumbrance. They had to be invested. If almost everyone is capable of using a large fortune, the difficulty comes when the sum is a small one. This woman remained faithful to herself. Close to death, she sought a shelter for her old bones. A real bargain came up. A lot had just fallen vacant in her town cemetery, and on this piece of land the owners had erected a magnificent, soberly designed, black-marble tomb, a genuine treasure in fact, which they were prepared to let her have for four thousand francs. She purchased this tomb. It was a safe investment, immune to fluctuations on the stock exchange and to political events. She had the inner grave prepared, and kept it in readiness to receive her own body. And, when everything was completed, she had her name carved on it in golden capitals.

This bargain satisfied her so completely that she was seized with a veritable love for her tomb. Initially, she went to see how the work was progressing. She ended up by paying herself a visit every Sunday afternoon. It was the only time she went out, and her only amusement. Towards two in the afternoon, she made the long trip that brought her to the city gates where the cemetery was situated. She would go into the little tomb, carefully close the door behind her, and kneel down on the *prie-dieu*. It was thus, set in her own presence, confronting what she was and what she would become, rediscovering the link of a constantly broken chain, that she effortlessly pierced the secret designs of Providence. A strange symbol even made her realize one day that she was dead in the eyes of the world. On All Saints' Day, arriving later than usual, she found the doorstep of her tomb piously strewn with violets. Some unknown and tender-hearted passers-by, seeing this tomb devoid of flowers, had had the kind thought of sharing their own, and had honoured the memory of this neglected corpse.

And now I think about these things again. I can see only the walls of the garden which lies on the other side of my window. And these few branches flowing with light. Higher still the foliage and higher still the sun. But all that I can perceive of the air rejoicing outside, of all this joy spread out over the world, are the shadows of branches playing on my white curtains. Also five rays of sunlight patiently pouring into the room the scent of dried grass. A breeze, and the shadows on the curtains come to life. If a cloud passes over the sun, the bright yellow of this vase of mimosas leaps from the shadow. It is enough: one light coming to birth, and I am filled with a confused and whirling joy. It is a January afternoon which thus places me in presence of the wrong side of the world. But the cold stays in the depths of the air. Everywhere a film of sunlight that would crack beneath your finger, but which clothes everything in an eternal smile. Who am I and what can I do but enter into the play of foliage and of light? Be this ray of sunlight in which my cigarette burns away, this softness and discreet passion breathing in the air. If I try to reach myself, it is in the very depths of this light. And if I try to understand and savour this delicate taste which reveals the secret of the world, it is myself that I find at the depth of the universe. Myself, that is to say this extreme emotion which frees me from my surroundings.

In a moment other things, other men and the graves they purchase. But let me cut out this minute from the cloth of time. Others leave a flower between pages, and enclose in them a walk where love has touched them with its wing. I also walk but am caressed by a god. Life is short, and it is a sin to waste one's time. They say that I am active. But being active is still wasting one's time, if in doing so one loses oneself. Today is a resting place, and my heart goes off in search of itself. If an anguish still clutches me, it is when I feel this impalpable moment slipping through my fingers like quicksilver. Then let those who wish turn their backs upon the world. I do not feel sorry for myself since I can see myself coming to birth. At this moment my whole kingdom is of this world. This sun and these shadows, this warmth and this cold rising from the depths of the air: why wonder at death and human suffering since everything is written on this window where the sun pours down its fullness as a greeting to my pity? I can say and in a moment I shall say that what counts is to be human and simple. No, what counts is to be true, and then everything fits in, humanity and simplicity. And when then am I truer than when I am the world? My cup brims over before I desire. Eternity is there and I was hoping for it. What I now wish for is no longer happiness but simply awareness.

One man contemplates and another digs his grave: how can we separate them? Men and their absurdity? But here is the smile of the heavens. The light swells and soon summer will be here. But here are the eyes and the voice of those whom I must love. I hold to the world through all my gestures, to men through all my gratitude and pity. I do not want to choose between these two sides of the world, and I do not like a choice to be made. People don't like you to be lucid and ironic. They say: 'That shows that you are not nice.' I can't see that this follows. Certainly, if I hear a man saying that he is an immoralist, I translate this by saying that he needs to give himself an ethic; if I hear another saying that he despises intelligence, I realize that he cannot bear his doubts. But because I don't like people to cheat. Great courage still consists of gazing steadfastly at the light as on death. Besides, how can I define the thread which leads from this all-consuming love of life to this secret despair? If I listen to the voice of irony,[6] crouching underneath things, it slowly shows itself. Winking its small, clear eye: 'Live as if ...' Even though I've searched hard, that is all I know.

After all, I am not sure that I am right. But that is not what is important if I think of that woman whose story I heard. She was

6. That 'guarantee of freedom' spoken of by Barrès.

going to die, and her daughter dressed her for her tomb while she was alive. It would in fact appear that it is easier to do this when the limbs are not stiff. But it's odd, all the same, how everyone around us is in a hurry.

2
NUPTIALS
1939

Note to the 1950 edition

These essays were originally written in 1936 and 1937, and a small number of copies of them published in Algiers in 1938. This new edition reproduces them without any changes, in spite of the fact that their author has not ceased to consider them as essays, in the precise and limited meaning of the term. [There is a further note on p. 297 : ed.]

'The hangman strangled Cardinal Carrafa with a silken rope which broke: two further attempts were necessary. The Cardinal looked at the hangman without deigning to utter a word.'

Stendhal, *La Duchesse de Palliano*

NUPTIALS AT TIPASA

In spring Tipasa is inhabited by gods and the gods speak in the sun and the scent of absinthe leaves, the silver-armoured sea, the blue glare of the sky, the flower-covered ruins and the light in great bubbles among the heaps of stone. At certain hours of the day the countryside is black with sunlight. The eyes try in vain to glimpse anything but drops of light and colours trembling on the lashes. The voluminous scent of aromatic plants tears at your throat and suffocates you in the vast heat. Far off I can just make out the black bulk of the Chenoua, rooted in the hills around the village, and moving with a slow and heavy rhythm until it finally squats down in the sea.

The village that we pass through on our way there already opens out on to the sea. We enter a blue and yellow world where we are greeted by the odorous sigh of the Algerian summer earth. Everywhere pinkish bougainvillaeas hang over the villa walls; in the garden the hibiscus plants are still pale red, the tea roses foam as thick as cream, and long, blue irises stand in delicate flower-beds. All the stones are warm. As we step off the buttercup-yellow bus, the butchers in their little red vans are making their morning rounds and calling to the villagers with their trumpets.

To the left of the port a stairway of dry stones leads to the ruins, through the mastic-trees and broom. The path goes in front of the small lighthouse before plunging into the open country. At the foot of this lighthouse large red and yellow cactus plants already go down towards the first rocks sucked at by the kissing sound of the sea. As we stand in the slight breeze, with the sun warming one side of our faces, we watch the light coming down from the sky, the smooth sea smiling with its glittering teeth. Before entering the ruins' kingdom we stand for the last time as mere spectators.

After a few steps the smell of absinthe seizes you by the throat.

Their grey wool covers the ruins as far as the eye can see. Their oil ferments in the heat, and the whole earth gives off a heady alcohol which makes the sky quiver. We stride to the meeting-place of love and desire. We are not seeking lessons or the bitter philosophy required from greatness. Nothing matters here but the sun, kisses and the wild scents of the earth. I myself do not seek to be alone there. I have often been there with those I loved and read on their features the clear smile taken by the face of love. Here I leave others to concern themselves with order and with moderation. The great free love of nature and the sea absorbs me completely. In this marriage between ruins and springtime the ruins have become stones again, and, losing the polish imposed on them by men, have gone back to nature. Nature has celebrated the return of these prodigal daughters by laying out a profusion of flowers. The heliotrope pushes its red and white head between the flagstones of the forum, and red geraniums spill their blood over what were houses, temples and public squares. Like those men whom much knowledge brings back to God, many years have brought these ruins back to their mother's house. Today their past has finally left them, and nothing distracts them from that deep force which draws them back to the centre of the things which fall.

How many hours spent crushing absinthe leaves, caressing ruins, trying to match my breathing to the tumultuous sighs of the world! Deep among wild scents and concerts of somnolent insects, I open my eyes and heart to the unbearable grandeur of this heat-soaked sky. It is not so easy to become what we are, to rediscover our deepest measure. But as I watched the solid backbone of the Chenoua, my heart grew calm with a strange certainty. I was learning to breathe, I was fitting into the mould and fulfilling myself. Each of the hills, as I climbed them one by one, kept me a reward, like that temple whose columns measure the course of the sun and which has a view over the whole village with its white and pink walls and green verandas. As also had this basilisk on the East hill, which has kept its walls and is surrounded by a great circle of uncovered ornamented coffins, most of them scarcely emerging from the earth whose nature they still share. They used to contain corpses; now, sage and wallflowers grow in them. The Sainte-Salsa basilica is Christian, but each time we look out through a gap in the walls we are greeted by the song of the world: hillsides planted with pine and cypress-trees, or the sea rolling its white horses twenty yards away. The hill on which Sainte-Salsa is built has a flat top and the wind blows more strongly through the portals. Under the morning sun a great happiness hovers in space.

Those who need myths are indeed poor. Here the gods serve as beds or resting places as the day races across the sky. I describe and say: 'This is red, this blue, this green. This is the sea, the mountain, the flowers.' And what need have I to speak of Dionysus to say that I love to crush mastic bowls under my nose? Is the old hymn, which will later come to me quite spontaneously, even addressed to Demeter: 'Happy is he alive who has seen these things on earth'? How can we forget the lesson of seeing, and of seeing on this earth? All one had to do at the mysteries of Eleusis was watch. Yet even here I know that I shall never come close enough to the world. I must be naked and dive into the sea, still scented with the perfumes of the earth, wash these off in the sea, and consummate on my flesh the embrace for which sun and sea, lips to lips, have so long been sighing. I feel the shock of the water, rise up through a thick cold glue, then dive back with my ears ringing, my nose streaming and the taste of salt in my mouth. As I swim, my water-varnished arms flash out to turn gold in the sunlight, and then plunge back with a twist of all my muscles; the water streams along my whole body as my legs take tumultuous possession of the waves – and the horizon disappears. On the beach I flop down on the sand, yield to the world, my flesh and bones heavy again. Besotted with sunlight, I occasionally glance at my arms where the water slides off and patches of salt and soft blond hair appear on my skin.

Here I understand what is called glory: the right to love without restraint. There is only one love in this world. Embracing a woman's body also means holding in your arms this strange joy which descends from sky to sea. In a moment, when I throw myself down among the absinthe plants to bring their scent into my body, I shall know, whatever prejudice may say, that I am fulfilling a truth which is that of the sun and which will also be that of my death. In a sense, it is indeed my life that I am playing out here, a life which tastes of warm stone, is full of the sighs of the sea and the rising song of the crickets. The breeze is cool and the sky blue. I love life with abandon and wish to speak of it with freedom: it makes me proud of my human condition. Yet people have often told me: there's nothing to be proud of. Yes, there is: this sun, this sea, my heart leaping with youth, the salt taste of my body, and the vast landscape where tenderness and glory merge in blue and yellow. It is this conquest that requires my strength and my resources. Everything here leaves me intact, I give up nothing of myself, I put on no mask: it is enough for me patiently to acquire the difficult knowledge of how to live which is worth all their arts of living.

Shortly before midday, we would come back through the ruins towards a little café by the side of the port. How cool was the welcome of the tall glass of iced green mint as I entered the well-shadowed room, my head ringing with colours and with the cymbals of the sun! Outside lie the sea and the road burning with dust. Sitting at the table I try to blink my eyelids so as to catch the multi-coloured dazzle of the white-hot sky. Our faces damp with sweat, but our bodies cool in our light garments, we all stretch out the happy weariness of a day of nuptials with the world.

The food is poor in this café, but there is plenty of fruit — peaches especially, whose juice drips down your chin as you bite into them. With my teeth closing inside the peach I gaze avidly before me as I listen to the blood pounding in my ears. Over the sea hangs the vast silence of noon. Every beautiful thing has a natural pride in its own beauty, and today the world allows its pride to seep from every pore. Why, in its presence, should I deny the joy of living, if I can avoid enclosing everything in this joy? There is no shame in being happy. But today the fool is king, and I call fools those who fear pleasure. We have heard so much about pride: you know, it's the sin of Lucifer. Beware, they cried, you will lose your soul, and your vital force. I have in fact

Nuptials at Tipasa

learnt since then that a certain pride. ... But at other times I cannot prevent myself from claiming the pride of life which the whole world conspires to give me. At Tipasa 'I see' equals 'I believe', and I am not stubborn enough to deny what my hands can touch and my lips caress. What I feel is not the need to make it into a work of art, but to describe, which is different. Tipasa appears to me like one of those characters whom one describes in order to give indirect expression to a general attitude. Like them, it bears witness, and in a virile fashion. It is the character I am describing today, and it seems to me that by dint of caressing and describing it my delight will have no end. There is a time for living and a time for bearing witness to life. There is also a time for creating, which is less natural. It is enough for me to live with my whole body and bear witness with my whole heart. Live Tipasa, bear witness, and the work of art will come later. There lies a freedom.

*

I would never stay more than one day at Tipasa. A moment always comes when we have looked too long at a landscape, in the same way as it is a long time before we have looked at it enough. Mountains, the sky, the sea are like faces whose barrenness or splendour we discover by looking rather than seeing. But if it is to speak to us, every face should come to be seen afresh. And, when we complain of growing tired too quickly, we should rather be filled with admiration that the world should appear new simply because we have forgotten it.

Towards evening I would go to a more formal section of the park, set out as a garden, just off the main road. As I left the tumult of scents and sunlight, in the now cool evening air, my mind grew calm and my relaxed body enjoyed the inner silence stemming from love satisfied. I sat on a bench watching the countryside fill out with light. I was replete. Above me a pomegranate tree drooped down its flower buds, closed and ribbed like tight fists containing every hope of spring. Rosemary was growing behind me, and all I could smell was the scent of alcohol. The hills were framed about with trees, and beyond them stretched a band of sea on which the sky, like a sail becalmed, lay resting with all its tenderness. In my heart was a strange joy, the very joy which stems from a clear conscience. There is a feeling familiar to actors when they know that they have played their part well, that is to say when they have, literally, made their gestures coincide with those of the ideal character they embody, entering a ready-made pattern and bringing it to life with their own heartbeats. That was exactly what I felt: I had played my part well. I had performed my task as a man, and the fact that I had known joy all one livelong day seemed to me not an exceptional success but the intense fulfilment of a condition which, in certain circumstances, makes it our duty to be happy. We are then alone again, but this time in satisfaction.

*

The trees had now become peopled with birds. The earth gave a slow sigh before sliding into darkness. In a moment, with the first star, night will fall on the theatre of the world. The dazzling gods of day will return to their daily death. But other gods will come. And, although they will be darker, their ravaged faces will nonetheless have been born deep in the earth.

But, for the moment, the unending bursting of the waves on the shore was reaching me across a whole space dancing with golden pollen. Sea, landscape, silence, scents of this earth, I drank my fill of a scent-laden life and bit into the already golden fruit of the world, overwhelmed by the feeling of its strong sweet juice flowing along my lips. No, it was neither I nor the world that counted, but solely the harmony and silence that gave birth to the love between us. A love that I was not weak enough to claim for myself alone, proudly aware that I shared it with a whole race born of the sun and sea, alive and full of character, which draws its greatness from its simplicity, and standing on the beaches smiles in complicity to the glittering smile of its heavens.

THE WIND AT DJEMILA

THERE are places where the mind dies so that a truth which is its very denial may be born. When I went to Djemila, there was wind and sun, but that is another story. What must be said first of all is that there reigned a heavy unbroken silence – something like a perfectly balanced pair of scales. The cry of birds, the soft sound of a three-hole flute, goats trampling, murmurs from the sky, these sounds made up the silence and desolation of these places. Now and then a sharp clap, a piercing cry, marked the upward flight of a bird huddled among the rocks. Wherever you walk, along the paths through the ruined houses, along wide paved roads under shining colonnades, along the vast forum between the triumphal arch and the temple set upon a hill, you always end up at the ravines which surround Djemila on every side, like a pack of cards opened out under a limitless sky. And you stand there, absorbed, face to face with stones and silence, as the day moves on and the mountains grow purple and surge upwards. But the wind blows across the plateau of Djemila. This great confusion of wind and sunlight, that mixes light with the ruins, forges something which gives man the measure of his identity with the solitude and silence of this dead city.

It takes a long time to go to Djemila. It is not a town where you stop and then move farther on. It leads nowhere and is a gateway to no other country. It is a place from which the traveller returns. The dead city lies at the end of a long, winding road where every turning seems the last and thus appears all that much longer. When, yellowish as a forest of bones, its skeleton at last looms up against the faded colours of the plateau, Djemila then symbolizes that lesson of love and patience which alone can lead us to the beating heart of the world. There, among a few trees and some dried grass, it uses all its mountains and all its stones to protect itself against vulgar admiration, quaintness or the delusions of hope.

We had wandered the whole day among this arid splendour. Then the wind, which we had scarcely felt at the beginning of the afternoon, seemed to grow little by little as the hours went by and fill the whole countryside. It blew from a gap in the mountains, far away towards the East, rushing from beyond the horizon, leaping and cascading among the stones and sunlight. It whistled with endless power among the ruins, whirled round inside an amphitheatre of stones and earth, bathed the heaps of pockmarked blocks of stone, clasped each column with its breath and shed itself in endless cries on the forum which lay open to the heavens. I felt myself whipping in the wind like a mast. Hollowed out at the waist, with burning eyes and cracking lips, my flesh dried out until it no longer belonged to me. Beforehand it had been by my flesh that I deciphered the handwriting of the world. On it the world had inscribed the signs of its tenderness or anger, warming it with its summer breath or biting it with its frosty teeth. But the wind had rubbed against me for so long, shaking me for more than an hour, stunning me with its resistance, that I lost consciousness of the pattern traced by my body. Like the pebble polished by the tides, I was polished by the wind, worn through to my very soul. I grew from being a little of that great force on which I drifted, until I gradually became the force itself, mingling the throbbing of my own heart with the great sonorous heartbeats of this omnipresent heart of nature. The wind was fashioning me in the likeness of the burning nakedness around me. And its fleeting embrace gave me, stone among stones, the solitude of a column or an olive-tree in the summer sky.

This violent bath of sun and wind drained me of all my vital force. I scarcely felt that quiver of wings inside me, the complaint of life, the weak rebellion of the mind. Soon, scattered to the four corners of the earth, self-forgetful and self-forgotten, I become one with this wind and live within it, am one with these columns and that archway, one with these flagstones warm to the touch, one with these pale mountains around the deserted city. And never

The Wind at Djemila

have I been at one and the same time so detached from myself and so present in the world.

Yes, I am present. And what strikes me at this moment is that I can go no farther. Like a man sentenced to life imprisonment, to whom everything is present. But also like a man who knows that tomorrow will be the same, and every other day. For when a man becomes conscious of what he is now, it means that he expects nothing further. If there are landscapes which are like moods, they are the most vulgar. For what I was following through this country was something that belonged not to me but to it, like a taste for death common to us both. Between the columns with their now lengthening shadows, anxieties melted into the air like wounded birds. And, in their place, came an arid lucidity. Anxiety is born from the heart of the living. But calm will cover over this living heart: that is all I can see clearly. As the day moved forward, as the noises and lights were muffled by the ashes falling from the sky, deserted by myself, I felt defenceless against the slow forces in my own being that were saying no.

Few people realize that there is a refusal which has nothing to do with renunciation. What meaning do words like future, improvement, good job, mean here? What is meant by the heart's progress? If I obstinately refuse all the 'later ons' of this world, it is because I have no desire to give up my present wealth. I do not want to believe that death is a gateway to another life. For me, it is a closed door. I do not say that it is a step that we must all take: but that it is a horrible and dirty adventure. Everything people suggest seeks to deliver man from the weight of his own life. But as I watch the great birds flying heavily through the sky at Djemila, it is precisely a certain weight of life that I ask for and obtain. When I am at one with this passive passion the rest ceases to concern me. I have too much youth in me to be able to speak of death. But it seems to me that, if I were to speak of it, it is here that I should find the precise word that would express, between horror and silence, the conscious certainty of a death without hope.

We live with a few familiar ideas. Two or three. With the worlds and the men we happen to meet, we polish and transform them. We need ten years to have an idea that really belongs to us – that we can talk about. Naturally, it is a little discouraging. But through it man gains a certain familiarity with the beautiful visage of the world. Until then, he has seen it face to face. Now he needs to step to one side to see its profile. A young man looks at the world face to face. He has not had time to polish the idea of death or of nothingness, though he has chewed over their full horror. That is what youth must be like, this harsh confrontation with death, this physical terror of the animal that loves the sun. Whatever people may say, youth has no illusions on this score, at any rate. It has had neither the time nor the piety to build itself any. And, I don't know why, but faced by this ravined landscape, by this solemn and lugubrious cry of stone, by Djemila inhuman at nightfall, by this death of colours and of hope, I was certain that when they reach the end of their lives, men worthy of the name must rediscover this confrontation, deny the few ideas which they had, and recover the innocence and truth which shine in the eyes of Greeks and Romans in face of their destiny. They regain their youth, but by embracing death. There is nothing more despicable in this respect than illness. It is a remedy against death. It prepares us for it. It creates an apprenticeship whose first stage is self-pity. It supports man in his great effort to avoid the certainty that he will die completely. But Djemila ... and I then feel certain that the true, the only progress of civilization, the one to which a man devotes himself from time to time, lies in creating conscious deaths.

What always amazes me, when we are so swift to elaborate on other subjects, is the poverty of our ideas on death. It is a good thing or a bad thing, I fear it or I summon it (they say). But also this proves that everything that is simple goes beyond us. What is blue, and how can we think 'blue'? The same difficulty arises for death. Death and colours are things that we cannot discuss. And, nevertheless, the important thing is this man before me, heavy as earth, who prefigures my future. But can I really think about it? I say to myself: I am going to die, but this means nothing since I cannot manage to believe it and can experience only other people's death. I have seen people die. Above all, I have

The Wind at Djemila

seen dogs die. It was touching them that overwhelmed me. I then think of flowers, smiles, desire for women, and realize that my whole horror of death lies in my fervour to live. I am jealous of those who will live and for whom flowers and the desire for women will have their full flesh-and-blood meaning. I am envious because I love life too much not to be selfish. What does eternity matter to me? You can lie in bed one day and hear someone tell you: 'You are strong and I owe it to you to be sincere: I can tell you that you are going to die'; lie there, with the whole of your life clasped in your hands, all your fear in your bowels and a look of stupidity in your eyes. What does the rest matter? Waves of blood come throbbing to my temples and I feel I could crush everything around me.

But men die in spite of themselves, in spite of their surroundings. They are told: 'When you are cured ...', and they die. I want none of that. For if there are days when nature lies, there are others when she tells the truth. Djemila is telling the truth this evening, and with what sad and insistent beauty! In the presence of this world I have no desire to lie or for other people to lie to me. I want to keep my lucidity to the last, and gaze upon my death with all the fullness of my jealousy and horror. It is when I cut myself off from the world that I fear death most, attaching myself to the fate of living men instead of contemplating the unchanging sky. Creating conscious deaths means lessening the distance which separates us from the world, and entering joylessly into fulfilment, alert to the exalting images which belong to a world for ever lost. And the sad song of the Djemila hills plunges the bitterness of this lesson deeper into my soul.

*

Towards evening we were climbing the slopes leading to the village and, retracing our steps, listening to our guide: 'Here is the pagan town; this area outside the field is where the Christians lived. Later on ...' Yes, it is true. Men and societies have succeeded one another in this place; conquerors have marked this country with their non-commissioned officer's civilization. They entertained a vulgar and ridiculous idea of greatness, and mea-

80 *Nuptials*

sured that of their empire by the surface which it covered. The miracle is that the ruins of their civilization should constitute the very negation of their ideal. For this skeleton town, seen from such a height, as evening fell and white pigeons flew around the triumphal arch, engraved no signs of conquest or ambition on the sky. In the end, the world always conquers history. I well know the poetry of the great cry of stone which Djemila utters among the mountains, the heavens and the silence: lucidity, indifference, the true signs of beauty or despair. Our heart tightens as we behold this greatness which we must already leave. Djemila stays behind us with the sad water of its sky, the song of a bird from the other side of the plateau, the sudden, quick scurrying of goats along the mountainside, and, in the calmed and sonorous dusk, the living face of a horned god on the frontal of an altar.

SUMMER IN ALGIERS
to Jacques Heurgon

THE love affairs we have with towns are often secret ones. Cities like Paris, Prague and even Florence are closed in upon themselves and thus restrict the world peculiar to them. But Algiers, like other privileged places such as coastal towns, lies open to the sky like a mouth or like a wound. What you can love in Algiers is what everybody lives off: the sea visible from every corner, a certain weight of sunlight, the beauty of the race. And, as always, this generosity and lack of modesty also hold a more secret flavour. In Paris you can feel nostalgic for space and for the beating of wings. Here, at least, man has everything he needs and, thus assured of his desires, can measure up his wealth.

You doubtless need to spend a long time in Algiers to understand how desiccating an excess of nature's blessings can be. There is nothing here for people seeking knowledge, education or self-improvement. This land contains no lessons. It neither promises nor reveals. It is content to give, but does so profusely. Everything here is revealed to the naked eye, and is known the very moment it is enjoyed. Its pleasures have no remedies and its joys remain without hope. What it demands are clear-sighted souls, that is to say those without consolation. It asks us to make an act of lucidity as we make an act of faith. Strange country, which gives the men it nourishes both their wretchedness and their greatness! It is not surprising that the sensual wealth heaped on the man of feeling in this country should coincide with the most extreme deprivation. There is no truth that does not carry its bitterness within itself. Why then should it be surprising if I never love the face of this country more than in the midst of its poorest inhabitants?

Throughout their youth men find here a life which matches

their beauty. Then, afterwards, come decline and forgetfulness. They have wagered on the flesh, but they knew that they would lose. In Algiers everything is a refuge and an occasion for triumphs for those who are young and alive: the bay, the sun, the games marked out in red and white on the terraces over towards the sea, the flowers and stadia, the cool-legged girls. But for the man who has lost his youth there is nothing to hang on to, and no place where melancholy can escape from itself. Elsewhere, the terraces in Italy, the cloisters of Europe or the shape of the hills in Provence, are all places where man can flee from his humanity and gently be saved from himself. But everything here demands solitude and young men's blood. Goethe on his deathbed called for light and this is a historic remark. In Belcourt and Bab-el-Oued the old men sitting at the back of cafés listen to young men with brilliantined hair boasting of their exploits.

It is the summer which grants us these beginnings and ends in Algiers. During these months the town is deserted. But the poor and the sky are always with us. With the first we go down together towards the port and its human treasures: the gentle warmth of the water and the brown bodies of the women. In the evening, crammed with these riches, they go back to the oilskin cloth and oil-lamp that are the only background that they know.

*

In Algiers you don't say 'to go swimming' but 'to dive in for a swim'. I won't insist. People bathe in the port and rest on the buoys. When you go close to a buoy on which a pretty girl is already sitting, you shout to your friends: 'I tell you it's a sea-gull.' These are healthy pleasures. They obviously constitute the ideal for these young men, since most of them continue to live like this during the winter, and each day at noon strip themselves bare in the sun for a frugal lunch. Not that they have read the boring sermons of our nudists, those protestants of the body (there is a way of systematizing the body which is as infuriating as systems for the soul). But they 'like being in the sun'. We shall never give enough importance to what this custom represents for our time. For the first time in two thousand years, the body has

Summer in Algiers

been shown naked on the beaches. For twenty centuries, men have tried to impose decency on the insolence and simplicity of the Greeks, to play down the flesh and complicate our clothes. Today, reaching back over this history, the young men sprinting on the Mediterranean beaches rediscover the magnificent gestures of the athletes of Delos. And by thus living close to the body, and living by the body, we learn that it has its own nuances, its life, and, to venture an absurdity, its own psychology.[1] The evolution of the body, like that of the mind, has its history, its reversals, its gains and its losses. With only this nuance: colour. When you go to swim in the port during summer, you notice that everybody's skin is changing at the same time from white to gold, then to brown, and, finally, to a tobacco colour which represents the final stage which the body can manage in this quest for transformation. The Kasbah's pattern of white cubes dominates the whole port. When you are at water level, people's bodies form a bronzed frieze against the glaring white background of the Arab town. And, as you move into the month of August and the sun grows stronger, the white of the houses becomes more blinding and skins take on a darker glow. How then can you fail to identify yourself with this dialogue between stone and flesh which keeps pace with the seasons and the sun? You spend the whole morning diving in the sea, with garlands of laughter among spouts of water, in long paddling trips around red and black cargo vessels (the ones from Norway smell of all kinds of wood, the ones from Germany reek of oil, the ones going from port to port along the coast smell of wine and old casks). When the sun is brimming over from every corner of the sky, the orange-coloured canoe

---

1. May I be so foolish as to say that I do not like the way Gide exalts the body? He asks it to hold back his desire in order to make it more intense. He thus brings himself close to those who, in the slang of brothels, are termed weirdies or kinkies. Christianity also seeks to suspend desire. But, more naturally, sees this a mortification. My friend Vincent, who is a cooper and junior breast-stroke champion, has an even clearer view of things. He drinks when he is thirsty, if he wants a woman tries to sleep with her, and would marry her if he loved her (this hasn't happened yet). Then he always says: 'That's better' – an energetic summary of the apology one could write for satiety.

laden with sunburnt bodies brings us back in a mad race. And when, in a sudden pause in the rhythmic stroke of the fruit-coloured blades of the double paddle, we glide smoothly into the harbour, how can I help but know that I am carrying across the smooth waters a tawny cargo of gods in whom I recognize my brothers?

But, at the other end of the town, the summer already offers us the contrast of its other wealth: I mean its silences and boredom. These silences do not always have the same quality, according to whether they are born of shadow or of sun. There is the silence of noon on Government Square. In the shade of the trees that grow each side Arabs sell penny glasses of iced lemonade, perfumed with orange blossom. Their cry of 'cool, cool' echoes across the empty square. When it fades away, silence falls again under the sun: in the merchant's pitcher, the ice moves and I can hear it tinkling. There reigns the silence of the siesta. In the streets round the docks, in front of the squalid barbers' shops, you can measure the silence by the melodious buzzing of the flies behind the hollow reed curtains. Elsewhere, in the Moorish cafés in the Kasbah, it is men's bodies which are silent, which cannot drag themselves away, leave the glass of tea, and rediscover time through the pounding of their own pulse. But there is, above all, the silence of the summer evenings.

These brief moments when day swings over into night must swarm with signs and secret calls for Algiers to be linked so closely to them in my heart. When I have been away from this country for some time, I imagine its dusks as promises of happiness. On the hills looking down over the town there are paths among the mastic-trees and olive-trees. And it is towards them that my heart then turns. I can see sheaves of black birds rising up against the green horizon. In the sky, suddenly emptied of its sun, something releases its hold. A whole flock of red clouds stretches up until it melts into the air. Almost immediately afterwards, there appears the first star that has been forming and growing harder in the thickness of the heavens. And then, sudden and all-consuming, night. What is so unique in these fleeting evenings of Algiers that it releases so many things in me? They leave a sweetness on my lips, but before I have time to weary of it, it has already vanished into darkness. Is this the secret of its persistence? The tenderness of this country is furtive and overwhelming. But once we feel it, then our heart at least surrenders. On the Padovani beach the dance-hall is open every day. And in this immense rectangular box which stands open to the sea all along one side, the penniless youth of the district come to dance until evening. Often I would wait there for one particular moment. In the daytime the dance-hall is protected by a sloping wooden roof. When the sun has gone in, this is removed. The hall is then filled with a strange green light, born of the double shell of the sky and sea. When you sit a long way from the windows, you can see only the sky, and, like puppets in a shadow-theatre, the faces of the dancers floating past one after another. Sometimes the musicians play a waltz and the dark profiles then revolve like cut-out figures placed on a record player. Night comes quickly then, and, with it, the lights. But I shall never be able to describe the secret enchantment of this subtle moment. What I do remember is a magnificent, tall girl who had danced all one afternoon. She was wearing a jasmine necklace on her close-fitting blue dress, which was damp with sweat right down the back. She was laughing and throwing back her head as she danced. When she passed in front of the tables, she left behind her a mingled scent of flowers and flesh. When evening came, I could no longer see her body pressed against her partner, but the white of her jasmine and the black of her hair were revolving one after the other against the sky, and when she threw back her full throat I could hear her laugh and see her partner's silhouette lean suddenly forward. It is to evenings such as these that I owe my idea of innocence. And I am learning not to separate these beings charged with violence from the sky in which their desires revolve.

*

In the local cinemas in Algiers there are often mint pastilles on sale with red letters engraved on them expressing everything needed for the birth of love : (1) questions : 'When will you marry me?'; 'Do you love me?'; (2) replies : 'Madly'; 'Next spring'. After having prepared the ground, you pass them to your neighbour who replies in the same vein or simply plays the fool. In Belcourt there have been marriages arranged like this and whole lives decided by an exchange of mint-flavoured sweets. And this gives a good picture of the childlike people of this country.

The hallmark of youth is perhaps a magnificent vocation for easy pleasures. But, above all, it lies in a haste to live that borders on extravagance. In Belcourt, as in Bab-el-Oued, people marry young. They start work very early, and exhaust the range of human experience in ten years. A workman of thirty has already played all his cards. He waits for the end with his wife and children around him. His delights have been swift and merciless. So has his life. And you then understand why he should be a child of this country where everything is given to be taken away. In this abundance and profusion life follows the curve of the great passions, sudden, demanding, generous. It is not to be built up but to be burned away. Reflection or self-improvement are quite irrelevant. The notion of hell, for example, is here nothing more than an amusing joke. Only the very virtuous are allowed such fancies. And I believe that virtue is a meaningless word throughout the whole of Algeria. Not that these men lack principles. They have their code of morality, which is very well defined. You 'don't let your mother down'. You see to it that your wife is respected in the street. You show consideration to pregnant women. You don't attack an enemy two to one, because 'that's dirty'. If anyone fails to observe these elementary rules, 'He's not a man' and that's all there is to it. This seems to me just and strong. There are still many of us who observe the highway code, the only disinterested one I know. But at the same time the shopkeeper's ethic is unknown. I have always seen the faces around me take on an expression of pity when a man goes by between two policemen. And, before finding out whether the man was a thief, a parricide, or simply an eccentric, people said: 'Poor fellow', or again, with a touch of admiration: 'He's a pirate.'

There are peoples born for pride and for life. It is they who nourish the most singular vocation for boredom. It is also they who look upon death with most repulsion. Apart from sensual delights, the Algerians' amusements are idiotic. For years now the entertainment of the over-thirty age group has been fully catered for by a bowling club, by friendly society dinners, cheap cinemas and communal celebrations. Sundays in Algiers are of the gloomiest. How could this mindless people disguise the deep horror of its life with myths? In Algiers everything associated with death is either ridiculous or detestable. These people have neither religion nor idols and die alone after having lived in a crowd. I know nowhere more hideous than the cemetery of the Boulevard Bru, which stands facing one of the most beautiful landscapes in the world. A fearful sadness rises from the black setting where, in aesthetic horror piled on aesthetic horror, death reveals its true face. 'Everything fades away', say the heart-shaped ex-votos, 'except memory.' And they all insist upon that ridiculous eternity which the heart of those who loved us provides at so low a cost. The same phrases serve all forms of despair. They address the deceased in the second person singular: 'Our memory will never abandon thee' – a gloomy pretence by means of which one lends a body and desires to what is at best a black liquid. Elsewhere, in the midst of a stupefying display of flowers and marble birds, you find this reckless vow: 'Never shall thy grave lack flowers.' But you are quickly reassured: the words are carved around a gilded stucco bouquet, a great time-saver for the living (like those flowers termed everlasting which owe their pompous name to the gratitude of those who still jump on moving buses). Since one must move with the times, the classical warbler is sometimes replaced by a breath-taking pearl aeroplane, piloted by a simpering angel who, in defiance of all logic, has been provided with a magnificent pair of wings.

Yet how can one explain that these images of death never cut themselves off from life? Here, values are closely linked together. The favourite joke of the Algerian undertakers, when they have no one in the hearse, is to shout: 'Like a ride, honey?' to the pretty girls they meet on the way. This may well have symbolic, if somewhat tasteless, implications. It can also seem blasphemous to acknowledge the news of someone's death by winking your left eye and saying: 'Poor chap, he won't sing any more.' Or, like that woman from Oran who had never loved her husband: 'God gave him to me, God has taken him away.' But when all is said and done, I don't see what is sacred about death, and I am, on the contrary, very aware of the difference between fear and respect. Everything here breathes the horror of dying in a country which is an invitation to life. And yet it is under the very walls of this cemetery that the young men of Belcourt arrange their meetings, and the girls let themselves be kissed and fondled.

I fully realize that such a people cannot be accepted by everyone. Here, intelligence occupies nothing like the place it does in Italy. This race is uninterested in the mind. It worships and admires the body. From this it derives its strength, its naïve cynicism,[2] and a puerile vanity that leads it to be severely criticized. People frequently criticize it for its 'mentality', that is to say for particular mode of life and set of values. And it is true that a certain intensity of life involves some injustice. Here, nevertheless, is a people with no past, no tradition, and yet which is not lacking in poetry. But it is a poetry whose hard and sensual quality I know very well, a poetry that is far from tenderness, even from the tenderness of the Algerian sky, the only poetry which in fact moves me and makes me one with myself. The opposite of a civilized people is a creative one. These barbarians lounging on the beaches give me the unreasoned hope that, perhaps without knowing it, they are modelling the face of a culture where man's greatness will finally discover its true visage. This people, plunged wholly in the present, lives with neither myths nor consolation. It has placed all its goods on this earth and hence remains defenceless against death. The gifts of physical beauty have been heaped upon it. And with them that strange greed which always accompanies this futureless wealth. Everything that people do in Algiers indicates a disgust for stability and a lack of regard for the future. People hasten to live, and if an art were to be born here, it would conform to that hatred of permanence which led the Dorians to carve their first column out of wood. And yet it is true that one can find a certain moderation as well as a constant excess in the strained and violent faces of this

2. See note on page 91.

people, in this summer sky emptied of tenderness, beneath which all truths can be told and on which no deceitful divinity has traced the signs of hope or of redemption. Between this sky and the faces looking up to it there is nothing on which to hang a mythology, a literature, an ethic or a religion; only stones, flesh, stars and those truths which the hand can touch.

*

A man who can feel his links with one country, his love for a few men, who knows that there is always a place where his heart will find its resting place, already owns many certainties in his life. And yet, certainly, this can be insufficient. But everything, at certain moments, yearns for that land of the soul. 'Yes, it is there that we must return.' What is strange in finding here on earth the union for which Plotinus yearned? Unity expresses itself here in terms of sun and sea. The heart feels it through a certain taste of flesh which constitutes its bitterness and greatness. I learn that there is no superhuman happiness, no eternity outside the curve of the days. These paltry and essential goods, these relative truths, are the only ones that can move me. I have not enough soul to understand the other, 'ideal' ones. Not that we should behave as beasts, but I can see no point in the happiness of angels. All I know is that this sky will last longer than I shall. And what can I call eternity except what will continue after my death? What I am expressing here is not the creature's self-satisfaction with its own condition. It is something quite different. It is not always easy to be a man, even less to be a man who is pure. But to be pure means rediscovering that country of the soul where the throbbing of our blood mingles with the violent pulsations of the afternoon sun. It is a well-known fact that we always recognize our homeland when we are about to lose it. Those whose self-torments are too great are those whom their homeland rejects. I have no desire here to be brutal or to appear exaggerated. But what in fact denies me in this life is first of all what kills me. Everything that exalts life at the same time increases its absurdity. In the summer of Algiers I learn that only one thing is more tragic than suffering, and that is the life of a happy man. But this can also be the path to a greater life, since it can teach us not to cheat.

Many people, in fact, affect a love of life in order to avoid love itself. They try to enjoy themselves and 'make experiments'. But this is an intellectual attitude. You need a rare vocation to become a sensualist. A man lives out his life without the help of his mind, with its triumphs and defeats, its simultaneous loneliness and companionship. I think that we can often feel a secret shame at the sight of these men from Belcourt who work, defend their wives and children, often without a word of reproach. I certainly have no illusions. There is not much love in the lives that I am describing. I should rather say that there is no longer very much. But at least they have eluded nothing. There are words which I have never really understood, like that of sin. I nevertheless believe that these men never sinned against life. For if there is a sin against life, it lies perhaps less in despairing of it than in hoping for another life, and evading the implacable grandeur of the one we have. These men have not cheated. They were gods of the summer at twenty in their thirst for life, and they are still gods today, stripped of all hope. I have seen two of them die. They were full of horror, but silent. It is better like that. From the mass of evils swarming in Pandora's box, the Greeks brought out hope as the very last, as the most terrible of all. I know of no more moving symbol. But hope, contrary to popular belief, is tantamount to resignation. And living means not being resigned.

This at least is the bitter lesson of summers in Algiers. But already the season is trembling and summer dips away. The first September rains, after so much violence and tension, come like the first tears shed by a liberated land, as if for a few days this country were bathed in tenderness. Yet at the same time the carob trees are casting the scent of love over the whole of Algeria. In the evening after the rain the whole earth lies with its belly moistened by an almond-flavoured seed, and after yielding to the sun throughout the summer lies at rest. And once again this scent lays its blessing upon the nuptials between man and the earth, and raises in us the only truly virile love that this world holds: one that is generous and will die.

Summer in Algiers

Note: Here, as an illustration, is the account of a fight overheard in Bab-el-Oued and reproduced word for word. (The narrator does not always speak the language of Musette's Cagayous. This is not surprising. The Cagayous' language is often a literary one, that is to say a reconstruction. Members of the 'underworld' do not always use slang. They use slang expressions, which is different. The Algerian uses a typical vocabulary and a special syntax. But it is by their introduction into French that these creations find their flavour.)

So then Coco comes forward and tells him: 'Just hold it a minute now, hold it.' Up comes the other fellow and says: 'Now what?' Then Coco says to him: 'I'll be letting you have it.' *'You'll* be letting *me* have it?' Then he puts his hand behind his back, but that was it. So then Coco says to him: 'Now keep your hands in front, because I'll be having your 45 and you'll be biting the dust all the same.'

So the other one kept his hand in front. And Coco gave him one, just one, not two, just one. The other man was on the deck, going 'Ow, Ow.' Then everybody came. And the bundle was on. One of them went up to Coco, then two, then three. But I said to him: 'Here, you're going to hit my brother, are you?' 'What do you mean, he's your brother?' 'If it's not my brother then he's as good as.' Then I thumped him. Coco was thumping, I was thumping, Lucien was thumping. I'd got one of them in the corner and was giving him the head. Then the law arrived. They put the chains on us, you know. Red with shame, I was, going all the way through Bab-el-Oued. In front of the *Gentlemen's Bar* there were some of my pals and some little girls as well. Red with shame, I was. But afterwards, Lucien's father told us: 'You were right to do it.'

THE DESERT
to Jean Grenier

LIVING, of course, is slightly the opposite of expressing. If I am to believe the great Tuscan masters, it means bearing triple witness, in silence, flames and immobility.

It is a long time before we realize that the people in their paintings can be encountered every day of the week in the streets of Florence or of Pisa. But it is equally true that we no longer know how to look at the real faces of those around us today. We no longer look at our contemporaries, and are eager only for what serves our aims and determines our behaviour. We prefer its most vulgar poetry to the face itself. But Giotto and Piero della Francesca are perfectly aware that a man's feelings are nothing. And, indeed, everyone has a heart. But the simple and eternal emotions round which revolves the love of living – hatred, love, tears and joys – grow deep inside a man and model the face of his destiny — like the grief which makes Mary clench her teeth in Giottino's *Entombment*. In the immense friezes of the Tuscan churches I see a crowd of angels whose faces are but lightly traced, and yet whose silent passion still reveals a loneliness all of its own.

What matters are not picturesque qualities, episodes, shades of colour or emotional effects. What counts is not poetry. What counts is truth. And I call truth anything that continues. There is a subtle lesson in thinking that, in this respect, only painters can satisfy our hunger. This is because they have the privilege of making themselves novelists of the body. Because they work in that magnificent and trivial matter that is called the present. And the present always shows itself in a gesture. They do not paint a smile, a fleeting moment of modesty, of regret or expectation, but a face with the shape of its bones and the colour of its blood.

The Desert

What they have expelled from these faces moulded for eternity is the curse of the mind: at the price of hope. For the body knows nothing of hope. All it knows is the beating of its own heart. Its eternity consists of indifference. As in the *Scourging of Christ* by Piero della Francesca, where, in a freshly washed courtyard, both the tortured Christ and the thickset executioner reveal the same detachment in their attitudes. This is because the torment has no sequel. Its lesson ends at the frame around its canvas. Why should a man who expects nothing of the morrow feel emotion? This impassibility and this greatness, which man shows when he has no hope, this eternal present, is precisely what perceptive theologians have called hell. And hell, as everyone knows, also consists of bodily suffering. The Tuscan painters stop at the body and not at its destiny. There are no prophetic paintings. And it is not in the museum that we must seek reasons to hope.

The immortality of the soul, it is true, preoccupies many intelligent people. But this is because they reject the only truth given to them, the body, before exhausting all its strength. For the body sets them no problems or, at least, they know the only solution it proposes: it is a truth which must perish and which, because of that, acquires a bitterness and nobility which they dare not contemplate directly. Intelligent people would sooner have poetry, for poetry is the soul's concern. Clearly I am playing on words. But it is also clear that all I wish to do by calling it truth is consecrate a higher poetry: that dark flame which Italian painters from Cimabue to Francesca have raised up amid the Tuscan scenery as the lucid protestation of men cast into a land whose splendour and light speak ceaselessly to them of a non-existent God.

It can happen that indifference and sensitivity may lead a face to merge with the mineral grandeur of a landscape. Just as certain Spanish peasants come to resemble their own olive-trees, so the faces in Giotto's pictures, shorn of the insignificant shadows which reveal the soul, finally merge with Tuscany itself in the only lesson which it freely offers: the exercise of passion at the expense of feeling, a mixture of asceticism and pleasure, a resonance common to both man and the earth and by which man, like the earth, defines himself as halfway between wretchedness and love. There are not so many truths of which the heart can be assured. And I recognized how obvious a truth this was on an evening when the shadows were beginning to drown the vines and olive-trees of the Florentine countryside in a vast and silent sadness. But sadness in this country is never anything but a commentary on beauty. And as the train travelled on through the evening, I felt a tension in me slowly giving way. And today, can I doubt that with the face of sadness this also bore the name of happiness?

Yes, Italy also lavishes in every landscape the lesson illustrated by its men. But it is easy to miss our chance of happiness, for it is always undeserved. The same is true of Italy. And if its grace is sudden, it is not always immediate. More than any other country, it invites us to deepen an experience which yet seems complete on first acquaintance. This is because it begins by lavishing its poetry in order better to disguise its truth. Its first spells are rites of forgetfulness: the oleanders of Monaco, Genoa full of flowers and the smell of fish, and blue evenings on the Ligurian coast. Then finally Pisa, and with it an Italy which has lost the rather tatty charm of the Riviera. But it is still a country of easy virtue, and why should we not lend ourselves for a time to its sensual grace? There is nothing urging me on while I am here (I am deprived of the joys of the 'hunted traveller' since a cheap ticket compels me to spend a certain time in the town 'of my choice'), and my patience for love and understanding seems endless on this first evening when, tired out and starving, I enter Pisa, and am greeted in Station Avenue by ten bellowing loudspeakers pouring out a flood of sentimental songs over a crowd in which almost everyone is young. I already know what I expect. After this life has surged around me, the strange moment will come when, with the cafés closed and the silence suddenly restored, I shall walk through the short, dark streets towards the centre of the town. How can I describe the trick whereby the empty town of Pisa, with its green and yellow monuments, the black and gold of the Arno, changes so swiftly and so skilfully into a strange setting of silence, water and stones. 'In such a night as this, Jessica!' Here, on this singular stage, gods appear with the voices of Shakespeare's lovers. ... We must learn how to lend ourselves to dreams when dreams lend themselves to us. In the depths of this Italian night, I can already hear the strains of this more private song which people come to look for here. Tomorrow, and only tomorrow, will the countryside fill out in the morning light. But this evening I am a god among gods, and as Jessica flies off 'on the swift steps of love', I mingle my voice with that of Lorenzo. But Jessica is only a pretext, and this upsurge of love goes beyond her. Yes, I believe that Lorenzo is less in love with her than grateful to her for allowing him to love. But why should I dream this evening of the Lovers of Venice and forget Verona? Because there is nothing here that invites us to cherish unhappy lovers. Nothing is vainer than to die for a love. What we ought to do is live. And a living Lorenzo is better than a Romeo in his grave, and this despite his rose-bush. How then can we refrain from dancing in these feasts of living love – and from sleeping in the afternoon on the short grass of the Piazza del Duomo, surrounded by monuments that there will always be time enough to visit, from drinking at the town fountains where the water was slightly lukewarm but so fluid, from seeing again the face of the woman who was laughing, with her long nose and proud mouth? All we must realize is that this initiation prepares us for higher illuminations. These are the dazzling processions leading to the Dionysian mysteries at Eleusis. It is in joy that man prepares his lessons and, when its ecstasy is at its highest pitch, the flesh becomes conscious and consecrates its communion with a sacred mystery whose symbol is black blood. It is here that the self-forgetfulness drawn from the ardour of that first Italy prepares us for the lesson which frees us from hope and takes us from our history. These twin truths of the body and of the moment in time, this spectacle of beauty, are things we should cling to as we cling to the only happiness we can expect, one that will enchant us but perish in the act.

*

The most repulsive materialism lies not where people think, but in the effort to pass off as living truths ideas which are dead, diverting on to sterile myths the stubborn and clear-sighted gaze which we should cast on what in us must die for ever. I remember that in Florence, in the cloister of the dead, at the Santissima Annunziata, I was carried away by something which I mistook for distress and which was only anger. It was raining. I was reading inscriptions on the tombstones and the ex-votos. This man had been a tender father and a faithful husband; another, at the same time as the best of husbands, a skilful merchant. A young woman, a model of all the virtues, had spoken French '*si come il nativo*'. There a young girl was the hope of her whole family, '*ma la gioia è pellegrina sulla terra*'. But nothing of all that affected me. Almost all of them, according to the inscriptions, had resigned themselves to dying, doubtless because they accepted their other duties. On that day children had invaded the cloister and were playing leap-frog over the tombstones which strove to perpetuate their virtues. Night was then falling, and I had sat down on the ground, my back against a column. A priest smiled at me as he went by. In the church, an organ was playing softly, and the warm colour of its pattern sometimes reappeared behind the children's shouts. Alone against the column, I was like someone seized by the throat and who shouts out his faith as if it were his last word. Everything in me protested against such a resignation. 'You must,' said the inscriptions. But no, and my revolt was right. This joy that travelled indifferent and absorbed like a pilgrim on the earth was something that I had to follow step by step. And, as far as the rest was concerned, I said no. I said no with all my strength. The tombstones taught me that it was pointless, that life is '*col sol levante, col sol cadente*'. But today I cannot see what my revolt loses by being pointless, and I am well aware of what it gains.

Besides, that is not what I set out to say. I should like to define a little more clearly a truth which I then felt at the very heart of my revolt and of which this revolt was only an extension, a truth which stretched from the small late roses in the cloister of Santa Maria Novella to the women on that Sunday morning in Florence, their breasts free beneath their light dresses, and their moist lips. At every church corner that Sunday morning stood displays of

The Desert

flowers, their petals thick and shining, bejewelled with spots of water. What they then offered me was a kind of 'naïvety' as well as a reward. There was a generous opulence in these flowers as there was in these women, and I could not see that desiring the latter was very different from longing for the former. The same pure heart sufficed for both. It is not often that a man feels his heart is pure. But when he does, his duty is to give the name of truth to what has so singularly purified him, even if this truth may seem a blasphemy to others. This is what I thought on that particular day. I had spent my morning at Fiesole, in a Franciscan convent, full of the scent of laurel. I had stood for a long time in the little courtyard overflowing with red flowers, sunlight and black and yellow bees. In a corner stood a green watering can. Before going there I had visited the monks' cells, and seen their little tables each adorned with a skull. Now, this garden bore witness to the sources of their inspiration. I had turned back towards Florence, down the hill which led towards the town lying open with all its cypress trees. I felt that this splendour of the world, these women and these flowers offered a kind of justification for these men. I was not sure that they were not also the justification for all those men who know that an extreme level of poverty always rejoins the wealth and luxury of the world. Between the life of these Franciscans, enclosed among columns and flowers, and the life of the young men of the Padovani beach in Algiers, who spend the whole year in the sun, I felt that there was a common resonance. If they strip themselves bare, it is for a greater life (and not for another one). This is at least the only valid meaning of expressions such as 'deprivation' and 'stripping oneself bare'. Being naked always has a sense of physical liberty and of that harmony between hand and flowers – this loving understanding between the earth and a man delivered from humanity – ah! I would be a convert to this if it were not already my religion. No, what I have just said cannot be a blasphemy – any more than if I say that the inner smile of Giotto's portraits of Saint Francis justifies those who have a taste for happiness. For myths are to religion what poetry is to truth, ridiculous masks laid on the passion to live.

Shall I go further? The same men who at Fiesole live among red flowers also keep in their cell the skull that nourishes their meditations. Florence at their window and death on their table. A certain continuity in despair can give birth to joy. And when life reaches a certain temperature, our soul and our blood mingle together and live at ease in contradiction, as indifferent to duty as to faith. I am no longer surprised that a cheerful hand should have thus resumed its strange notion of honour on a wall in Pisa: '*Alberto fa l'amore con la mia sorella.*' I am no longer surprised that Italy should be the land of incests, or at least, which is more significant, of admitted incests. For the path which leads from beauty to immorality is tortuous but certain. Plunged deep in beauty the mind feeds off nothingness. When he faces landscapes whose grandeur clutches him by the throat, each of his thoughts is a scratch on man's perfection. And soon, crossed out, scarred and rescarred by so many overwhelming certainties, he ceases to be anything at all in face of the world except a formless stain knowing only passive truths, the world's colour or its sun. Landscapes as pure as this dry up the soul and their beauty is unbearable. The message of these gospels of stone, sky and water is that there are no resurrections. Henceforth, from the depths of these deserts which the heart sees as magnificent, the men of these countries begin to feel temptation. Why is it surprising if minds brought up before the spectacle of nobility, in the rarefied air of beauty, remain unconvinced that greatness and goodness can live together? An intelligence with no god to carry it to completion seeks for a god in what denies it. Borgia on his arrival in the Vatican exclaims: 'Now that God has given us the papacy, let us hasten to enjoy it.' And he behaves accordingly. Hasten is indeed the word. There is already a hint of the despair so characteristic of those filled with all good things.

Perhaps I am mistaken. For I was in fact happy in Florence like many others before me. But what is happiness except the simple harmony between a man and the life he leads? And what more legitimate harmony can link a man to life than the twin awareness of his longing to endure and the death which awaits him? At least he learns to count on nothing and to see the present

The Desert

as the only truth given to us 'as a bonus'. I realize that people talk about Italy, the Mediterranean, as classical countries where everything is on a human scale. But where is this, and where is the road leading to it? Let me open my eyes to seek my measure and my satisfaction! What I do see is Fiesole, Djemila and ports in the sunlight. The human scale? Silence and dead stones. All the rest belongs to history.

And yet this is not the end. For it has not been laid down that happiness should be for ever inseparable from optimism. It is linked with love – which is not the same thing. And I know of times and places where happiness can seem so bitter that we prefer its promise. But this is because in these times or places I lacked the heart to love, that is to persevere. What we must talk of here is man's entry into the feasts of earth and beauty. For now, like the neophyte shedding his last veils, he lays down before his god the small change of his personality. Yes, there is a higher happiness where happiness seems trivial. At Florence I went up to the top of the Boboli gardens to a terrace from which my gaze could travel right across Mount Oliveto and the upper part of the town over to the horizon. On each of these hills the olive-trees were pale as little wisps of smoke, while the cypress-trees were like darker shoots against their slight mist, the nearer ones green, the more distant ones black. Heavy clouds cast stains on the deep blue of the sky. As the afternoon drew to its close, there came a silver light in which everything fell silent. The top of the hills had first of all been shrouded in clouds. But a breeze had risen whose breath I could feel on my cheek. As it blew, the clouds behind the mountains drew apart like the two sides of a curtain. At the same time the cypress-trees on the summit seemed to shoot up in a single jet against the sudden blue of the sky. With them the whole hillside and landscape of stones and olive-trees rose slowly back into sight. Other clouds came. The curtain closed. And the hill with its cypress-trees and houses vanished anew. Then the same breeze, which was closing the thick folds of the curtain over other hills, scarcely visible in the distance, came and drew them apart again here. As the world thus filled and emptied its lungs, the same breath ceased a few seconds away and then, far off, resumed the theme of a fugue which stone and air composed on the world's scale. Each time the theme was repeated in a slightly lower key. As I followed it into the distance, I became a little calmer. And as I reached the end of this perspective which the heart could feel, I saw in one glance the whole range of hills moving with the same breath, and with them, it seemed, the song of the whole earth.

Millions of eyes, I know, have gazed at this landscape, and for me it was like the first smile of the sky. It took me out of myself in the deepest sense of the word. It assured me that except for my love and the wondrous cry of these stones there is no meaning in anything. The world is beautiful, and outside it there is no salvation. The great truth that it patiently taught me is that the mind is nothing, nor even the heart. And that the stone warmed by the sun or the cypress-tree shooting up against the suddenly clear sky mark the boundary of the only universe in which 'being right' is meaningful: nature without men. And this world annihilates me. It carries me through to the end. It denies me without anger. As this evening fell over the Italian countryside, I was on my way to a wisdom where everything had already been overcome, had not tears come into my eyes and had not the great sob of poetry welling up within me made me forget the truth of the world.

*

It is on this moment of balance that I must end: the strange moment when spirituality rejects ethics, where happiness is born of the absence of hope, where the mind finds its justification in the body. If it is true that every truth bears its bitterness within it, it is also true that every denial contains a flourish of affirmations. And this song of hopeless love which is born of contemplation can also form the most effective guide for action. As he emerges from the tomb, the risen Christ of Piero de la Francesca has no human expression on his face – only a fierce and soulless grandeur that I cannot help taking for a resolve to live. For the wise man, like the idiot, expresses little. This return delights me.

The Desert

But do I owe this lesson to Italy, or have I drawn it from my own heart? It was doubtless in Italy that I became aware of it. But this is because Italy, like other privileged places, offers me the spectacle of a beauty in which men nevertheless die. Here again truth must decay and what is more exalting? Even if I long for it, what have I in common with a truth that is not destined to decay? It is not on my scale. And to love it would be pretence. People rarely understand that it is never through despair that a man gives up what constituted his life. Impulses and moments of despair lead towards other lives, and merely indicate a quivering attachment to the lessons of the earth. But it can happen that when he reaches a certain degree of lucidity a man feels his heart is closed, and without protest or rebellion turns his back on what up to then he had taken for his life, that is to say his restlessness. If Rimbaud dies in Abyssinia without having written a single line, this is not because he prefers adventure or has renounced literature. It is because 'that's how things are', and because when we reach a certain stage of awareness we finally acknowledge something which each of us, according to our particular vocation, seeks not to understand. This clearly involves undertaking the survey of a certain desert. But this strange desert is accessible only to those who can live there without ever slaking their thirst. Then, and only then, is it peopled with the living waters of happiness.

Within reach of my hand in the Boboli gardens hung enormous golden Chinese persimmons whose skin had burst and which were oozing with thick syrup. Between this light hill and these juicy fruits, between the secret brotherhood which linked me to the world and the hunger which urged me to seize the orange-coloured flesh above my hand, I could feel the movement which leads certain men from spiritual purity to sensual delights and from self-denial to the fullness of desire. Both then and now I admired the link which rivets man to the world, this double image in which my heart can intervene and dictate its happiness to the exact point where the world can either carry it to fruition or destroy it. Florence! One of the few places in Europe where I realized that a consent lay sleeping at the heart of my revolt.

In its sky mingled with tears and sunlight, I learned to say yes to the earth and to burn in the dark flame of its feast days. I felt ... but what word can I use? what excess? How can I consecrate the harmony between love and revolt? The earth! In this great temple deserted by the gods all my idols have feet of clay.

3
SUMMER

1954

'But you are born
For a limpid day.'
         Hölderlin

MINOTAUR OR THE HALT
AT ORAN

to Pierre Galindo

This essay dates from 1939, something which should be borne in mind if the reader is to judge what Oran could be like today. Violent protests emanating from this beautiful town have in fact assured me that all these imperfections have been (or will be) remedied. The beauties celebrated in this essay have, on the other hand, been jealously protected. Oran, a happy and realistic city, no longer needs writers. It is waiting for tourists.

(1953)

THERE are no more deserts, there are no more islands. Yet the need for them makes itself felt. If we are to understand the world, we must turn aside from it; if we are to serve men better, we must briefly hold them at a distance. But where can we find the solitude necessary to strength, the long breathing-space in which the mind can gather itself together and courage take stock of itself? We still have large towns. But these must fulfil certain conditions.

The cities that Europe can offer are too full of rumours from the past. A practised ear can still detect the rustling of wings, the quivering of souls. We feel the dizziness of centuries, of glory and of revolutions. There, we remember the clamour in which Europe was forged. There is not enough silence.

Paris is often a desert for the heart, but sometimes, as we stand looking over it from the Père-Lachaise, a wind of revolution suddenly fills this desert with flags and vanquished grandeurs. This same is true of certain Spanish towns, of Florence or of Prague. Salzburg would be peaceful without Mozart. But, from time to time, there runs across the Salzach the great cry of Don Juan plunging into hell. Vienna seems more silent, a maiden among cities. The stones there are no more than three centuries old, and their youth has known no sadness. But Vienna stands at a crossroads of history. The clash of empires rings round about her. On certain evenings, when the sky veils itself in blood, the stone horses on the monuments of the Ring seem about to take flight. In this fleeting moment, when everything tells of power and history, you can distinctly hear the Ottoman empire crashing under the charge of the Polish cavalry squadrons. Here, likewise, there is not enough silence.

It is, without doubt, this well-peopled solitude which men come to seek in the towns of Europe. Men who know the task awaiting them, that is. Here they can choose their company, take it and leave it. How many minds have been tempered by that walk between their hotel room and the old stones of the Île Saint-Louis! It is true that others have died there of loneliness. But it was there, in any case, that those who survived learned why they should grow and assert themselves. They were alone and yet not alone. Centuries of history and beauty, the burning evidence of a thousand past lives, walked with them along the Seine, and spoke to them both of traditions and of conquests. But their youth urged them to summon up this company. There comes a time, there come times in history, when such company is a crowd. 'It's between us two now,' exclaims Rastignac as he confronts the vast mouldering heap of the town of Paris. Yes, but two can be a crowd as well!

Deserts themselves have taken on meaning, have been overladen with poetry. They have become sacred places for all the sufferings of this world. But what the heart requires at certain moments is, on the contrary, a place without poetry. Descartes, for his meditations, chooses his desert: the busiest commercial city of his time. There he finds his loneliness, and the chance to write what is perhaps the greatest of our virile poems: 'The first [precept] was never to accept anything as true unless I knew without the slightest doubt that it was so.' One can have less ambition and yet the same nostalgia. But in the last three centuries Amsterdam has been covered with museums. To escape from poetry and rediscover the peacefulness of stones, we need other deserts, and other places with neither souls nor resting places. Oran is one of these.

The Street

I have often heard people from Oran complaining about their town: 'There is no interesting society here.' But you wouldn't want one if there were! A number of high-minded people have tried to acclimatize the customs of another world to this desert, faithful to the principle that no one can be of genuine service to art or to ideas without co-operation from others.[1] The result has been that the only instructive society is that of poker-players, boxing enthusiasts, bowling fanatics and regional societies. There, at least, the atmosphere is natural. After all, there is a certain kind of greatness which does not lend itself to elevation. It is infertile by nature. And anyone who wants to find it leaves interesting society behind him and goes down into the street.

The streets of Oran are abandoned to dust, pebbles and heat. If it rains, there is a flood and a sea of mud. But rain or shine, the shops have the same absurd and extravagant air. All the bad taste of Europe and the East has chosen Oran as its meeting place. There, piled on top of one another, you find marble greyhounds, swan-lake ballet dancers, Diana the Huntress in green galalith, discus-throwers and harvesters, everything that serves for wedding or birthday presents, the whole depressing population which a commercial and joking genie ceaselessly summons to our chimney-pieces. But this perseverance in bad taste here assumes a baroque extravagance where all can be forgiven. Behold, in a jewel-case of dust, the contents of one shop-window: ghastly plaster-cast models of tortured feet, a batch of Rembrandt sketches 'given away at 150 francs each', a quantity of 'practical jokes and tricks', tricolour wallets, an eighteenth-century pastel drawing, a mechanical plush donkey, bottles of *eau de Provence* for preserving green olives, and an ignoble-looking wooden virgin

[1]. In Oran, you meet Gogol's Klestakoff. He yawns and then: 'I feel that we shall have to concern ourselves with higher things.'

with an indecent smile. (So that no one shall remain ignorant, the 'management' has placed a label at its feet: 'Wooden virgin'.)

*

You can find in Oran:

1. Cafés whose grease-covered counters are strewn with the feet and wings of flies, where the proprietor never stops smiling although the place is always empty. A 'small black' used to cost twelve sous and a 'large one' eighteen;

2. Photographers' shops where the technique has not progressed since the invention of sensitized paper. They display a singular fauna, never encountered in the street, which ranges from the pseudo-sailor leaning with one elbow on a console-table, to the marriageable maiden, dress belted at the waist, standing with dangling arms against a sylvan scene. It can be assumed that these are not copies from nature but original creations;

3. An edifying plethora of undertakers. This is not because people die more frequently in Oran, but simply because, I suppose, they make more fuss about it.

The endearing simplicity of this nation of shop-keepers extends even to their advertisements. The future programme of a cinema in Oran gives details of a third-class film. I note the adjectives 'magnificent', 'splendid', 'extraordinary', 'marvellous', 'overwhelming' and 'stupendous'. To conclude, the management informs the public of the considerable sacrifices it has had to make in order to be able to present this astonishing 'production'. However, the price of the seats will remain the same.

It would be wrong to think that this merely shows the taste for exaggeration peculiar to Mediterranean countries. What the authors of this miraculous prospectus are really doing is giving proof of their psychological perspicacity. They need to overcome the indifference and deep apathy which men feel in this country as soon as they have to choose between two entertainments, two jobs, and even, quite frequently, between two women. You decide only when compelled to do so. And the advertisers are perfectly aware of this. They will go to the same extremes as in America, having the same reasons for exasperation in both places.

Finally, the streets of Oran tell us about the two essential pleasures of the local youth: having its shoes shone, and parading these same shoes along the boulevard. To gain a correct idea of the first of these two delights, you must entrust your shoes at ten o'clock on a Sunday morning to the shoe-shiners of the Boulevard Gallieni. There, perched on a high stool, you can enjoy that peculiar satisfaction which even the profane can receive from the spectacle of men as deeply and visibly in love with their work as are the shoe-cleaners of Oran. Everything is worked out to the last detail. Several brushes, three kinds of polishing rag, shoe-polish mixed with petrol: one might believe that the operation has been concluded when a perfect shine comes to birth beneath the application of the soft brush. But the same eager hand puts a second coat of polish on the gleaming surface, rubs it, dulls it, drives the cream into the very heart of the leather and then brings out, with the same brush, a double and truly definitive shine which emerges from the innermost depths.

The marvels thus obtained are then exhibited to the connoisseurs. Really to appreciate the pleasures offered by the boulevard, you must attend the fancy-dress dances organized by the youth of Oran every evening in the town's main thoroughfares. Between the ages of sixteen and twenty, in fact, the 'fashionable' young Oranais choose to model their elegance on the American cinema and disguise themselves before going to dine. With curly brilliantined hair flowing from under a felt hat which is cocked over the left ear while its brim obliterates the right eye, neck encircled in a collar generous enough to receive the continuation of the hair, the microscopic knot of the tie held in place by the strictest of pins, jacket hanging half-way down the thighs and nipped in at the hips, light-coloured trousers hanging short, shoes gleaming above triple soles, these youths parade along the pavement their unshakeable self-confidence and the steel tips of their shoes. They attempt to imitate, in all matters, the gait, the self-confidence and superiority of Mr Clark Gable. Consequently, the more critically-minded members of the town normally baptize these young men, by the grace of unaffected pronunciation, 'Clarques'.

However that may be, the main boulevards of Oran are invaded late every afternoon by an army of agreeable adolescents who take the greatest pains to look like gangsters. Since the young girls of Oran know that they have been destined since birth to marry these tender-hearted rogues, they also flaunt the make-up and elegance of the great American actresses. The same cynics consequently christen them 'Marlenes'. Thus when on the evening boulevards the chirping of birds rises from the palm-trees to the sky, scores of Clarques and Marlenes meet, casting appreciative and evaluating glances, happy to live and to appear, absorbed for an hour in the bliss of perfect existences. What we then behold, in the words of the jealous, are the meetings of the American commission. But these words reveal the bitterness of the over-thirties who have no part in such games. They fail to recognize these daily congresses of youth and romantic love for what they are – the parliaments of birds found in Hindu literature. But no one on the boulevards of Oran discusses the Problem of Being, or is concerned with the way to perfection. All that remains is the fluttering of wings, the flaunting of outspread tails, flirtations between victorious graces, all the rapture of a careless song that fades with the coming of night.

I can already hear Klestakoff saying: 'We must concern ourselves with higher things.' Alas, he is quite capable of doing so. A little encouragement, and in a few years' time he will people this desert. But, for the time being, a gently secretive soul can find rest in this facile town, with its parade of made-up maidens who have no disguise for feelings, who make so poor a pretence at coquetry that we immediately see through their wiles. Concern ourselves with the higher life! We should do better to use our eyes: Santa Cruz carved out of the rock, the mountains, the flat sea, the violent wind and the sun, the tall cranes in the docks, the sheds, the quays and the gigantic flights of stairs which scale the rock on which the town is set, and in the town itself these games and this boredom, this tumult and this solitude. Perhaps none of this is high enough. But the great value of these overpopulated islands is that in them the heart can strip itself bare. Silence is now possible only in noisy towns. From Amsterdam Descartes wrote to Balzac, now old, 'Each day I stroll through the confusion of a great people, with as much freedom and quiet as you find in your lanes.'

The Desert in Oran

Compelled to live in the presence of an admirable landscape, the Oranais have overcome this formidable trial by screening themselves behind extremely ugly buildings. You expect a town opening out on to the sea, washed and refreshed by the evening breeze. And, except for the Spanish district, you find a city which has its back to the sea, which has been built turning in upon itself, like a snail. Oran is a long, circular yellow wall topped with a hard sky. At first, men wander round the labyrinth, looking for the sea as for Ariadne's thread. But they turn round and round in the yellow, stifling streets until, in the end, the Oranais are devoured by the Minotaur of boredom. The Oranais have long since ceased wandering. They let the monster eat them.

No one can know what stone really is until he has been to Oran. In this dustiest of cities the pebble is king. It is so well loved that merchants display it in their windows, either as a paperweight or simply for its appearance. People pile them up along the streets, doubtless for pure visual pleasure, since a year later the pile is still there. Things which elsewhere derive their poetry from being green here take on a face of stone. The hundred or so trees which can be found in the business quarter of the town have been carefully covered over with dust. They have become trees from a petrified forest, their branches exuding an acrid, dusty smell. In Algiers the Arab cemeteries have their well-known gentleness. In Oran above the Ras-el-Aïn ravine, facing the sea for once, what you see laid out against the blue sky are fields of chalky, crumbly pebbles set blindingly on fire by the sun. In the midst of these dead bones of the earth, scattered patches of crimson geraniums give the landscape its life and fresh blood. The whole town is held fast in a clamp of stone. Seen from the Planters, the cliffs which hold it in their grip are so thick that the landscape loses its reality between the stone. Man is an outlaw. So much heavy beauty seems to come from another world.

If what we call a desert is a place without a soul in which the sky alone is king, then Oran awaits its prophets. All around and above the town the brutal nature of Africa is, in fact, resplendent in its most burning glory. It splits open the ill-chosen décor which men have laid upon it, utters its violent cries between each house and over all the housetops. If you go up on to one of the roads running along the side of the Santa Cruz mountain, what you see first of all are the scattered and brightly coloured blocks of Oran. But as soon as you go a little higher, the jagged cliffs surrounding the plateau seem to be crouching in the sea like red beasts. From higher still, great whirlpools of sun and wind swirl over the untidy town, blowing and battering through it as it lies scattered in confusion over all four corners of the rocky landscape. You see the clash between the magnificent anarchy of men and the permanence of an unchanging sea. This gives the road along the mountain-side an overwhelming scent of life.

Deserts have something implacable about them. The mineral sky of Oran, its trees and streets in their layer of dust, all join forces to create this thick and impassive world in which the mind and heart cannot be turned from themselves, nor from their one subject, which is man. Here I am speaking of harsh refuges. People write books about Florence and Athens. These towns have formed so many European minds that they must have a meaning. They keep the power to sadden or excite. They calm a certain hunger of the soul whose proper food is memory. But how can one feel tender in a town where nothing appeals to the mind, where ugliness itself is anonymous, where the past is reduced to nothingness? What can be the attraction of emptiness, of boredom, of an indifferent sky? Solitude, without a doubt, and perhaps human beings as well. There is a certain race of men for whom human beings, wherever they are beautiful, make up a bitter homeland. Oran is one of the thousand capitals such men possess.

Sport

The Central Sporting Club in the Rue du Fondouk in Oran is presenting an evening of boxing which it proclaims will be appre-

The Minotaur or the Halt at Oran

ciated by those who really love the sport. What this actually means is that the boxers whose names are on the posters are far from being champions, that some of them will be stepping into the ring for the first time, and that you can therefore count on the courage if not on the skill of the contestants. An Oranais having electrified me by the formal undertaking that 'blood will flow', I find myself this evening among the real lovers of the sport.

It would appear that the latter never demand comfort. A ring has in fact been erected at the far end of a kind of whitewashed, garishly-lit garage with a corrugated iron roof. Folding chairs have been set up on all four sides of the ropes. These are the 'ringside seats'. Other seats have been set up in the body of the hall, and at the far end there is a wide-open space known as the 'free area', so named because not one of the five hundred people standing there can take out his pocket handkerchief without causing a serious accident. This rectangular box contains a thousand men and two or three women – of the type who, according to my neighbour, 'always want to show off'. Everyone is sweating ferociously. While we wait for the 'white hopes' to step into the ring, an immense loudspeaker grinds out Tino Rossi. Ballads before butchery.

The true lovers of the sport possess limitless patience. The fights promised for nine o'clock have not yet started at half-past, and yet no one complains. It is a warm spring evening, and the smell of humanity in its shirt-sleeves is intoxicating. Violent discussions are accompanied by the periodic popping of lemonade bottle corks and the tireless lamentations of the Corsican singer. A few new arrivals are fitted in, when a projector casts a blinding light on to the ring. The white hopes step into the ring.

These white hopes, or beginners, who fight for pleasure, are always anxious to prove it by massacring each other at the first opportunity, with a fine disregard for technique. None of them has ever lasted more than three rounds. The hero of the evening in this respect is a certain 'Aero the Kid' who normally sells lottery tickets on café terraces. His opponent, in fact, has taken an unlucky dive out of the ring at the beginning of the second round under the impact of a fist that whirled like a propeller.

The crowd has grown a little more excited, but still out of politeness. It takes deep, grave breaths of the sacred odour of embrocation. It contemplates this series of slow rites and confused sacrifices which are made even more authentic by the propitiatory patterns cast by the struggling shadows on the whiteness of the wall. These are the formal prologue of a savage and calculated religion. The trance will come only later.

And, at this very moment, the loudspeaker introduces Amar, 'the tough Oranais who never gives up', against Pérez, 'the Algerian puncher'. The profane might well misinterpret the howls which greet the presentation of the boxers in the ring. They might think that this was some sensational fight in which the two rivals were going to settle a personal quarrel known to the public. It is indeed a quarrel that they are going to settle, but one that for the last hundred years has cast a mortal division between Algiers and Oran. A few hundred years ago, these two North African towns would have already bled each other white, as Florence and Pisa did in happier times. Their rivalry is all the stronger from being based on absolutely nothing. Having every reason to love each other, their hatred is all the fiercer. The Oranais accuse the Algerians of being 'stuck-up'. The Algerians insinuate that the Oranais are ill-bred. These are bloodier insults than one might think, since they are metaphysical. And because they cannot besiege each other, Oran and Algiers meet, struggle and exchange insults in the field of sport, statistics and public works.

It is consequently a page of history that is unfolding itself in the ring. And the tough Oranais, supported by a thousand howling voices, is defending against Pérez a way of life and the pride of a province. Truth compels me to say that Amar is putting his points badly. His arguments are out of order: he lacks reach. The Algerian puncher, on the other hand, is long enough in the arm and makes his points persuasively on his opponent's eyebrow. The Oranais bears his colours triumphantly, amidst the howls of the frenzied spectators. In spite of repeated encouragement from the gallery and from my neighbour, in spite of the fearless 'Bash him', 'Give him what for', the insidious cries of 'Foul', 'Oh, the ref. never saw him', the optimistic 'He's shagged', 'He's had it',

The Minotaur or the Halt at Oran

the Algerian is declared winner on points to the accompaniment of interminable booing. My neighbour, who likes to talk about the sporting spirit, applauds ostentatiously, whispering to me meanwhile in a voice made hoarse by so much shouting, 'Like this, they won't be able to say *down there* that the Oranais are savages.'

But in the body of the hall a number of fights that were unlisted on the programme have already broken out. Chairs are waved in the air, the police force their way through, the excitement is at its height. To calm these good people and contribute to the restoration of silence, the 'management' instantly entrusts the loudspeaker with the thunderous march of *Sambre- et-Meuse*. For a few moments the hall takes on a wondrous aspect. Confused bunches of fighters and indulgent referees wave to and fro beneath the policemen's grasp, the gallery is delighted and urges them to further efforts with wild cries, cock-a-doodle-doos or ironic mewing, soon submerged in the irresistible flood of military music.

But the announcement that the main fight is about to start is sufficient to restore calm. This happens quickly with no flourishes, as when actors leave the stage as soon as the play is over. In the most natural way in the world hats are dusted, chairs put back in their place, and every face immediately assumes the benign expression of the respectable spectator who has paid for his seat at a family concert.

The last fight of the evening confronts a French naval champion with an Oranais boxer. This time, it is the latter who has the advantage of reach. But during the initial rounds his advantage makes little appeal to the crowd. It is digesting its excitement, convalescing. It is still short of breath. Its catcalls lack animosity. If it applauds, it is with no vigour. The spectators split into two camps, as they must do if order is to prevail. But each man's choice is guided by that indifference which succeeds great weariness. If the Frenchman holds on in the clinches, if the Oranais forgets that one does not attack with the head, the boxer is bowled over by a broadside of hisses but immediately put back on his feet by a salvo of applause. It is not until the seventh round that sport comes back to the surface, accompanied by the emergence from their fatigue of its true lovers. The Frenchman, in fact, has been put down on the canvas, and, anxious to win back points, has charged at his opponent. 'Here we go,' says my neighbour. 'This will be murder.' And, in fact, that is what it is. Covered in sweat beneath the implacable lights, the two boxers open their guard, close their eyes and swing. They push with their knees and shoulders, exchange their blood and snort with fury. Instantaneously the spectators stand erect and punctuate each hero's effort with their cries. They receive the blows, return them, swell them by a thousand harsh and panting voices. The same men who had chosen their favourite in indifference stick to their choice through obstinacy and endow it with passion. Every ten seconds my right ear is pierced by a shout from my neighbour 'Go on, bluejacket! Bash him, matelot', while a spectator in front of us shouts '¡Anda, hombre!' to the Oranais. The hombre and the bluejacket comply, escorted, in this whitewashed temple of cement and corrugated iron, by a crowd in frenzied worship of these low-browed gods. The dull thud of every blow echoes in enormous vibrations through the very body of the crowd, which gasps its last breath with the boxers themselves.

In this atmosphere the announcement of a draw is badly received. It runs contrary to what, in the crowd, is an utterly Manichean vision: there is good and evil, the victor and the vanquished. One is either right or wrong. The conclusion of this impeccable logic is immediately provided by two thousand energetic lungs which accuse the judges of being either bought or sold. But the bluejacket has gone to embrace his opponent in the ring and drinks his fraternal sweat. This is enough to make the crowd effect an immediate volte-face and explode in applause. My neighbour is right: they are not savages.

The crowd which now flows out beneath a sky filled with silence and with stars has just fought the most exhausting of battles. It says nothing, fades furtively away, too exhausted for exegesis. There is good and evil, this religion is merciless. The cohort of the faithful is now nothing more than a gathering of black and white shadows disappearing into the night. The reason is that strength and violence are lonely gods. They give nothing to the memory. On the contrary, they scatter miracles by handfuls in the present. They are on the same scale as this people which lacks a past and celebrates its communions round boxing rings. They are slightly difficult rites, but which simplify everything. Good and evil, the victor and the vanquished: at Corinth two temples stood side by side, the one of Violence, the other of Necessity.

Monuments

For many reasons connected as much with economy as with metaphysics, one can say that Oranais style, if such a thing exists, finds clear and powerful expression in that singular edifice known as the *Maison du Colon*. Oran has, indeed, no lack of monuments. The town has its quota of Imperial Marshals, and of ministers and local benefactors. You come across them in little dusty squares, resigned to rain as to sun, converted like everything else to stone and boredom. But they nevertheless represent something imported. In this happy barbarity they stand as regrettable traces of civilization.

Oran, on the contrary, has erected altars and rostrums to itself. When the Oranais had to construct a building to be shared by the innumerable agricultural organizations which provide the country with its livelihood, they decided to erect, using the most solid materials, and placing it at the centre of their business city, a convincing representation of their virtues: *La Maison du Colon*. To judge by this building, these virtues are three in number: boldness of taste, love of violence, and a sense of historical synthesis. Egypt, Byzantium and Munich have collaborated in the delicate construction of a pastry-cake representing an immense inverted cup. Multicoloured stones, of the most startling effect, have been set along each side of the roof. The brightness of these mosaics is so persuasive that all one can discern at first is a shapeless dazzle. But on closer inspection they do reveal their meaning to the fully awakened attention: a gracious settler, wearing a bow tie and a solar topee, is receiving the homage of a procession of slaves clad as nature intended.[2] Finally, the edifice has been erected, with all its illuminations, at the centre of a crossroads, amid the bustle of the tiny gondola-shaped tramways whose squalor is one of the charms of the town.

Oran is, moreover, very attached to the two lions which stand on its main square. Since 1888 they have sat majestically on either side of the staircase leading up to the town hall. Their creator was called Cain. They look majestic and are short in the body. It is said that, at night, they descend one after the other from their pedestal and pad silently round the darkened square, stopping on occasion to urinate at length between the tall dusty fig-trees. These are, naturally, rumours to which the Oranais lend an indulgent ear. But it is unlikely.

In spite of some researches I have not been able to develop any great enthusiasm for Cain. All I have discovered is that he enjoyed the reputation of a skilful depicter of animals. Nevertheless, I often think about him. This is a tendency which the mind acquires in Oran. Here is a sonorously named artist who gave this town a work of no importance. Several hundred thousand men have grown familiar with the jovial lords of the jungle that he placed in front of a pretentious town hall. It is one kind of artistic success. These lions doubtless bear witness, as do thousands of other works of the same kind, to something very different from talent. Men have painted *The Night Watch*, *Saint Francis Receiving the Stigmata*, *The Exaltation of the Flower*, or carved the statue of David. What Cain did was erect two grinning felines in the town square of a trading province overseas. But one day the statue of David will crumble into ruin with the town of Florence, and these lions will perhaps be saved from the disaster. Once again, they bear witness to something else.

Can I clarify this idea? These statues contain both insignificance and solidity. The mind has made no contribution, and matter an enormously large one. Mediocrity seeks to endure by every means, including bronze. We refuse it the right to eternity, but it takes it every day. Is it not itself eternity? In any case,

2. Another of the qualities of the Algerian race is, as can be seen, frankness.

The Minotaur or the Halt at Oran

there is something moving in this perseverance, and it bears its lesson, which is the one offered by all the monuments of Oran and by Oran itself. For an hour a day, for once in a while, it compels you to take an interest in something which is not important. The mind can profit from such moments of calm. This is how it takes the cure and, since it must pass through these moments of humility, I feel that this opportunity to stultify itself is better than others. Everything perishable seeks to endure. Let us then admit that everything wishes to endure. The works of man have no other meaning, and in this respect Cain's lions have the same chance of succeeding as the ruins at Angkor. This encourages modesty.

There are other monuments in Oran. This, at least, is what we must call them, since they too bear witness for their town, in perhaps a more significant way. They are the excavations which, at the moment, cover the coastline over a distance of ten kilometres. The apparent aim is to transform the brightest of bays into an enormous port. In fact, it is yet another opportunity for man to pit himself against stone.

In the canvases of certain Flemish masters you see the insistent recurrence of an admirably spacious theme: the construction of the Tower of Babel. You see immense landscapes, rocks reaching up into the sky, escarpments teeming with workmen, animals, ladders, strange machines, ropes and beams. Men, in fact, are in the picture only to bring out the inhuman vastness of the buildings. It is this that comes to your mind on the coast road running to the west of Oran.

There, clinging to immense slopes, are rails, tip-trucks, cranes, and miniature railways.... Under a devouring sun toy-like locomotives circumnavigate vast blocks of stone to the accompaniment of whistles, dust and smoke. Night and day a nation of ants swarms over the smoking carcass of the mountain. Scores of men, hanging from the same rope against the cliff face, their bellies pressed to the handles of pneumatic drills, quiver day after day in mid-air, unloosing whole sections of stone that crash down in a roar of dust. Farther along, the trucks tip their load from the top of the slopes, and the rocks suddenly launched towards the sea roll and dive into the water, each heavy block followed by a shower of lighter stones. At regular intervals, at dead of night or in the middle of the day, explosions shake the whole mountain and lift up the sea itself.

What man is doing, in these excavations, is making a head-on attack against stone. And if we could for a moment forget the harsh slavery which makes this work possible, we should be filled with admiration. These stones, wrenched from the mountain, help man in his projects. They pile up beneath the first waves, gradually emerge, and finally take shape as a jetty that will soon be covered with men and machines moving daily farther out to sea. Vast steel jaws gnaw unceasingly at the cliff's belly, swivel round and disgorge their excess rubble into the sea. As the cliff face sinks lower, the whole coast pushes the sea relentlessly backwards.

Stone, of course, cannot be destroyed. All that can be done is move it around. Whatever happens, it will always outlast the men who use it. For the moment it lends itself to their determination to act. Even that determination is doubtless quite gratuitous. But it is man's task to move things around: he must choose between doing that or doing nothing at all.[3] Clearly, the Oranais have chosen. Before that indifferent bay, they will still go on for years piling up heaps of pebbles along the coast. In a hundred years, that is to say tomorrow, they will have to start again. But today these piles of rock bear witness for the men who wend their way among them, their faces set in a mask of dust and sweat. The true monuments of Oran remain its stones.

Ariadne's Stone

It seems that the Oranais are like that friend of Flaubert who, on his deathbed, cast a last look at this irreplaceable earth and cried out: 'Close the window, it's too beautiful.' They have closed the

---

3. This essay deals with a particular temptation. One must have experienced it. One can then choose to act or not to act, but with full awareness of what is involved.

The Minotaur or the Halt at Oran

window, they have walled themselves in, they have exorcized the landscape. But Le Poittevin is dead, and now that he is gone tomorrow has followed tomorrow. Similarly, beyond the yellow walls of Oran the earth and sea pursue their indifferent dialogue. This permanence which the world possesses has always held a contradictory charm for man. It inspires him and casts him into despair. The world never has more than one thing to say, it is interesting, then boring. But, in the long run, it conquers through obstinacy. It is always right.

As soon as you leave the gates of Oran, nature takes on a harsher note. Towards Canastel lie immense stretches of waste land, covered with scented bushwood. There, the wind and sun speak only of solitude. Above Oran stands the Santa Cruz mountain, with its plateau and the thousand ravines leading to it. Roads, along which in former times one could travel in a coach, cling to the hillsides overlooking the sea. In January some are covered in flowers. Buttercups and daisies turn them into sumptuous paths, woven with white and yellow. On Santa Cruz there is no more to be said. But if I had to speak of this mountain, I should forget the sacred processions which climb its harsh slopes on the great feast days and evoke other pilgrimages. They travel in solitude through the red stone, rise above the motionless bay, before descending to consecrate a perfect and shining hour to frugality.

Oran also has its deserts of sand: its beaches. The ones near the city gates are empty only in winter and in spring. Then they are plateaux covered with asphodels and peopled with small bare villas among the flowers. The sea growls a little, lower down. But the sun, the slight wind, the whiteness of the asphodels, the harsh blue of the sky already foreshadow the summer and the golden youth which then covers the beach, long hours on the sand and the sudden gentleness of evening. Each year sees a new harvest of flower-maidens on these shores. Apparently, they last only for one season, since the following year other warm corollas take their place, who the previous summer were still little girls with bodies hard as buds. Coming down from the plateau at eleven in the morning, all this young flesh, scarcely covered by its motley garments, flows over the sand like a multicoloured wave.

One must go farther off (and strangely near, in fact, to that place where two hundred thousand men walk round in their own tracks) to find a landscape that is still untouched: long empty dunes on which the passage of men has left no trace but a worm-eaten hut. From time to time an Arab shepherd leads across the top of the dunes the black and beige stains made by his herd of goats. On these beaches in the province of Oran each summer morning feels like the first morning of the world. Each dusk feels like the last, a solemn death proclaimed at sunset by a final light which darkens every shade. The sea is ultramarine, the road the colour of dried blood, the beach yellow. Everything vanishes with the green sun; an hour later the dunes are flowing with moonlight. Then comes night, boundless beneath a shower of stars. Storms drift occasionally across the night, and flashes of lightning flow along the dunes, turn the sky pale, and cast an orange-coloured glow upon the sand or on our eyes.

But this cannot be shared through speech. It must be lived. So much solitude and grandeur give these places an unforgettable appearance. In the mild early dawn, beyond the small, still black and bitter waves, a new being cleaves the waters of night that are so heavy to bear. The memory of these joys gives me no regret, and this is how I know that they were good. After so many years, they are still there, somewhere in this heart which finds fidelity so hard. And I know that today, if I want to visit them, the same sky will still pour down its cargo of stars and breezes upon the deserted dunes. These are the lands of innocence.

But innocence needs sands and stones. And man has forgotten how to live with them. This, at least, appears to be the case, since he has shut himself up in this strange town of slumbering boredom. It is nevertheless this confrontation which gives Oran its value. The capital of boredom, besieged by innocence and beauty, is hemmed in by an army as rich in soldiers as in stones. Yet, at certain times, how tempted one feels in this town to pass over to the enemy! How tempted to merge oneself with these stones, to become indistinguishable from this burning and impassive uni-

The Minotaur or the Halt at Oran

verse which stands as a challenge to history and its agitations! A vain temptation, no doubt. But there is in every man a deep instinct which is neither that of destruction nor that of creation. It is simply the longing to resemble nothing. In the shade of the warm buildings of Oran, on its dusty asphalt, one sometimes hears this invitation. It seems that, for a time, the minds which yield to it are never disappointed. They find the shades of Eurydice and the sleep of Isis. These are the deserts where thought refills its lungs, the cool hand of evening on a troubled heart. No vigil can be kept upon this Mount of Olives; the mind joins and approves the sleeping Apostles. Were they really wrong? They did have their revelation after all.

Let us think of Sakia-Mouni in the desert. He spent long years there, crouching motionless and looking up to heaven. The gods themselves envied him this wisdom and this fate of stone. In his stiff and outstretched hands, the swallows had made their nest. But, one day, they flew away to follow the call of distant lands. And the man who had killed in himself desire and will, glory and sadness, began to weep. Thus it happens that flowers grow from the rock. Yes, let us consent to stone when we must. It too can give us the secret and the rapture that we seek in faces. Of course, this cannot last. But what is there that can? The face's secret fades, and we must tread once more the closed paths of desire. And if stone can do no more for us than can the human heart, it can at least do just as much.

'To be nothing!' For thousands of years this cry has inspired millions of men in revolt against desire and suffering. Its echoes have travelled all the way across centuries and oceans, before coming to rest upon the oldest sea in the world. They still echo softly against the solid cliffs of Oran. Everyone, in this country, follows this advice without knowing it. Naturally, it is practically in vain. Nothingness is no more in our grasp than is the absolute. But since we welcome as evidence of grace the eternal signs which roses or the sufferings of men can bring us, let us also not reject the rare invitations to sleep which are granted to us by the earth. The second have as much truth as the first.

This, perhaps, is the Ariadne's thread of this frenzied and sleep-walking town. We acquire the virtues, the wholly provisional virtues, of certain boredom. To be spared, we must say 'yes' to the Minotaur. It is an old and fecund wisdom. Above the sea, lying silent at the foot of the red cliffs, we need only to hold ourselves exactly balanced between the two massive headlands which, to right and left, stand bathed in the clear water. In the chugging of a coastguard vessel crawling out to sea, bathed in radiant light, you can now distinctly hear the stifled call of glittering and inhuman forces: it is the Minotaur's farewell.

It is midday, the day itself stands at a point of balance. His rite accomplished, the traveller receives the price of his deliverance: the little stone, dry and soft as an asphodel, that he picks up on the cliff. For the initiate the world is no heavier to carry than that stone. The burden of Atlas is easy; all you need do is choose your time. You then understand that for an hour, a month, a year, these shores can lend themselves to freedom. They offer the same uncritical welcome to the monk, the civil servant and the conqueror. There were days when I used to expect, in the streets of Oran, to meet Descartes or Cesare Borgia. This did not happen. But perhaps another will be more fortunate that I. A great action, a great undertaking, virile meditation required in days gone by the solitude of a desert or a convent. There men kept vigil over the weapons of their mind. Where better could we keep this vigil now than in the emptiness of a large town built to last in the midst of mindless beauty?

Here is the small stone, soft as an asphodel. It lies at the beginning of everything. Flowers, tears (if you insist), departures and struggles are for tomorrow. In the middle of the journey, when the heavens open their fountains of light in vast, resounding space, the headlands all along the coast look like a fleet of ships impatient to weigh anchor. These heavy galleons of rock and light lie trembling on their keels as if in preparation for a voyage to the islands of the sun. Oh, mornings in Oran! From high on the plateaux the swallows swoop down into the immense cauldrons of simmering air. The whole coast is ready for departure, a thrill of adventure runs along it. Tomorrow, perhaps, we shall set sail together.

THE ALMOND-TREES

'Do you know,' Napoleon once said to Fontanes, 'what fills me most with wonder? The powerlessness of force to establish anything. There are only two powers in the world: the sword and the mind. In the end the sword is always conquered by the mind.'

Conquerors, we see, are sometimes melancholy. They must pay something for so much vainglory. But what, a hundred years ago, was true of the sword, is no longer true today for the tank. The conquerors have made progress, and the dismal silence of mindless places has established its long reign over a lacerated Europe. At the time of the hideous wars of Flanders Dutch painters could perhaps still paint the cockerels in their farmyards. The Hundred Years War has likewise been forgotten, and yet the prayers of the Silesian mystics still inhabit some men's hearts. But today things have changed, the painter and the monk are mobilized: we are one with this world. The mind has lost that regal certainty which a conqueror could acknowledge; it now exhausts itself in cursing force, for want of knowing how to master it.

There are noble souls who keep deploring this, and saying it is evil. We do not know if it is evil, but we know it is a fact. The conclusion is that we must come to terms with it. All we then need to know is what we want. And what indeed we want is never again to bow down before the sword, never more to declare force to be in the right when it is not serving the mind.

This, it is true, is an endless task. But we are here to pursue it. I do not have enough faith in reason to subscribe to a belief in progress, or to any philosophy of History. But I do at least believe that men have never ceased to grow in the knowledge of their destiny. We have not overcome our condition, and yet we know it better. We know that we live in contradiction, but that we must refuse this contradiction and do what is needed to reduce it. Our task as men is to find those few first principles that will calm the infinite anguish of free souls. We must stitch up what has been torn apart, render justice imaginable in the world which is so obviously unjust, make happiness meaningful for nations poisoned by the misery of this century. Naturally, it is a superhuman task. But tasks are called superhuman when men take a long time to complete them, that is all.

Let us then know our aims, standing steadfast on the mind, even if force dons the mask of ideas or of comfort to lure us from our task. The first thing is not to despair. Let us not listen too much to those who proclaim that the world is ending. Civilizations do not die so easily, and even if this world were to collapse, it will not have been the first. It is indeed true that we live in tragic times. But too many people confuse tragedy with despair. 'Tragedy', Lawrence said, 'ought to be a great kick at misery.' This is a healthy and immediately applicable idea. There are many things today deserving of that kick.

When I lived in Algiers, I would wait patiently all winter because I knew that in the course of one night, one cold, pure February night, the almond trees of the Vallée des Consuls would be covered with white flowers. I was then filled with delight as I saw this fragile snow stand up to all the rain and resist the wind from the sea. Yet every year it lasted, just long enough to prepare the fruit.

This is not a symbol. We shall not win our happiness with symbols. We shall need something more weighty. All I mean is that sometimes, when life weighs too heavily in this Europe still overflowing with its misery, I turn towards those shining lands where so much strength is still untouched. I know them too well not to realize that they are the chosen lands where courage and contemplation can live in harmony. The contemplation of their example then teaches me that if we would save the mind we must pass over its power to groan and exalt its strength and wonder. This world is poisoned by its misery, and seems to wallow in it. It has utterly surrendered to that evil which Nietzsche called the spirit of heaviness. Let us not contribute to it. It is vain to weep over the mind, it is enough to labour for it.

But where are the conquering virtues of the mind? This same

Nietzsche listed them as the mortal enemies of the spirit of heaviness. For him they are strength of character, taste, the 'world', classical happiness, severe pride, the cold frugality of the wise. These virtues, more than ever, are necessary today, and each can choose the one that suits him best. Before the vastness of the undertaking, let no one in any case forget strength of character. I do not mean the one accompanied on electoral platforms by frowns and threats. But the one that, through the virtue of its whiteness and its sap, stands up to all the winds from the sea. It is that which, in the winter of the world, will prepare the fruit.

1940

PROMETHEUS IN THE UNDERWORLD

'I felt that the Gods lacked something so long as there was nothing to set against them.'

Prometheus in the Caucasus. Lucian

WHAT is the meaning of Prometheus for the man of today? It would doubtless be said that this God-defying rebel is the model for contemporary man, and that his protest, raised thousands of years ago in the deserts of Scythia, is culminating today in an unparalleled historical convulsion. But, at the same time, something tells us that this victim of persecution is still among us, and that we are still deaf to the great cry of human rebellion of which he gives the solitary signal.

Modern man indeed endures a multitude of suffering over the narrow surface of the earth, lacks foods and warmth, and sees liberty as merely a luxury that can wait; and all that he can do is suffer a little more, even as all that liberty and its last witnesses can do is vanish a little farther. Prometheus was the hero who loved men enough to give them fire and liberty, technology and art. Today mankind needs and cares only for technology. It rebels through its machines, holding art and what art implies as an obstacle and symbol of slavery. What, on the contrary, characterizes Prometheus is that he cannot separate machines from art. He believes that both souls and bodies can be freed at the same time. The man of today believes that we must first of all free the body, even if the mind must suffer a provisional decease. But can the mind die provisionally? Indeed, if Prometheus were to come back to earth, the men of today would behave as the gods did long ago: they would nail him to the rock, in the name of that very humanism which he was the first to symbolize. The hostile voices that would then insult the defeated victim would be the very ones which echo on the threshold of Aeschylan tragedy: those of Force and Violence.

Am I yielding to the meanness of the times, to naked trees and the winter of the world? But this very nostalgia for light is my justification: it speaks to me of another world, of my true country. Does this nostalgia still mean something for some men? In the year the war began, I was to take ship and follow the voyage of Ulysses. At that time, even a penniless young man could form the sumptuous project of crossing the sea in quest of sunlight. But I then did as everyone else. I did not take ship. I took my place in the queue shuffling towards the open mouth of hell. Little by little, we entered. At the first cry of murdered innocence, the door slammed shut behind us. We were in hell, and we have not left it since. For six long years, we have been trying to come to terms with it. We now catch glimpses of the warm ghosts from the islands of the blessed only across the long, cold, sunless years which are still to come.

How then, in this damp, dark Europe, can we avoid trembling with regret and sharing this cry which in his old age Châteaubriand uttered to Ampère departing for Greece: 'You will rediscover neither a leaf of the olive-trees nor a pip of the grapes which I saw in Attica. I regret even the grass that grew there in my day. I have not had the strength to make a patch of heather grow.' And we too, sunk in spite of our youthful blood in the terrible old age of this last century, sometimes regret the grass which always grew, the olive leaf we shall no longer gaze on for itself, and the grapes of liberty. Man is everywhere, and everywhere we find his cries, his suffering and his threats. When so many men are gathered together, the grasshopper can find no space. History is a sterile earth where the heather will not grow. Yet the men of today have chosen history, and they neither could nor should have turned their faces from it. But instead of mastering it, they agree a little more each day to be its slave. It is here that they betray Prometheus, this son 'both bold in thought and light of heart'. It is here that they go back to the wretchedness of the men whom Prometheus tried to save. 'They saw without seeing, heard without listening, like figures in a dream.'

Yes, one evening in Provence, one whiff of salt is enough to show us that everything still lies before us. We need to reinvent fire, to reinstall those crafts which calm the body's hunger. Attica, the vine-harvest of liberty, the bread of the soul, must come later. What can we do but cry to ourselves: 'They will never more return, or they will return for others', and do what we must to see that others at least do not lack them? And what of us, who feel this painfully, and who yet try to accept it without bitterness? Are we lagging behind, or are we forging ahead? Shall we have the strength to make the heather grow again?

We can imagine how Prometheus would have replied to this question which arises in our country. Indeed, he has already given his answer: 'I promise you, O mortals, both improvement and repair, if you are skilful, virtuous and strong enough to achieve them with your own hands.' If, then, it is true that salvation lies in our own hands, I shall say Yes to the questions of this century, because of the wise strength and informed courage that I still feel in some of those I know. 'O Justice, O my mother,' cries Prometheus, 'you see what I am made to suffer.' And Hermes mocks the hero: 'I am amazed that, being half a god, you did not foresee the torment you now undergo.' 'I foresaw it,' replies the rebel. Those I have mentioned are, like him, the sons of justice. They too suffer from the misery of all men, knowing what they do. They indeed know that blind justice does not exist, that history has no eyes, and that we must therefore reject its justice in order to put in its place, in so far as this can be done, the justice invented by the mind. It is here that Prometheus comes once more back into our century.

Myths have no life of their own. They wait for us to clothe them in flesh. If one man in the world answers their call, they give us their strength in all its fullness. We must preserve this myth, and ensure that its sleep is not mortal so that resurrection may become possible. I sometimes doubt whether the men of today can be saved. But it is still possible to save their children, in both their body and their mind. It is possible to offer them at one and the same time the chances of happiness and those of beauty. If we must resign ourselves to living without beauty, and the liberty which it implies, the myth of Prometheus is one of those which remind us that any mutilation of man can only be temporary, and that we serve nothing in man if we do not serve the whole of man. If he is hungry for bread and for heather, and if it is true that bread is the more necessary, let us learn how to keep the memory of heather alive. At the darkest heart of history the men of Prometheus, without ceasing from their harsh calling, will keep watch over the earth and over the unwearying grass. The enchained hero maintains, amid the thunder and lightning of the Gods, his quiet faith in man. This is how he is harder than his rock and more patient than his vulture. More than his rebellion against the gods, it is this long stubbornness which is meaningful for us. It accompanies this admirable determination to separate and exclude nothing, and which always has and always will unite the suffering heart of men and the springtimes of the world.

1946

SHORT GUIDE TO TOWNS WITHOUT A PAST

THE gentleness of Algiers is rather Italian. The cruel glare of Oran is more like Spain. Perched high on a rock above the Rummel gorges, Constantine is reminiscent of Toledo. But Spain and Italy are overflowing with memories, with works of art and educative ruins. And Toledo has had its Greco and its Barrès. The cities I am discussing are, on the contrary, towns without a past. They are towns which offer neither relaxation nor tenderness. When the siesta hours bring their boredom, there is neither compassion nor melancholy in their sadness. In the morning light, or in the natural luxury of the evenings, their delights are, on the contrary, without gentleness. These towns give nothing to the mind and everything to the passions. They are suited neither to wisdom nor to the refinements of taste. A Barrès and those like him would be crushed to pieces.

Passionate travellers (of other people's passions), over-sensitive minds, aesthetes and newly-weds have nothing to gain from going to Algiers. And, unless he has an absolute vocation, no one could be recommended to retire and live there for ever. Sometimes, in Paris, when people I esteem ask me about Algiers, I feel like crying out: 'Don't go there.' Such a joke would have some truth in it. For I can see what they are expecting and know they will not obtain it. And, at the same time, I know the charms and the subtle power of this country, its insinuating hold on those who linger there, how it immobilizes them, first of all by ridding them of questions, and finally by rocking them to sleep in everyday life. When the light hits you, so glaring that it turns black and white, it almost stops you breathing. You give way to it, settle down in it, and then realize that this too long splendour holds nothing for the soul and is merely an excessive delight. You would then like to turn back to the mind. But the men of this

Short Guide to Towns without a Past

country, and that is their strength, seem stronger in heart than mind. They can be your friends (and what friends!), but you can never tell them your secrets. Such a thing might be considered rather fearsome here in Paris, where souls are poured out so lavishly and where the water of secrets flows softly and endlessly along among the fountains, statues and the gardens.

What this land most resembles is Spain. But with no traditions, Spain would be merely a beautiful desert. And unless they happen to have been born there, there is only one race of men who can think of withdrawing for ever to the desert. Since I was born in this desert, I cannot in any case consider discussing it as a visitor. Can one number the charms of a dearly loved woman? No, you love her all of a piece, if I may use the expression, with one or two precise reasons for tenderness such as a favourite pout or a particular way of shaking the head. I thus have a long-standing liaison with Algeria, one that will doubtless never end, and which prevents me from being completely lucid. All you can do in such a case is, by perseverance, to make a kind of abstract list of what you love in the thing you love. It is this academic exercise that I can undertake here in respect of Algeria.

First of all comes the beauty of its young people. The Arabs, of course, and then the others. The French of Algeria are a bastard race, made up of unforeseen mixtures. Spaniards and Alsatians, Italians, Maltese, Jews and Greeks have come together there. As in America this brutal interbreeding has had happy results. As you walk through Algiers, look at the wrists of the women and the young men, and then think of the ones you see in the Paris *métro*.

The traveller who is still young will also notice that the women there are beautiful. The best place to take full note of this is the terrace of the Café des Facultés, in the Rue Michelet, in Algiers, on a Sunday morning in April. Cohorts of young women, sandals on their feet, wearing light, brightly coloured dresses, walk up and down the street. You can admire them without inhibitions: that is why they are there. At Oran the Cintra bar on the Boulevard Gallieni is also a good observatory. At Constantine you can always walk round the bandstand. But since the sea is several hundred kilometres away, there is something lacking in the people you meet there. In general, and because of this geographical location, Constantine offers fewer attractions, though its boredom has a rather more delicate quality.

If the traveller arrives in summer, the first thing he must obviously do is go down on to the beaches which surround the towns. He will see the same young people, more dazzling because less clothed. The sun then gives them the somnolent eyes of great beasts. In this respect the beaches of Oran are the finest, for nature and women are both wilder there.

As far as picturesqueness is concerned, Algiers offers an Arab town, Oran a Negro village and a Spanish district, and Constantine a Jewish quarter. Algiers has a long necklace of boulevards along the sea; you must walk there at night. Oran has few trees, but the finest stones in the world. Constantine has a suspension bridge where the thing to do is have your photograph taken. On very windy days the bridge sways to and fro above the deep gorges of the Rummel, and you have a feeling of danger.

I recommend the sensitive traveller, if he goes to Algiers, to go and drink *anisette* under the archways around the port, to go in the morning to La Pêcherie and eat freshly caught fish grilled on charcoal stoves; to go and listen to Arab music in a little café in the Rue de la Lyre whose name I have forgotten; to sit on the ground at six in the evening at the foot of the statue of the Duc d'Orléans in Government Square (not for the sake of the duke, but because there are people walking by, and it is pleasant there); to go and lunch at the Padovani restaurant, which is a kind of dance-hall on stilts, on the sea shore, where life is always easy; to visit the Arab cemeteries, first of all to find calm and beauty there, and then to appreciate at their true value the ignoble cities where we stack our dead; to go and smoke a cigarette in the Rue des Bouchers, in the Kasbah, in the midst of the spleens, livers, mesenteries and bleeding lungs that are dripping everywhere (the cigarette is necessary, since these middle ages have a strong smell).

For the rest, you must be able to speak ill of Algiers when in Oran (insisting on the commercial superiority of Oran as a port), make fun of Oran when in Algiers (have no hesitation in accepting the idea that the Oranais 'do not know how to live'), and, at every opportunity, humbly acknowledge the superiority of Algiers over metropolitan France. Once these concessions have been made, you will be able to appreciate the real superiority of the Algerian over the Frenchman, that is to say his limitless generosity and his natural hospitality.

It is perhaps here that I could stop all irony. After all, the best way of talking about what you love is to speak of it lightly. As far as Algeria is concerned, I am always afraid to lean on this matching inner chord, whose blind and serious song I know so well. But I can at least say that it is my true country, and that anywhere in the world I recognize its sons and my brothers by the friendly laughter that seizes me when I meet them. Yes, what I love about the towns of Algiers does not cut me off from the men who live in them. That is why I prefer to be there at that evening hour when the shops and offices pour out into the streets, still dark from the sun, a chattering crowd which flows right along to the boulevards facing the sea. There, it begins to grow silent as the night falls, and as the lights from the sky, from the lighthouses in the bay and from the streetlamps, merge gradually into the same quivering glow. A whole people then stands meditating on the sea shore, and the crowd splits up into a thousand solitudes. Then begin the great African nights, royal exile, and the exaltation of despair which awaits the solitary traveller.

No, you must certainly not go there if you feel a lukewarm heart and if your soul is weak and weary! But for those who know what it is like to be torn between yes and no, between noon and midnight, between revolt and love, and finally for those who love funeral-pyres along the shore, there is a flame awaiting them in Algiers.

1947

HELEN'S EXILE

THE Mediterranean has its sunlit tragedy which is not that of the mists. On certain evenings, on the sea, at the foot of the mountains, night falls on the perfect curve of a little bay, and an anguished fullness rises from the silent waters. We realize in such places that, if the Greeks experienced despair, it was always through beauty and its oppressive quality. Tragedy, in this golden sadness, reaches its highest point. Our own time, on the contrary, has nourished its despair in ugliness and in convulsions. That is why Europe would be ignoble if grief could ever have this quality.

We have exiled beauty, the Greeks took up arms on its behalf. A first but a long-standing difference. Greek thought always took its stand upon the idea of limit. It carried nothing to extremes, neither religion nor reason, because it denied nothing, neither reason nor religion. It gave everything its share, balancing light with shade. Our Europe, on the contrary, eager for the conquest of totality, is the daughter of excess. It denies beauty, as it denies everything which it does not extol. And, although in diverse ways, it extols only one thing: the future empire of reason. In its madness it pushes back the eternal limits, and at once dark Furies swoop down upon it to destroy. Nemesis is watching, goddess of moderation, not of vengeance. All those who go beyond the limit are by her pitilessly chastised.

The Greeks, who spent centuries asking themselves what was just, would understand nothing of our idea of justice. Equity, for them, supposed a limit, while our whole continent is convulsed by the quest for a justice which it sees as absolute. At the dawn of Greek thought Heraclitus already conceived justice as setting its bounds to the physical universe itself. 'The sun will not go beyond its bounds, for otherwise the Furies which watch over justice will find it out.' We, who have cast both the universe and

Helen's Exile

the mind from their proper orbit, laugh at such threats. We light up in a drunken sky what suns we please. But these bounds nevertheless exist and we know it. In our wildest madness we dream of a balance that we have lost, and which in our simplicity we think we shall rediscover when our errors cease. An infantile presumption, and one which justifies the fact that childish peoples, inheriting our madness, should guide our history today.

A fragment attributed to this same Heraclitus states simply: 'Presumption, regression of progress.' And, many centuries after the Ephesian, Socrates, threatened by the death penalty, granted himself no other superiority than this: that he did not presume to know what he did not. The most exemplary life and ideas which these centuries can offer end on a proud acknowledgement of ignorance. And, in forgetting this, we have forgotten our virility. We have preferred the power which apes greatness, Alexander first of all, and then the Roman conquerors, which our school history books, by an incomparable vulgarity of soul, teach us to admire. We have conquered in our turn, have set aside the bounds, mastered heaven and earth. Our reason has swept everything away. Alone at last, we finally hold empire over a desert. How could we conceive this higher balance in which nature balanced history, beauty and goodness, and which carried the music of poetry even into the tragedy of blood? We turn our back upon nature, we are ashamed of beauty. Our miserable tragedies stink of offices, and the blood they run with has the colour of dirty ink.

That is why it is indecent to proclaim today that we are the sons of Greece. Or, if we are, we are sons turned renegade. Putting history on the throne of God, we are marching towards theocracy, like those whom the Greeks called barbarians and whom they fought to the last in the waters of Salamis. If we really want to grasp our difference, we must address ourselves to the man who, among our philosophers, is the true rival of Plato. 'Only the modern town', Hegel dares write, 'can offer the mind the ground where it can achieve awareness of itself.' Thus we live in the time of great cities. The world has been deliberately cut off from what gave it permanence: nature, the sea, hills, evening meditations. Awareness can now be found only in the streets, because there is history only in the streets, so runs the decree. And, consequently, our most significant works bear witness to the same prejudice. One seeks in vain for landscapes in major European writers since Dostoyevsky. History explains neither the natural universe which came before it, nor beauty, which stands above it. It has consequently chosen to know nothing of them. Whereas Plato contained everything, nonsense, reason and myths, our philosophers contain nothing except either nonsense or reason, because they have closed their eyes to the rest. The mole is meditating.

It was Christianity that began to replace the contemplation of the world by the tragedy of the soul. But Christianity at least referred to a spiritual nature, and consequently maintained a certain fixity. Now that God is dead, all that remains is history and power. For a long time now, the whole effort of our philosophers has been aimed solely at replacing the idea of human nature by the idea of situation, and ancient harmony by the confused upsurge of chance, or by the pitiless movement of reason. While the Greeks used reason to restrain the will, we have ended by placing the upsurge of the will at the heart of reason, and reason has therefore become murderous. For the Greeks, values were pre-existent to every action, and marked out its exact limits. Modern philosophy places its values at the end of action. They are not, but they become; and we shall know them completely only at the end of history. When they disappear, limits do as well, and since ideas differ on what these will be, since there is no struggle which, unhindered by these same values, does not extend indefinitely, we are now witnessing a conflict of Messianisms whose clamours merge in the shock of empires. Excess is a fire, according to Heraclitus. The fire is gaining ground; Nietzsche has been overtaken. It is no longer with hammer blows but with cannon shots that Europe philosophizes.

Nature is still there, nevertheless. It sets up its calm skies and its reasons against the folly of men. Until the atom too bursts into flame, and history ends in the triumph of reason and the death agony of the species. But the Greeks never said that the limit

Helen's Exile

could not be crossed. They said that it existed and that the man who dared ignore it was mercilessly struck down. There is nothing in the history of today that can contradict them.

Both the historical spirit and the artist seek to remake the world. But the artist, through an obligation of his very nature, recognizes the limits which the historical mind ignores. This is why the latter aims at tyranny while the passion of the first is liberty. All those who are fighting today for liberty are in the final analysis fighting for beauty. Of course, no one thinks of defending beauty solely for its own sake. Beauty cannot do without man, and we shall give our time its greatness and serenity only by accompanying it into its misery. We shall never again stand alone. But it is equally true that man cannot do without beauty, and this is what our time pretends to forget. It tenses itself to achieve empires and the absolute, it seeks to transfigure the world before having exhausted it, to set it to rights before having understood it. Whatever it may say, it is turning its back on this world. Ulysses, on Calypso's island, is given the choice between immortality and the land of his fathers. He chooses this earth, and death with it. Such a simple greatness is today foreign to our minds. Others will say that we lack humility. But this word, all things considered, is ambiguous. Like those buffoons in Dostoyevsky who boast of everything, rise up to the stars and end by flaunting their shame in the first public place, we lack simply the pride of the man who is faithful to his limitations and perceptively in love with his condition.

'I hate my time,' said Saint-Exupéry before his death, for reasons that are not far removed from those which I have mentioned. But, however overwhelming this cry may be, coming from him who loved men for their admirable qualities, we shall not take it as our own. Yet what a temptation, at certain times, to turn our back upon this gaunt and gloomy world. But this is our time and we cannot live hating ourselves. It has fallen so low as much by the excess of its virtues as by the greatness of its faults. We shall fight for the one amongst its virtues that comes from far off. Which virtue? Patroclus's horses weep for their master, dead in battle. All is lost. But Achilles returns to the fray and victory lies at the end because friendship has been murdered: friendship is a virtue.

It is by acknowledging our ignorance, refusing to be fanatics, recognizing the boundaries of man and the world, through the faces we love, in short, through beauty, that we shall rejoin the Greeks. In a way, the meaning of tomorrow's history will not be where men think it is. It lies in the struggle between creation and the inquisition. Whatever the price that artists will have to pay for their empty hands, we can hope for their victory. Once again, the philosophy of darkness will melt away above the dazzling sea. Oh, noonday thought, the Trojan war is fought far from the battle ground! Once again, the terrible walls of the modern city will fall to deliver, 'its soul serene as the untroubled waves', Helen's beauty.

1948

THE ENIGMA

WAVES of sunlight, pouring from the topmost sky, bounce fiercely on the countryside around us. All falls quiet with this din, and Mount Luberon, over there, is merely a vast block of silence which I listen to unceasingly. I listen carefully, someone runs to me from far off, invisible friends call to me, my joy grows, the same joy as years ago. Once again, a happy enigma helps me to understand everything.

Where is the absurdity of the world? In this shining glory, or in the memory of its absence? How, with so much sun in my memory, could I have wagered on nonsense? People around me are amazed; so, at times, am I. I could tell them, as I tell myself, that it was in fact the sun which helped me, and that the very thickness of its light coagulates the universe and its forms into a dazzling blackness. But there are other ways of saying this, and I should like, faced by this white and black clarity which for me has always been that of truth, to explain in simple terms what I feel about this absurdity which I know too well to allow anyone to speak about it in an oversimplified way. Moreover, the very fact of talking about it will lead us back to the sun.

No man can say what he is. But he can sometimes say what he is not. People want the man who is still seeking to have already reached his conclusions. A thousand voices are already telling him what he has found, and yet he knows that this is not the case. Should he carry on seeking and let them talk? Of course. But, from time to time, we must defend ourselves. I do not know what I am looking for, I name it prudently, I withdraw what I said, I repeat myself, I go backwards and forwards. People nevertheless call upon me to deliver the name, or names, once and for all. Then I object; are not things lost when they receive a name? Here, at least, is what I can try to say.

*

If I am to believe one of my friends, a man always has two characters: his own, and the one his wife thinks he has. If we replace his wife by society, we shall understand how a particular expression, used by a writer to describe a whole context of emotions, can be isolated by the way people comment on it and presented to its author every time he tries to talk about something else. Words are like actions: 'Are you the father of this child?' 'Yes.' 'Then he is your son.' 'It is not as simple as that, not at all!' Thus Gérard de Nerval, one filthy night, hanged himself twice, once for himself because he was unhappy, and a second time for his legend, which now helps some people to live. No one can write about real unhappiness, or about certain moments of happiness, and I shall not try to do so here. But, as far as legends are concerned, we can describe them, and, for a moment at least, believe that we have dispelled them.

A writer writes to a great extent to be read (as for those who say they don't, let us admire them but not believe them). Yet more and more, in France, he writes in order to obtain that final consecration which lies in not being read. From the moment, in fact, that he can provide the material for a picturesque article in one of our mass-circulation newspapers, there is every possibility that he will be known to a fairly large number of people who will never read his works because they will be content to know his name and to read what other people write about him. From then onwards, he will be known (and forgotten) not for what he is, but according to the image which a hurried journalist has given of him. To make a name in literature, it is consequently no longer indispensable to write books. It is enough to be thought to have written one book, mentioned in the evening papers, and on which one can repose for the rest of one's life.

There is no doubt that this reputation, great or small, will be undeserved. But what can be done about it? Let us rather admit that this inconvenience can be beneficial. Doctors know that certain illnesses are desirable: they provide, in their own way, a compensation for a functional disorder which, in their absence, would express itself in a more serious disturbance. Thus there are fortunate constipations and providential attacks of arthritis.

The Enigma

The flood of words and hasty judgements, which nowadays drowns all public activity in an ocean of frivolity, at least endows the French writer with a modesty that he constantly needs in a nation which, moreover, gives a disproportionate importance to his calling. To see your name in two or three newspapers I could mention is so harsh a trial that it must inevitably involve some spiritual benefit. Let us then praise society, which can so cheaply teach us every day, by its very homages, that the greatness which it honours is worthless. The louder the sound, the quicker it dies. It evokes that fire of tow which Alexander VI often had burned before him to remind him that all the glory of this world vanishes like smoke.

But that is enough irony. It is enough, in this respect, to say that an artist should cheerfully resign himself to allowing what he knows is an unworthy image of himself to lie about in dentists' and hairdressers' waiting-rooms. It was there that I read about a fashionable author who was considered to spend every night presiding over heady Bacchanalian orgies, where nymphs were clothed in nothing but their hair and fauns had dark and fatal nails. One might doubtless have wondered how he found the time to write a series of books that filled several library shelves. This writer, in fact, like many of his colleagues, sleeps at night in order to spend long hours every day working at his desk, and drinks Vichy water so as not to strain his liver. This does not prevent the average Frenchman, whose Saharan sobriety and mania for cleanliness are well known, from being indignant at the idea that our writers should teach men to drink and not to wash. There is no lack of examples. I can myself give an excellent recipe of how to secure a reputation for austerity very cheaply. I do in fact bear the weight of such a reputation, which is a source of great amusement to my friends (as far as I myself am concerned, it is more a source of embarrassment, for I know how little I deserve it). All you need do, for example, is decline the honour of dining with a newspaper editor of whom you do not have a high opinion. Even simple decency cannot be imagined except by reference to some twisted sickness of the soul. In any case, no one will ever imagine that, if you refuse this editor's dinner, this is not only because you do not have a very high opinion of him, but also because your greatest fear in the world is being bored – and what is more boring than a typically Parisian dinner?

We must therefore be resigned. But from time to time you can try to readjust the sights, and to repeat that you cannot always be a painter of the absurd and that no one can believe in a literature of despair. Of course, it is always possible to write, or to have written, an essay on the notion of the absurd. But, after all, you can also write about incest without having necessarily hurled yourself on your unfortunate sister; and I have nowhere read that Sophocles ever thought of killing his father and dishonouring his mother. The idea that every writer necessarily writes about himself and depicts himself in his books is one of the puerile notions that we have inherited from Romanticism. It is by no means impossible, on the contrary, that a writer should be interested first and foremost in other people, or in his time, or in familiar myths. Even if he does happen to put himself in the picture, it is only very exceptionally that he talks about what he is really like. A man's works often retrace the story of his nostalgias or his temptations, practically never his own story, especially when they claim to be autobiographical. No man has ever dared describe himself as he is.

As far as such a thing is possible, I would, on the contrary, have liked to be an objective writer. What I call an objective writer is an author who chooses themes without ever taking himself as the subject. But the modern mania of identifying the author with his subject-matter cannot allow him to enjoy this relative liberty. Thus one becomes a prophet of the absurd. Yet what did I do except reason about an idea which I found in the streets of my time? It goes without saying that both I and my whole generation have nourished this idea (and that a part of myself still does so). What I did, however, was to set it far enough from me to analyse it and decide on its logic. Everything that I have been able to write since then is sufficient proof of this. But it is more convenient to exploit a cliché than a nuance. They choose the cliché: so I am absurd as before.

What is the point of saying yet again that in the experience

The Enigma

which interested me, and on which I happened to write, the absurd can be considered only as a point of departure – even though the memory and feeling of it still accompany the later steps in the argument? Similarly, with all due sense of proportion, Cartesian doubt, which is systematic, is not enough to make Descartes into a sceptic. In any case, how could one restrict oneself to saying that everything is meaningless, and that we should plunge into absolute despair? Without going to the root of the matter, one can at least remark that in the same way as there is no absolute materialism, since simply to form this word there must be something in the world apart from matter, there is likewise no total nihilism. As soon as you say that everything is nonsense, you express something that is meaningful. Refusing to see the world all meaning amounts to abolishing all value judgements. But living and eating, for example, is in itself a value judgement. You choose to stay alive the moment you do not allow yourself to die of hunger, and you consequently recognize that life has at least a relative value. What, in fact, does a literature of despair mean? Despair is silent. Moreover, even silence is meaningful if your eyes speak. True despair is the agony of death, the grave or the abyss. If it speaks, if it reasons, above all if it writes, immediately a brother reaches out his hand, the tree is justified, love is born. A literature of despair is a contradiction in terms.

Of course, a certain optimism is not my speciality. Like all the men of my age, I grew up to the sound of the drums of the First World War, and our history since that time has remained murder, injustice or violence. But real pessimism, which does exist, lies in adding something to all this cruelty and shame. For my part, I have never ceased fighting against this dishonour, and I hate only the cruel. In our darkest nihilism I have sought only reasons to go beyond it. Not, I would add, through virtue, nor by a rare elevation of the soul, but by an instinctive fidelity to a light in which I was born, and in which for thousands of years men have learned to welcome life even in suffering. Aeschylus is often full of despair; yet he sheds light and warmth. At the centre of his universe, we find not fleshless nonsense but an enigma, that is to say a meaning which is difficult to decipher because it dazzles us. And, likewise, the unworthy but nevertheless stubborn sons of Greece who still survive in this emaciated century may still find this history too scalding hot, and yet they bear the pain because they want to understand it. At the centre of our work, dark though it may be, there shines an inexhaustible sun, the same sun which cries today across the hills and plain.

*

After this, the fire of tow can burn; what do our image and our usurpations matter? What we are, what we have to be, are enough to fill our lives and occupy our strength. Paris is a marvellous cave, and its men, seeing their own shadows reflected on the far wall, take them for the only reality there is. The same is true of the strange and fleeting fame this town awards. But we have learned, far from Paris, that there is a light behind us, and that we must turn round and cast off our chains if we are to look at it directly; that our task is, before we die, to seek for all the words we can to name it. Each artist is undoubtedly pursuing his truth. If he is a great artist, each work brings him nearer to it, or, at least, itself swings closer in towards this centre, this buried sun where everything must one day burn. If he is mediocre, each work takes him farther from it, the centre is then everywhere, the light disintegrates. But the only people who can help the artist in his obstinate quest are those who love him, and those who, themselves lovers or creators, find in their own passion the measure for all passion, and can then judge.

Yes, all this noise . . . when peace would be to love and create in silence! But we must learn to be patient. One moment more, the sun seals our mouths.

1950

RETURN TO TIPASA

'You have sailed with a furious soul far from your father's house, beyond the double rocks of the sea, and you live in a foreign land.'

Medea

For five days, the rain had been falling unceasingly on Algiers, and had finally drenched the sea itself. From the heights of an apparently inexhaustible sky, unending sheets of rain, so thick they were viscous, swooped down on the gulf. Soft and grey like a great sponge, the sea heaved in the shapeless bay. But the surface of the water seemed almost motionless beneath the steady rain. At long intervals, however, a broad and imperceptible movement raised a murky cloud of steam from off the sea and brought it into harbour, beneath a circle of soaking boulevards. The town itself, all its white walls running with damp, gave off another cloud of steam which moved out to meet the first. Wherever you turned when this happened, you seemed to be breathing water, and you could drink the very air.

Looking at this drowned sea, I walked about and waited, in this December Algiers which was still for me the town of summers. I had fled from the night of Europe, from a winter of faces. But the town of summers had itself been emptied of its laughter and offered me only hunched and shining backs. In the evening, in the violently lit cafés where I sought refuge, I read my age upon faces that I could recognize without giving them a name. All I knew was that these men had been young when I was, and that now they were young no more.

I stayed on, however, without any clear idea of what I was waiting for, except, perhaps, the moment when I could go back to Tipasa. It is, indeed, a great folly and one that is almost always punished, to go back to the places of your youth, and to seek to relive, at the age of forty, things which you loved or greatly enjoyed at twenty. But I knew about this folly. I had already come back to Tipasa for a first time, shortly after those wartime years that marked for me the end of my youth. I then hoped, I believe, to rediscover a liberty which I could not forget. Here, indeed, more than twenty years ago, I had spent whole mornings wandering among the ruins, breathing the scent of absinthe, warming myself against the stones, finding the small roses which survive in springtime and swiftly lose their leaves. Only at noon, when the very crickets fell silent in the heat, would I flee before the avid blaze of an all-devouring light. Sometimes at night I would sleep open-eyed beneath a sky flowing with stars. Then I was alive. Fifteen years afterwards I found my ruins again, a few steps from the first waves. I followed the streets of the forgotten city across the fields covered with bitter trees, and, on the hills overlooking the bay, could still caress the breadcrust-coloured pillars. But now the ruins were surrounded by barbed wire, and could be reached only through official entrances. It was also forbidden, for reasons which apparently enjoyed the blessing of morality, to walk there after dark; by day you met a sworn guardian. And that morning, doubtless by chance, it was raining over the whole area of the ruins.

Bewildered, walking through the lonely and rain-soaked countryside, I at least made an effort to rediscover that strength which has so far never failed me, and which helps me to accept what exists once I have recognized that I cannot change it. And I could not, in fact, travel backwards through time, restore to the world the face that I had loved and which had disappeared in the course of one day, many years ago. On the second of September, in fact, I had not gone to Greece, as I had planned. Instead, war had come to us, then had covered Greece itself. This distance, these years which separated the warm ruins from the barbed wire were also in myself, as I stood that lay before the sarcophagi filled with black water or under the dripping tamarisk trees. Brought up first of all in the spectacle of beauty, which was my only wealth, I had begun with fullness. What had followed was

Return to Tipasa

barbed wire: I mean tyrannies, war, police forces, the time of revolt. We had had to come to terms with the night: the beauty of the day was only a memory. And in this muddy Tipasa, the memory itself was growing dim. No talk now of beauty, fullness or youth! In the light cast by the flames, the world had suddenly shown its wrinkles and its wounds, both old and new. It had grown old in an instant, the twinkling of an eye, and we with it. I knew well enough that only men caught unawares could be inspired by the passion which I sought for here. Love cannot exist without a little innocence. Where was innocence? Empires were crumbling, men and nations tearing at one another's throats; our mouths were sullied. After being innocent in ignorance, we were now unintentionally guilty: the more we knew, the greater grew the mystery. This is why we busied ourselves, Oh! mockery of mockeries, with morality. Sick in spirit, I dreamed of virtue! In the days of innocence, I did not know that morality existed. I now knew that it did, and could not live up to it. On the promontory that I had loved in former days, between the drenched pillars of the ruined temple, I seemed to be walking behind someone whose footsteps I could still hear on the tombstones and mosaics, but whom I should never catch up with again. I went back to Paris, where I stayed for some years before coming back home.

During all these years, however, I had an obscure feeling that something was lacking. When you have once had the chance to love intensely, your life is spent seeking to find this light and ardour once again. To give up beauty and the sensual happiness it brings and devote myself exclusively to unhappiness requires a greatness that I do not have. But, after all, nothing is true which compels us to exclude. Isolated beauty ends in grimaces, solitary justice in oppression. Anyone who seeks to serve the one to the exclusion of the other serves nobody, not even himself, and in the end is doubly the servant of injustice. A day comes when, because we have held ourselves so stiff, nothing amazes us any more, and our life is spent in beginning again. These are days of exile, dryness and dead souls. To live again, we need grace, forgetfulness of ourselves, or else a homeland. On some mornings, as we turn a corner, an exquisite dew falls on our heart and then vanishes. But its freshness still remains, and it is always this which the heart demands. I had to leave once more.

And, in Algiers for a second time, still walking under the same downpour which I felt had not stopped since a departure which I had considered final, in the midst of this immense melancholy which smelled of rain and sea, in spite of this misty sky, these backs fleeing beneath the deluge, these cafés whose sulphurous light decomposed people's faces, I still persisted in my hopes. Did I not know, moreover, that rain in Algiers, although looking as if it is going on for ever, nevertheless does stop quite suddenly, like those rivers in my country which swell to a flood in two hours, devastate acres of land, and dry up again in an instant? One evening, in fact, the rain stopped. I waited for yet another night. A liquid morning rose, dazzling, over the pure sea. From the sky, fresh as a rose, washed and rewashed by the waters, reduced by each successive laundering to its most delicate and clearest texture, there fell a quivering light which gave each house, each tree, a palpable shape and a magic newness. The earth, on the morning the world was born, must have arisen in just such a light. Once again I set out for Tipasa.

There is not a single one of these sixty-nine kilometres that is not filled for me with memories and sensations. A violent childhood, adolescent day-dreams to the hum of the bus's engines, mornings, the freshness of young girls, beaches, young muscles always tensed to their highest effort, that slight anguish which evening brings to a heart of sixteen years, desire for life, glory, and always the same sky as companion to all the years, with its inexhaustible strength and light, a sky insatiable and continually devouring, for months on end, the victims lying crucified upon the beach at the funereal hour of noon. Always the same sea as well, almost impalpable in the morning air, which I glimpsed again on the horizon as soon as the road left the Sahel and the bronze-coloured vineyards on its hills, and plunged down towards the coast. But I did not stop to look at it. I wanted to see the Chenoua again, this heavy, solid mountain, carved in one piece and running along the west side of Tipasa Bay before plunging

Return to Tipasa

into the sea. You see it from far off, long before you arrive, as a light blue haze still mingling with the sea. But it gradually condenses as you come nearer, until it takes on the colour of the waters which surround it, like an immense and motionless wave brutally caught in the very act of breaking over a suddenly calm sea. Nearer still, almost at the gates of Tipasa, you see its beetling mass, brown and green, the old, unshakeable, mossgrown god, port and haven for its sons, of whom I am one.

I was gazing at it as I finally crossed the barbed wire and stood among the ruins. And, in the glorious December light, as happens only once or twice in lives that can henceforth see themselves as crowned with every blessing, I found exactly what I had come to seek, and which, in spite of time and in spite of the world, was given truly to myself alone in this deserted nature. From the olive-strewn forum you could see the village opposite. Not a sound came from it: wisps of smoke rose in the limpid air. The sea also lay silent, as if breathless beneath the unending shower of cold and glittering light. From the Chenoua a distant cock-crow alone extolled the fragile glory of the day. Across the ruins, as far as the eye could see, there lay nothing but pock-marked stones and absinthe plants, trees and perfect columns in the transparence of the crystal air. It was as if the morning stood still, as if the sun had stopped for an immeasurable moment. Amid this light and silence, years of night and fury melted slowly away. I listened to an almost forgotten sound within myself, as if my heart had long been stopped and was now gently beginning to beat again. And, now awake, I recognized one by one the imperceptible sounds that made up the silence: the continuous bass part of the birds, the short, light sighing of the sea at the foot of the rocks, the vibration of the trees, the blind song of the columns, the whispering of the absinthe plants, the furtive lizards. I could hear all that, while also listening to the waves of happiness rising up within me. I felt that I had at last come back to port, for a moment at least, and that from henceforth this moment would never end. But shortly afterwards the sun visibly rose a degree higher in the sky. A blackbird chirped its brief prelude and immediately, from all around, birds' voices exploded with a strength, a jubilation, a joyful discord, an infinite delight. The day moved on. It was to carry me through till evening.

At noon, on the half-sandy slopes, strewn with heliotropes as if by a foam which the furious waves of the last few days had left behind them in their retreat, I gazed at the sea, then gently rising and falling as if exhausted, and quenched the two thirsts that cannot long be neglected if all our being is not to dry up, the thirst to love and the thirst to admire. For there is only misfortune in not being loved; there is misery in not loving. We all, today, are dying of this misery. This is because blood and hatred lay bare the heart itself: the long demand for justice exhausts the love which nevertheless gave it birth. In the clamour in which we live love is impossible and justice not enough. This is why Europe hates the daylight and can do nothing but confront one injustice with another. But I rediscovered at Tipasa that, in order to prevent justice from shrivelling up, from becoming a magnificent orange containing only a dry and bitter pulp, we had to keep a freshness and a source of joy intact within ourselves, loving the daylight which injustice leaves unscathed, and returning to the fray with this reconquered light. Here once more I found ancient beauty, a young sky, and measured my good fortune as I realized at last that in the worst years of our madness the memory of this sky had never left me. It was this which in the end had saved me from despair. I had always known that the ruins of Tipasa were younger than our new buildings or our crumbling towns. There, the world was born again each morning in a light that was always new. O light! This is the cry of all the characters who, in classical tragedy, come face to face with their destiny. Their final refuge was also ours, and I now knew that this was so. In the depths of the winter I finally learned that there lay in me an unconquerable summer.

*

Once again I left Tipasa, returning to Europe and its struggles. But the memory of this day still bears me up and helps me greet with equanimity both joys and woes. What can I long for, at the difficult moment where now we stand, except the power to

Return to Tipasa

exclude nothing and learn to weave from strands of black and white one single rope that is stretched to breaking point? In everything which I have done or said up to now, I seem to recognize these two forces, even when they contradict each other. I have not been able to deny the light where I was born, and I have not wished to reject the servitudes of our time. It would be too easy to place here by the side of Tipasa other names which are more sonorous and more cruel: for the men of today there is an inner path which I know well through having travelled both ways upon it, and which leads from the hills of the mind to the capitals of crime. And, doubtless, we can always take rest, sleep on the hillside or settle down in crime. But if we give up a part of what exists, we must ourselves give up being; we must then give up living or loving except by proxy. Thus there is a will to live while refusing nothing of what life offers which is the virtue that I honour most in all this world. From time to time, at least, it is true that I should like to have exercised it. Since few epochs more than our own require us to be equal to the best as to the worst, I should like, in fact, to elude nothing and keep a double memory alive. Yes, there is beauty and there are the humiliated. Whatever difficulties the enterprise may present, I should like never to be unfaithful either to the second or the first.

But this still sounds like ethics, and we live for something that goes beyond them. If we could name it, what silence would ensue! On the hill of Sainte-Salsa, to the east of Tipasa, the evening is inhabited. Darkness, it is true, has not yet come, but an invisible waning of the light foreshadows sunset. A wind rises, gentle as the night, and suddenly the untroubled sea chooses its way and flows like a great barren river across the horizon. The sky grows darker. What follows is mystery, the gods of night, and what lies on the other side of pleasure. But how can this be expressed? The small coin that I take away from here has one clear side, the face of a beautiful woman which constantly repeats all I have learned today, and a side which is eaten away and which I feel under my fingers during my return. What can this lipless mouth do except repeat what another, mysterious voice within me says, a voice which daily teaches me my ignorance and happiness:

'The secret that I am looking for is buried in a valley of olive-trees under the grass and cold violets, around an old house that smells of vines. For more than twenty years I have wandered over this valley, and over others like it, questioning dumb goat-herds, knocking at the door of uninhabited ruins. Sometimes, when the first star shines in a still clear sky, beneath a rain of delicate light, I have thought that I knew. I did know, in fact. Perhaps I still know. But no one wants this secret, doubtless I myself do not desire it, and cannot cut myself off from my own people. I live with my family, which believes that it reigns over rich and hideous towns, built of stones and fogs. Day and night it raises its voice, and everything yields while it bows down before nothing: it is deaf to all secrets. Its power, which bears me up, nevertheless bores me, and I come to be weary of its cries. But its unhappiness is my own, we are of the same blood. I too am sick, and and am I not a noisy accomplice who has cried out among the stones? Thus I try to forget, I march through our towns of iron and fire, I smile bravely at the night, I welcome storms, I shall be faithful. In fact, I have forgotten: henceforth, I shall be deaf and active. But perhaps one day, when we are ready to die of ignorance and exhaustion, I shall be able to give up our gaudy tombs, go and lie down in the valley, under the unchanging light, and learn for a last time what I know.'

1953

THE SEA CLOSE BY
Logbook

I grew up in the sea and poverty was sumptuous, then I lost the sea and found all luxuries grey and poverty unbearable. Since then, I have been waiting. I wait for the homebound ships, the house of the waters, the limpidity of day. I wait patiently, am polite with all my strength. Men see me walk by in fine and learned streets, I admire landscapes, applaud like everyone else, shake hands, but it is not me speaking. Men praise me, I dream a little, they insult me, I scarcely show surprise. Then I forget, and smile at the man who insulted me, or am too courteous in greeting the person I love. What can I do if all I can remember is one image? Finally they call upon me to tell them who I am. 'Nothing yet, nothing yet ...'

It is at funerals that I excel myself. I do, indeed. I walk slowly through the iron-strewn paths of suburbs, travelling along wide lanes planted with cement trees and leading to holes in the cold earth. There, beneath the scarcely reddening bandage of the sky, I watch bold workmen inter my friends beneath six feet of earth. If I then cast the flower which a clay-covered hand holds out to me, it never misses the grave. My piety is exact, my feelings as they should be, my head is suitably inclined. I am admired for finding just the right word. But I have no merit in this: I am waiting.

I have been waiting for a long time. Sometimes, I stumble, I lose my touch, success evades me. What does it matter, for I am then alone. It is thus that I wake up at night, and, still half-asleep, think I hear the sound of waves and the breathing of the waters. Fully awake, I recognize the wind in the trees and the sad murmur of the empty town. I then need all my art to hide my distress or clothe it in the prevailing fashion.

At other times, on the contrary, I am helped. On certain days in New York, lost at the bottom of those wells of stones and steel where wander millions of men, I would run from one to another, without seeing where they ended, exhausted, until I was sustained only by the human mass seeking its way out. But, each time, the distant siren of a tug-boat came to remind me that this town, this empty well, was an island, and at the tip of the Battery the water of my baptism was awaiting me, black and rotting, covered over with hollow corks.

Thus, though I possess nothing, have given away my fortune, camp by the side of all my houses, I can still be blessed with all riches when I choose, set sail at every hour, unknown to despair. There is no country for those who despair, but I know that the sea comes before and after me, and hold my madness ready. Those who love and are separated can live in grief, but this is not despair: they know that love exists. This is why I suffer, dry-eyed, in exile. I am still waiting. A day comes, at last...

*

The bare feet of the sailors beat softly on the deck. It is dawn, and we are setting sail. The moment we leave harbour, a short, gusty wind vigorously brushes the sea which curls backwards in small, foamless waves. A little later the wind freshens and scatters the sea with swiftly vanished camellias. Thus throughout the morning we hear our sails slapping over a cheerful pond. The waters are heavy, scaly, covered with cool foam. From time to time the waves yap against the bow; a bitter, unctuous foam, the God's saliva, flows along the wood and loses itself in the water where it scatters into shapes that die and are reborn, the hide of a white and blue cow, an exhausted beast which drifts a long way behind our wake.

*

Since our departure the seagulls have been following our ship, apparently without effort, almost without moving their wings. Their fine straight navigation scarcely leans upon the breeze. Suddenly, a loud plop at the level of the kitchens casts a greedy

The Sea Close By

alarm among the birds, throws their fine flight into confusion and sends up a fire of white wings. The seagulls whirl madly in every direction, and then without any loss of speed drop away from the fight one by one and dive down to the sea. A few seconds later they are together again on the water, a quarrelsome farmyard that we leave behind us, nestling in the hollow of the wave, and slowly plucking through the manna of scraps.

*

At noon, under a deafening sun the sea, exhausted, scarcely finds the strength to rise. When it falls back on itself, it makes the silence whistle. It cooks for an hour and the pale water, a vast white-hot iron sheet sizzles. In a minute it will turn and offer its damp side, now hidden in waves and darkness, to the sun.

*

We pass by the gates of Hercules, the headland where Antaeus died. Beyond, the Ocean lies everywhere, on one side we pass by the Horn and the Cape of Good Hope, the Meridians wed the Latitudes, the Pacific drinks the Atlantic. Once our course is set for Vancouver, we plunge slowly towards the South Seas. A few cables' lengths away Easter Island, Desolation and the New Hebrides file past us in convoy. Suddenly one morning the seagulls disappear. We are far from any land, and alone, with our sails and our engines.

*

Alone also with the horizon. The waves come from the invisible East, patiently, one by one; they reach us, and then, patiently, set off again for the unknown West, one by one. A long voyage, with no beginning and no end. . . . Rivers and streams pass by, the sea passes and remains. This is how we must love it, faithful and fleeting. I wed the sea.

*

The high seas. The sun sinks down, is swallowed by the mists long before it reaches the horizon. For one brief moment, the sea is pink on one side and blue on the other. Then the waters grow darker. The schooner slides, minute, over the surface of a perfect circle of thick, tarnished metal. And at the most peaceful hour, as evening comes, hundreds of porpoises emerge from the water, play around us for a moment, then flee to the horizon where there are no men. They leave behind them the silence and anguish of primitive waters.

*

A little later still, we meet an iceberg on the Tropic. Doubtless invisible after its long voyage in these warm waters, but still effective: it passes to starboard, where the rigging is briefly covered with a frosty dew, while to port the day dies without moisture.

*

Night does not fall at sea. Rather, from the depths of the waters, which an already submerged sun gradually darkens with its thick ashes, it rises towards the still pale sky. For a brief moment Venus shines alone above the black waves. In the twinkling of an eye, stars swarm in the liquid night.

*

The moon has risen. First it gently illuminates the surface of the waters, then mounts higher and writes upon the supple water. At last at its zenith it lights up a whole corridor of sea, a rich river of milk which, with the motion of the ship, flows inexhaustibly towards us through the dark ocean. Here is the faithful night, the cool night which I called for amid the noise of lights, drink and the tumult of desire.

*

We sail across spaces so vast they seem unending. Sun and moon rise and fall in turn, on the same thread of light and night. Days at sea, even and indistinguishable as happiness...

*

This life rebellious to forgetfulness, rebellious to memory, of which Stevenson speaks.

*

The Sea Close By

Dawn. We sail perpendicularly across the Tropic of Cancer, the waters groan and are convulsed. Day breaks over a surging sea, full of steel spangles. The sky is white with mist and heat, with a dead but unbearable glare, as if the sun had turned liquid in the thickness of the clouds, over the whole stretch of the celestial vault. A sick sky over a decomposing sea. As the day draws on, the heat grows in the white air. All day long the bow noses out clouds of flying fish, small iron birds, forcing them from their bushes in the waves.

*

In the afternoon we meet a steamer going back towards the towns. Our sirens exchange greetings in three great hoots, like prehistoric animals. Passengers lost at sea are warned that other men are present and exchange greetings with them, the two ships draw slowly farther apart upon the malevolent waters; all this fills the heart with sadness. What man who cherishes the sea and loneliness will ever stop himself from loving these obstinate madmen who, clinging to planks and tossed by the mane of immense oceans, chase after islands long adrift?

*

In the very midst of the Atlantic we bend beneath savage winds blowing endlessly from pole to pole. Each cry we utter is lost, flies off into limitless space. But this cry, carried day after day on the winds, will finally reach land at one of the flattened ends of the earth and echo timelessly against the frozen walls until a man, lost somewhere in his shell of snow, hears it and consents to smile with happiness.

*

I was half asleep in the early afternoon sun when a terrible noise awoke me. I saw the sun in the depths of the sea, the waves reigning in the surging heavens. Suddenly the sea was alight, the sun flowed in long icy draughts down my throat. Around me the sailors were laughing and crying. They loved one another, yet with no forgiveness. On that day I recognized the world for what it was, I consented that its good should also do evil and its drawback carry benefits. On that day I realized that there were two truths, of which one must never be told.

*

The curious Austral moon, slightly pared, accompanies us for several nights and then slides rapidly from the sky down to the sea which swallows it. There remains the Southern Cross, the infrequent stars, the porous air. At the same instant, the wind also ceases completely. The sky rolls and pitches above our immobile masts. Engine dead, sails hove to, we whistle in the warm night while the water beats amicably against our sides. No commands, the machines are silent. Why indeed should we carry on and why should we return? Our cup runneth over, and a mute, invincible madness rocks us to sleep. A day comes like this which draws everything to a close; we must then let ourselves sink, like those who swim until exhausted. What do we accomplish? For ever, I have held it secret from myself. O bitter bed, princely couch, the crown lies at the bottom of the seas.

*

In the morning the lukewarm water foams gently under our propeller. We put on speed. Towards noon, travelling from distant continents, a herd of sea cows cross our path, overtake us and swim rhythmically northwards, followed by multicoloured birds which, from time to time, rest upon their horns. This rustling forest slowly vanishes on the horizon. A little later, the sea is covered over with strange, yellow flowers. Towards evening, for hour after hour, we are preceded by an invisible song. I go to sleep, at home.

*

All our sails stretched in a keen breeze, we race across a clear and rippling sea. At top speed our helm goes hard to port. And towards nightfall, correcting our course again, listing so far to starboard that our sails skim the water, we sail rapidly along the side of a southern continent which I recognize for having in former days flown blindly across it in the barbarous coffin of an aeroplane. I was an idle king and my chariot dawdled; I waited for the sea but it never came. The monster roared, took off from the guano fields of Peru, hurled itself above the beaches of the Pacific, flew over the fractured white vertebrae of the Andes and then above the herds of flies which cover the immense Argentinian plain, linked with one swoop the milk-flowing Uruguyan meadows to the black rivers of Venezuela, landed, roared again, quivered with greed at the sight of new empty spaces to devour, and yet never ceased failing to move forward or at least did so only with a convulsed, obstinate slowness, a fixed, weary and intoxicated energy. I felt then that I was dying in my metallic cell and dreamed of bloodshed and of orgies. Without space there is neither innocence nor liberty! When a man cannot breathe, prison means death or madness; what can he do there but kill and possess? Today, on the contrary, I have all the air I need, all our sails slap in the blue air, I am going to cry out with speed, we throw our sextants and compasses into the sea.

*

Under the imperious wind our sails are like iron. The coast drifts at full speed before our eyes, forests of royal coconut trees whose feet are bathed by emerald lagoons, a quiet bay, full of red sails, moonlit beaches. Great buildings loom up, already cracking under the pressure of the virgin forest which begins in the servants' courtyard; here and there a yellow ipeca or a tree with violet branches burst through a window. Rio finally crumbles away behind us and the monkeys of Tijuca will laugh and gibber in the vegetation that has overgrown its new ruins. Still faster, along wide beaches where the waves spread out in sheaves of sand, still faster, where the Uruguyan sheep plunge into the sea and at once turn it yellow. Then on the Argentinian coast great crude piles of faggots, set up at regular intervals, raise slowly grilling halves of oxen to the sky. At night the ice from Tierra del Fuego comes and beats for hours against our hull; the ship barely loses speed and tacks about. In the morning the single wave of the Pacific, whose cold foam boils green and white for thousands of kilometres along the Chilean coast, slowly lifts us up and threatens to wreck us. The helm avoids it, overtakes the Kerguelen Islands. In the sweetish evening the first Malayan ships come out to meet us.

*

'To sea! To sea!' shouted the magical boys in one of my childhood books. I have forgotten everything of the book except this cry. 'To sea!', and from across the Indian Ocean to the banks of the Red Sea, where in the silent nights you can hear the stones in the desert, scorched in the daytime, cracking one by one, we come back to the antique sea in which all cries are hushed.

*

Finally one morning we drop anchor in a bay filled with a strange silence, beaconed with fixed sails. All we can see are a few sea birds quarrelling in the sky over scraps of reeds. We swim ashore to an empty beach; we spend all day swimming and drying ourselves in the sand. When evening comes, under a sky that turns green and fades into the distance, the sea, so calm already, becomes still more peaceful. Short waves blow a vaporous foam on to the lukewarm shore. The sea birds have disappeared. All that is left is a space, lying open to a motionless voyage.

*

The knowledge that certain nights of prolonged gentleness will return to the earth and sea when we have gone can indeed help us in our death. Vast sea, forever virgin and forever ploughed, my religion with the night! It washes and feeds us in its sterile furrows, frees us and holds us upright. Each wave brings its promise, always the same. What does the wave say? If I were to die, in the midst of cold mountains, unknown to the world, cast off by my own people, my strength at last exhausted, the sea would at the final moment flood into my cell, come to raise me above myself and help me die without hatred.

*

At midnight, alone on the shore. One moment more and then I shall set sail. The sky itself has weighed anchor, with all its stars, like those ships which at this very hour gleam throughout the world with all their lights and illuminate dark harbour waters. Space and silence weigh equally upon the heart. A sudden love, a great work, a decisive act, a thought which transfigures, all these at certain moments bring the same unbearable anxiety, linked with an irresistible charm. Is living like this in the delicious anguish of being, in exquisite proximity to a danger whose name we do not know the same as rushing to our doom? Once again, without respite, let us go.

*

I have always felt that I was living on the high seas, threatened, at the heart of a royal happiness.

1953

PART TWO
CRITICAL ESSAYS

LA NAUSÉE [Nausea]

by Jean-Paul Sartre

A NOVEL is never anything but a philosophy put into images. And, in a good novel, the whole of the philosophy has passed into the images. But if once the philosophy overflows the characters and action, and therefore looks like a label stuck on the work, the plot loses its authenticity and the novel its life.

Nevertheless, a work that is to last cannot dispense with profound ideas. And this secret fusion between experiences and ideas, between life and reflection on the meaning of life, is what makes the great novelist (as we see him in a work such as *La Condition humaine* [*Man's Estate*] for example).

The work in question today is a novel where this balance has been broken, where theories damage life. For some time now, this has happened quite frequently. But what is striking in *La Nausée* is the fact that the author has remarkable gifts as a novelist as well as the most lucid and cruellest of minds, and that these gifts are at one and the same time both lavished and squandered.

Taken individually, in fact, each of the chapters of this extravagant meditation reaches a kind of perfection in bitterness and truth. The novel which is sketched out in it – a small port in the North of France, a middle class composed of ship-owners who combine religious observance with the pleasures of the table, a restaurant where the exercise of eating resumes its repugnant aspect in the narrator's eyes – in short everything that concerns the mechanical side of existence is depicted with a sureness of touch in which lucidity leaves no place for hope.

Similarly, the reflections on time, which is embodied by an old woman trotting aimlessly along a narrow street, are, taken in isolation, one of the most telling illustrations of the philosophy of anguish, as expressed in the thought of Kierkegaard, Chestov,

Jaspers or Heidegger. Thus the two sides of the novel are both equally convincing. But they do not, when joined together, make up a work of art, and the passage from one to the other is too swift, too unmotivated, for the reader to be carried away as he is by a genuine novel.

Indeed, the book itself reads less like a novel than a monologue. A man judges his life, and by so doing judges himself. I mean that he analyses his presence in the world, the fact that he moves his fingers and eats at regular hours – and what he finds at the bottom of the most elementary act is its fundamental absurdity.

In the best ordered of lives a moment always comes when the scenery collapses. Why this and that, this woman, this job and this appetite for a future? To put it all in a nutshell, why this fever for life in these legs that are going to rot?

We all have this feeling. And, in any case, for most men, the approach of dinner, the arrival of a letter or a smile from a passing girl, are enough to carry them along. But the man who likes to dig right down into ideas finds that if he looks directly at this idea his life become impossible. And to live knowing that life is pointless is what gives rise to anguish. And if you live against the stream, the whole of your being is seized with disgust and revolt, and this revolt of the body is what is called nausea.

A strange subject certainly, and yet the most banal of them all. M. Sartre carries it to its conclusions with a vigour and certainty that show how ordinary so apparently subtle a form of disgust can be. It is in this effort that the similarity between M. Sartre and another author whom, unless I am mistaken, no one has mentioned in connection with *La Nausée*, is to be found. I mean Franz Kafka.

But the difference is that, in M. Sartre's novel, there is some indefinable obstacle which prevents the reader from participating, and which holds him back when he is at the very threshold of consent. I myself explain this by the very noticeable lack of balance between the ideas that the work contains and the images in which these are expressed. But there is perhaps something further. For the mistake of a certain literature lies in thinking that life is tragic because it is wretched.

Life can be magnificent and overwhelming, that is its whole

tragedy. Without beauty, love or danger it would be almost easy to live. And M. Sartre's hero does not perhaps give us the real meaning of his anguish when he insists on those aspects of man which he finds repugnant, instead of basing his reasons for despair on certain of man's signs of greatness.

The realization that life is absurd cannot be an end in itself but only a beginning. It is a truth which nearly all great minds have taken as their starting point. It is not this discovery which is interesting, but the consequences and the rules for actions which can be drawn from it. At the end of this voyage to the frontiers of anxiety M. Sartre does seem to authorize one hope: that of the creator who achieves deliverance through writing.

There may perhaps emerge from primitive doubt a cry of 'I write, therefore I am.' And there is something rather comic in the lack of proportion between this final hope and the revolt which gave it birth. For, in the last resort, almost all writers know how trivial their work is when compared to certain moments of their life. M. Sartre's object was to describe these moments. Why not go right through to the end?

However that may be, this is the first novel by a writer from whom we can expect everything. So natural a suppleness in staying on the far boundaries of conscious thought, so painful a lucidity, indicate limitless gifts. This is enough for *La Nausée* to be welcomed as the first cry of an original and vigorous mind whose future works and lessons we are anxious to discover.

Review published in *Alger Républicain*
on 20 October 1938

LE MUR [The Wall]
by Jean-Paul Sartre

JEAN-PAUL SARTRE, whose *La Nausée* I reviewed in this column, has just published a collection of short stories in which the strange and bitter themes of his first novel recur under a different form. Men sentenced to death, a madman, a sexual pervert, a man suffering from impotence and a homosexual make up the characters in these stories. This choice of themes might seem rather peculiar. But already in *La Nausée* the aim was to turn an exceptional case into an everyday story. It is at the far boundaries of the heart and instincts that M. Sartre finds his inspiration.

But this needs further definition. It can be shown that the most ordinary of people is already a monster of perversity and that, for example, we all more or less wish for the death of those we love. This, at least, is the aim of a certain kind of literature. It does not seem to me that this is M. Sartre's aim. And, at the risk of being perhaps a shade over-subtle, I would say that his aim is to show that the most perverse of creatures acts, reacts and describes himself in exactly the same way as the most ordinary. And if there were a criticism to be made, it would concern only the use which the author makes of obscenity.

Obscenity in literature can attain a certain grandeur. It certainly contains an element of grandeur, as the example of Shakespeare can show. But at least it must be required by the work itself. And while, in *Le Mur*, this may be the case for 'Érostrate', it is not true for 'Intimacy', where the sexual descriptions often seem gratuitous.

*

There is in M. Sartre a certain taste for impotence, in the full meaning of the word and in its physiological sense, which leads

Le Mur

him to choose characters who have come to the end of their tether, and who stumble over an absurdity which they cannot overcome. The obstacle they encounter is their own life, and I will go so far as to say that they do so through an excess of liberty.

These people are quite rootless, have no principles, no Ariadne's thread, are so free that they disintegrate, and are deaf to the call of action or creation. One single problem preoccupies them, and they have not defined it. It is this which gives M. Sartre's stories both their immense interest and their absolute mastery.

Whether we look at the young Lucien, who begins by surrealism and ends in the Action Française, or at Eve, whose husband is insane, and who wants at all costs to penetrate into this mad domain from which she is excluded, or at the hero of 'Érostrate', everything they do, say or feel is unforseen. And nothing, at the moment when they are introduced to us, indicates what they will do in a minute's time. M. Sartre's art lies in the details he gives of his ridiculous creatures, and the way he observes their monotonous behaviour. He describes, making few suggestions, but patiently following his characters and attributing importance only to the most pointless of their acts.

It would not be surprising to learn that at the very moment when he begins his story, the author himself is not sure where it will lead him. But the fascination of such story-telling is undeniable. We are gripped by what is going to happen and the reader also identifies himself with that higher and ridiculous freedom which leads the characters to their own end.

For these characters are, in fact, free. But their liberty is of no use to them. This, at least, is what M. Sartre demonstrates. It is doubtless this which explains the emotion of these pages, which so often leave us breathless, as well as their cruel pathos. For in this universe man is freed from all the shackles of his prejudices, and sometimes even from his own nature. Then, reduced to self-contemplation, he becomes aware of his profound indifference to everything which is not himself. Man is alone, locked up in this liberty. It is a liberty which exists only in time, for death inflicts on it a swift and breathtaking denial. His condition is absurd. He will go no farther, and the miracles of those mornings where life begins again have lost all meaning for him.

How can one remain lucid when faced with such truths? It is normal that these beings, deprived of human amusements, the cinema, love or the Legion of Honour, should throw themselves into an inhuman world where they will this time forge their own chains: madness, sexual mania or crime. Eve wants to go mad. The character of 'Érostrate' wants to commit a crime, and Lulu wants to live with her impotent husband.

Those who avoid making this revolution or who do not complete it still feel nostalgic for the self-annihilation which it offers. And, in the best of these short stories, 'La Chambre', Eve watches her husband's delirium and tortures herself to discover the secret of this universe in which she would like to be absorbed, of this isolated room in which she would like to sleep with the door closed for ever.

This intense and dramatic universe, these garish and yet colourless sketches, are a good definition of M. Sartre's work and his appeal. And it is justifiable to speak of 'the work' of an author who, in two books, has succeeded in going straight to the essential problem and in bringing it to life through characters which haunt us. A great writer always brings with him his world and his message. M. Sartre's' message involves a conversion to nothingness, but also to lucidity. And the image, which he perpetuates through his characters, of a man sitting amid the ruins of his life, is a good illustration of the greatness and truth of this work.

Review published in *Alger Républicain*
On 12 March 1939

ENCOUNTERS WITH ANDRÉ GIDE

I WAS sixteen when I had my first encounter with André Gide. An uncle, who had taken part of my education in hand, sometimes gave me books. A butcher by trade, and with no shortage of customers, his only real passion was for reading and for ideas. He devoted his mornings to the meat trade, and the rest of the day to his library, to reading newspapers, and to interminable discussions in the local cafés.

One day he held out to me a small book with a parchment-like cover, assuring me that it 'would interest me'. I read everything indiscriminately, in those days; I probably opened *Les Nourritures terrestres* (*Fruits of the Earth*) after having finished *Lettres de femme* (*Letters of a Woman*) or a volume of the Pardaillan series. I found these invocations rather obscure. I shied away from this hymn to the goods of nature. In Algiers, at the age of sixteen, I was saturated with these riches; I longed for others, no doubt. And then 'Blida, little rose ...'. I knew Blida, unfortunately. I gave the book back to my uncle, telling him that it had in fact interested me. Then I went back to the beaches, to my listless studies and idle reading, and also to the difficult life that I led. The meeting had not come off.

The next year I met Jean Grenier. He too, among other things, held out to me a book. It was a novel by André de Richaud which was called *La Douleur* (*Suffering*). I have never met André de Richaud. But I have never forgotten his admirable book, which was the first to speak to me of what I knew: a mother, poverty, fine evening skies. He untied deep down inside me a tangle of obscure bonds, freed me from fetters whose hindrance I felt without being able to give them a name. I read it in one night, in the best tradition, and in the morning, secure in the possession of a new and strange liberty, went hesitatingly forward over an unknown land. I had just learned that books dispensed other things than forgetfulness and entertainment. My obstinate silences, these vague but all-embracing sufferings, the strange world that surrounded me, the nobility of my family, their poverty, my secrets, all this, I realized, could be expressed! There was a deliverance, an order of truth, in which poverty, for example, suddenly took on its true face, the one I had suspected it possessed, and that I obscurely revered. *La Douleur* gave me a glimpse of the world of creation, into which Gide was to be my guide. This is where my second encounter with him took place.

I began to read properly. A fortunate illness had taken me away from my beaches and my pleasures. I still read books in the same disorder, but with a new appetite. I was looking for something, I wanted to rediscover the world which I had glimpsed and which seemed to me to be my own. Between books and daydreams I was gradually discovering, alone or thanks to friendship, new dimensions to life. After so many years, I still keep in my heart the marvel of this apprenticeship. One morning I tumbled across Gides *Traités* (*Essays*). Two days later I knew by heart whole passages of *La Tentative amoureuse* (*The Attempt at Love*). As to *Retour de l'enfant prodigue* (*The Return of the Prodigal Son*) it had become the book of which I never spoke: perfection seals our lips. I merely made an adaptation, which together with a few friends I later put on the stage. In the meantime, I read the whole of Gide's work, and received, from *Les Nourritures terrestres*, in my turn, the upheaval of my whole being that has so often been described. But I received that on my second encounter, as can be seen, perhaps because when I read for the first time I was a young, unenlightened barbarian, but also because this revolution could not be, as far as I was concerned, in any way concerned with the senses. The shock was decisive in quite a different way. Long before Gide himself had confirmed this interpretation, I learned to read *Les Nourritures terrestres* as the gospel of self-deprivation that I needed.

*

From that point onwards Gide reigned over my youth, and it is impossible not to be always grateful to those whom we have admired at least once, for having hoisted us to the highest point that our soul can reach. In spite of all this, however, I never saw Gide as my master either in writing or in thinking; I had given myself others. Gide appeared to me rather, because of what I have just said, as the model of the artist, the guardian, the king's son, who kept watch over the gates of the garden in which I wanted to live. For example, there is almost nothing in what he has written about art with which I do not entirely agree, although our century has moved away from this conception. The reproach addressed to Gide's work is that it is distant from the anguish of our time. We choose to believe that, if a writer is to be great, he must be revolutionary. But if this is true, history proves that he keeps this quality only up to the revolution, and no farther. Moreover, it is by no means certain that Gide did move away from his time. What is more certain is that his time wanted to move away from what he represented. The question is whether it will ever succeed, or will do so only by committing suicide. Gide also suffers from that other prejudice of our day, which is that we have to parade our despair to be intelligent. Here discussion is easier: this prejudice is very silly.

I nevertheless did have to forget Gide's example, and, of necessity, to turn away very early from this world of innocent creation, at the same time as I left the land where I was born. History has forced itself upon my generation. I had to take my place in the line waiting before the porch of the black years. Then we fell into step, and have not yet reached our goal. How could I not have changed since? At least I have not forgotten the fullness and light in which I began my life, and I have placed nothing above them. I have not denied Gide.

In fact, I met him again at the end of our darkest years. I was then occupying part of his flat in Paris. It was a studio with a balcony, and its greatest peculiarity consisted of a trapeze which hung in the middle of the room. I had taken it down, I think, for I was tired of seeing the intellectuals who came to see me suspending themselves from it. I had been installed in this studio for a good number of months when Gide, in turn, came back from North Africa. I had never met him before; and yet it was as if we had always known each other. Not that Gide ever received me very intimately. He had a horror, as I already knew, of that noisy promiscuity which takes the place of friendship in our world. But the smile with which he greeted me was simple and joyful and, when he was with me, I never saw him on his guard.

As far as the rest as concerned, forty years' difference in age stood between us, together with our mutual horror of embarrassing each other. This is why I spent many weeks living close to Gide, almost without seeing him. He would sometimes knock at the double door which separated the studio from his library. At arms' length, he would be carrying Sarah, the cat, which had got into his room across the roof. Sometimes, the piano attracted him. On another occasion he listened by my side to the announcement of the armistice on the wireless. I well knew that war, which brings most people an end to their loneliness, was for him, as for me, the only true loneliness. For the first time, together round this radio set, we felt that we were sharing something of our times. On other days all I knew of his presence, on the other side of the door, was footsteps, rustlings, the gentle disturbance of his meditations and musings. But what did it matter? I knew that he was there, next door to me, and that he protected, with his unrivalled dignity, that secret realm into which I used to dream of entering, and towards which I have always turned, in the midst of our struggles and our cries.

*

Today, now that he has turned away from us, who could replace my old friend at the gates of this realm? Who will keep the garden until the day when we can go back to it? He kept watch, at least, until his death; it is therefore just that he should continue to receive the quiet gratitude that we owe to our true masters. The unpleasant noises made at his departure will in no way alter this. Of course, those who know how to hate are still furious over this death. He, whose privileges had been so bitterly envied, as if justice did not consist of sharing these privileges rather than lumping everything together in a general servitude, found himself in dispute to the very end, and found people indignant over such a serenity. Not a day goes by without his once again receiving the homage of hatred, of envy, or of that poor insolence which thinks it descends from Retz and which, in fact, comes from the pantry.

Yet what unanimity should have been realized around this little iron bed. To die is such appalling torture for some men that it seems to me as if a happy death redeems a small patch of creation. If I were a believer, Gide's death would bring me great relief. But if those believers I see do believe, what is the object of their faith? Those deprived of grace simply have to practise generosity amongst themselves. As far as the believers are concerned, they lack nothing, they are provided for; or at least they act as if that were the case. We, on the contrary, lack everything, except the fraternal hand. This is doubtless why Sartre was able to pay Gide, over and above their differences, an exemplary act of homage. Certain men thus find, in their reflections, the secret of a serenity which is neither miserly nor facile. Gide's secret lies in the fact that never, in the midst of his doubts, did he lose the pride of being a man. Dying also formed part of this condition, which he had wanted to assume to the very end. What would they have said of him if, after having lived surrounded by privileges, he had gone trembling to his death? It was then that he would have shown that he had stolen his moments of happiness. But no, he smiled at the mystery, and showed the abyss the same face which he had presented to life. Without ever knowing it, we were waiting for him at that moment, for one last time. And, for the last time, he did not fail us.

Essay published in the *Hommage de la Nouvelle Revue Française* to André Gide in November 1951

HERMAN MELVILLE
(Reprinted by permission of Éditions d'Art Lucien Mazenod)

IN the days when the whalers of Nantucket stayed at sea for several years, the young Melville, aged 22, took ship on one of them, then changed to a man-of-war and sailed the seas. On his return to America, he enjoyed a certain success with his traveller's tales, and then published his great books in the midst of indifference and incomprehension.[1] After the publication and failure of *The Confidence Man* (1857), Melville, discouraged, 'consents to annihilation'. Having become a customs officer and the father of a family, he entered into an almost complete silence (a few poems, very infrequently) which was to last thirty years. He then hastened to write a masterpiece, *Billy Budd* (completed in April 1891), and died, a few months later, forgotten (a three-line obituary in the *New York Times*). He had to wait until our own day for America and Europe finally to give him his place, among the greatest geniuses of the West.

It is scarcely easier to speak in a few pages of a work which has the tumultuous dimensions of the oceans where it was born than to summarize the Bible or condense Shakespeare. But to judge Melville's genius, if nothing else, we must recognize that his works depict a spiritual experience of unequalled intensity, and that they are to some extent symbolic. Certain critics[2] have questioned this obvious fact, which now scarcely seems open to doubt. His admirable books are numbered among those exceptional works that can be read in different ways, which are at one and the same time both obvious and obscure, as dark as the noon-

1. For a long time, *Moby Dick* was considered as an adventure story suitable as a school prize.
2. Let me in passing advise critics to read page 449 of *Mardi* in the French translation.

day sun and yet as clear as deep water. The wise man and the child can both draw sustenance from them. The story of Captain Ahab, for example, flying from the Southern to the Northern seas in pursuit of Moby Dick, the white whale who has taken off his leg, can doubtless be read as the fatal passion of a character driven mad by grief and loneliness. But it can also be seen as one of the most overwhelming myths ever invented on the subject of the struggle of man against evil, depicting the irresistible logic which finally leads the just man to take up arms first against creation and the creator, then against his fellows and against himself.[3] Let us have no doubt about it: if it is true that talent recreates life while genius has the additional gift of crowning it with myths, Melville is first and foremost a creator of myths.

I will add that these myths, contrary to what people say of them, are clear. They are obscure only in so far as the root of all suffering and all greatness lies buried in the darkness of the earth. They are no more obscure than Phèdre's cries, Hamlet's silences, or the triumphant songs of Don Giovanni. It seems to me, on the contrary (and this would deserve detailed development), that Melville never wrote anything but the same book, which he began again and again. This single book is the story of a voyage, inspired first of all solely by the joyful curiosity of youth (*Typee*, *Omoo*, etc.), then later inhabited by an increasingly wild and burning anguish. *Mardi* is the first, magnificent story in which Melville declares that this quest, which nothing can appease, and in which, finally, 'pursuers and pursued fly across a boundless ocean', now lies open. It is in this work that Melville becomes aware of the fascinating call which for ever echoes within him: 'I have undertaken a journey without maps.' And again: 'I am the restless hunter, the one who has no home.' *Moby Dick* simply carries to perfection the great themes of *Mardi*. But since artistic perfection is also inadequate to quench the kind of thirst with which we are confronted here, Melville will start once again, in

---

3. As an indication, here are some of the obviously symbolic pages of *Moby Dick* (French translation, Gallimard): pp. 120, 121, 123, 139, 173, 177, 191–3, 203, 209, 241, 310, 313, 339, 373, 415, 421, 452, 457, 460, 472, 485, 499, 503, 517, 520, 522. [For English edition, see note on p. 301.]

Pierre or Ambiguities, this unsuccessful masterpiece, to depict the quest of genius and misfortune whose sneering failure he will consecrate in the course of the long journey on the Mississippi which forms the theme of *The Confidence Man*.

This constantly rewritten book, this unwearying peregrination in the archipelago of dreams and bodies, on the ocean, 'of which each wave is a soul', this Odyssey beneath an empty sky, make Melville into the Homer of the Pacific. But we must immediately add that, with him, Ulysses never returns to Ithaca. The country in which Melville weighs anchor with *Billy Budd*, at the threshold of death, is a desert island. By allowing the young sailor, a figure of beauty and innocence, and whom he himself dearly loves, to be condemned to death, Captain Vere submits his heart to the law. And at the same time, by this flawless story which can be placed on the same level as certain Greek tragedies, Melville tells us, in his old age, of his acceptance that beauty and innocence should be put to death so that an order may be maintained, and the ship of men continue to move forward towards an unknown horizon. Has he then truly secured the peace and final dwelling-place which he nevertheless said could not be found in the Mardi archipelago? Or are we, on the contrary, faced with this final shipwreck that Melville in his despair asked of the gods? 'One cannot blaspheme and live,' he had proclaimed. At the height of consent, is not *Billy Budd* the highest blasphemy? This can never be known, any more than whether Melville did finally consent to a terrible order, or whether, in quest of the spirit, he allowed himself to be led, as he had asked, 'beyond the reefs, in sunless seas, into night and death'. But no one, in any case, measuring the long anguish which runs through his life and work, will fail to acknowledge the greatness, all the more anguished in being the fruit of self-conquest, of the reply which he has given.

But this, though it had to be said, should mislead no one as to the true genius of Melville and the sovereignty of his art. It is bursting with health, strength, upsurges of humour, and human laughter. It was not he who opened the shop of sombre allegories which nowadays hold our sad Europe spellbound. As a creator, he is for example at the farthest possible remove from Kafka, and he makes us aware of this writer's artistic limitations. However irreplaceable it may be, the spiritual experience in Kafka's work overflows the modes of expression and invention, which remain monotonous. In Melville this experience is balanced by expression and invention, and constantly finds its flesh and blood in them. Like the greatest artists, Melville constructed his symbols out of concrete things, not from the material of dreams. The creator of myths partakes of genius only in so far as he inscribes these myths in the denseness of reality, and not in the fleeting clouds of the imagination. In Kafka the reality which he describes is created by the symbol, the fact stems from the image, whereas in Melville the symbol emerges from reality, the image is born of what we see with our own eyes.[4] This is why Melville never cut himself off from flesh or nature, which are barely perceptible in Kafka's work. On the contrary, Melville's lyricism, which reminds us of Shakespeare's, makes use of the four elements. He mingles the Bible with the sea, the music of the waves with that of the spheres, the poetry of the days with the grandeur of the Atlantic. He is inexhaustible, like the winds which blow for thousands of miles across empty oceans and which, when they reach the coast, still have strength enough to destroy whole villages. He rages, like Lear's madness, over the wild seas where Moby Dick and the spirit of evil crouch among the waves. When the storm and total destruction have passed, a strange calm rises from the primitive waters, the silent pity which transfigures tragedies. Above the speechless crew, the perfect body of Billy Budd turns gently at the end of its rope in the pink and grey light of the approaching day.

T. E. Lawrence placed *Moby Dick* by the side of *The Possessed* or *War and Peace*. One can, without hesitation, place by its side *Billy Budd*, *Mardi*, *Benito Cereno*, and some others. These anguished books, which describe the destruction of man, but in which life is exalted on each page, are inexhaustible sources of

4. In Melville, the metaphor suggests the dream, but from a concrete, physical starting point. In *Mardi*, for example, the hero comes across 'huts of flame'. However, they are made of red tropical creepers, whose leaves had happened to be raised by the wind.

strength and pity. We find in them revolt and acceptance, unconquerable and endless love, passion for beauty, language of the highest order, in short, genius. 'To perpetuate one's name,' said Melville, 'one must carve it on a heavy stone and sink it to the depths of the sea: depths last longer than heights.' Depths do in fact have their painful virtue, as did the unjust silence in which Melville lived and died, and as did the ageless ocean which he unceasingly ploughed. From their endless darkness he one day drew his works, those visages of foam and night, carved by the waters, whose mysterious royalty has scarcely begun to shine upon us. Yet it already helps us to emerge effortlessly from our continent of shades and go once more down to the sea, towards its light and secret.

Article published in *Les Écrivains célèbres*,
Editions Mazenod, Volume III, 1952

ON FAULKNER

In his preface to *Sanctuary* André Malraux wrote that Faulkner had introduced the detective story into classical tragedy. This is true. Moreover, there is something of the detective story in every tragedy. Faulkner, who knows this, has had no hesitation in choosing his criminals and heroes in today's newspapers. The *Requiem* is thus, for me, one of the few modern tragedies there are.

In its original form *Requiem for a Nun* is not a play. It is a novel in dialogue form. But it has a dramatic intensity. First of all because a secret is gradually disclosed and tragic expectation constantly maintained. Secondly because the conflict which brings the characters face to face with their destiny, around the murder of a child, is a conflict that cannot be solved except through the acceptance of this destiny itself.

Faulkner here contributes to bringing forward the time when the tragedy at work in our history can also take up its place in our theatre. His characters belong to our own day, and yet they confront the same destiny which crushed Electra or Orestes. Only a great artist could thus attempt to introduce the great language of pain and humiliation into our apartments. Neither is it the work of chance that Faulkner's strange religion is experienced in this play by a Negress who has been a prostitute and is a murderess. This intense contrast does, on the contrary, sum up the human grandeur of his *Requiem* and of his whole work.

Let me add in conclusion that the great problem of modern tragedy is one of language. Characters in lounge suits cannot talk like Oedipus or Titus. Their language must be at one and the same time simple enough to be our own and lofty enough to be tragic. In my view, Faulkner has found this language. I have tried to restore this in French, and not to betray the work and the author that I admired.

> Programme note to Camus's own adaptation
> of *Requiem for a Nun*

INTELLIGENCE AND THE SCAFFOLD

IT is said that when Louis XVI, on his way to the guillotine, tried to give one of his escorts a message for the queen, he received the following reply: 'I am not here to run messages for you but to take you to the scaffold.' I feel that this excellent example of correct language and obstinate perseverance on the job in hand is perfectly applicable, if not to all the novels in our language, at least to a certain classical tradition of the French novel. Novelists belonging to this family do indeed refuse to carry messages, and their sole concern seems to be to lead their characters imperturbably to the meeting-place that awaits them, whether this be the convent of Madame de Clèves, the triumph of Juliette and the ruin of Justine, the solitude of Adolphe, the deathbed of Madame de Graslin, or that festival of old age which Proust finds in the salon of Madame de Guermantes. What really characterizes these authors is singleness of purpose, and it would be pointless to look in these novels for the equivalent of the interminable adventures of a Wilhelm Meister, for example; it is not that we are strangers to pedantry – but we have our own particular kind, which is not, fortunately, that of Goethe. All we can say is that, in art, an ideal of simplicity always requires fixity of intention. We can therefore place at the centre of the French novel a certain obstinacy.

This is why the novel sets primarily artistic problems. If our novelists have proved anything, it is that the novel, contrary to general belief, cannot easily dispense with perfection. However, it is a strange sort of perfection, which is not always formal. People imagine – wrongly – that novels do not require style. They do, in fact, demand style of the most difficult kind, the one which takes second place. But the problems which our great novelists set themselves did not concern form for form's sake. They dealt solely with the exact link these writers wished to introduce between their tone and their ideas. They had to find, halfway between monotony and chit-chat, a language to express their obstinacy. If this language is often lacking in outward show, this is because it is born of sacrifices. The messages have been omitted: everything is reduced to essentials. This is why minds as different as Stendhal and Madame de Lafayette look as if they belong to the same family: they have both worked hard to use the right language. The first problem which Stendhal sets himself is in fact the one which preoccupied the novelists of the great centuries. What he calls 'absence of style' is a perfect conformity between his art and his passions.[5] For what gives originality to all the novels of this kind, compared to those written in other countries, is that they are not only a school for life but a school for art: the liveliest flame crackles through their accurate language. Our great successes are born of a particular concept of strength, which can be called elegance, but which still has to be defined.

*

You need to be two men in order to write. In French literature the great problem is thus the translation of what we feel into what we want to make other people feel. What we call a bad writer is one who expresses himself by reference to an inner context that the reader cannot know. This leads the mediocre writer to say everything he pleases. The great rule of the artist, on the contrary, is to forget half of himself in favour of communicable expression. This inevitably involves sacrifices. And this quest for an intelligible language whose function is to mask the immensity of his fate, leads him to say not what he pleases but only what he must. A great part of the genius of the French novel lies in this conscious effort to give the order of a pure language to the cries of passion. In short, what triumphs in the works I am discussing is a certain preconceived idea, by which I mean intelligence.

This, however, needs to be defined. People always tend to think that this intelligence involves outward appearances, composition for example. Now it is curious to note that the composi-

5. 'If I am not clear, all *my world* is destroyed.' (Stendhal)

Intelligence and the Scaffold

tion of the typical novel of the seventeenth century, of *La Princesse de Clèves*, for example, is extremely loose. It launches out into several stories, begins in complexity even though it ends in unity. In fact, we have to wait until the nineteenth century to find in *Adolphe* the purity of line which we are very ready, in our imagination, to lend *La Princesse de Clèves*. Similarly, the composition of *Les Liaisons dangereuses* is purely chronological, with no artistic experiments. The composition of Sade's novels is elementary; philosophical dissertations alternate with erotic descriptions, and do so right to the end. Stendhal's novels offer curious evidence of carelessness, and there will always be constant reasons for surprise in the final chapter of *La Chartreuse de Parme* (*The Charterhouse of Parma*), in which the author, as if in sight of home, anxious to conclude, bundles in twice as many events as in the rest of the book. It is not, in any case, these examples which justify the claim that French novels possess an Apollonian perfection of form.

The unity, the profound simplicity, the classicism of these novels are thus to be found elsewhere. It is doubtless nearer to the truth to say merely that the great characteristic of these novelists lies in the fact that each one of them, in his own way, always says the same thing and always in the same tone. Being classical means repeating oneself. We thus find, at the heart of our great works of fiction, a certain conception of man which intelligence tries to illustrate by means of a small number of situations. And, of course, this could be said of any good novel, if it is true that the novel uses intelligence to create its universe in the same way that the theatre makes use of action. But what seems peculiar to this French tradition is that the plot and characters should in general be restricted to this one idea, and that everything should be arranged to send its vibrations everywhere. Here, intelligence not only contributes the original idea; it is, at the same time, a marvellously economical principle which produces a kind of passionate monotony. It is at one and the same time both creative and mechanical. Being classical means both repeating oneself and knowing how to repeat oneself. And this is the difference which I see between French novels and the fiction of other countries, where intelligence inspires works, but where it also allows itself to be carried away by its own reactions.[6]

*

To take a specific example, it seems to me that Madame de Lafayette's aim, since nothing else in the world concerns her, is solely to teach us a very particular conception of love. Her strange postulate is that this passion places man in peril. And although this is something which can be said in conversation, no one has ever had the idea of carrying logic quite so far as Madame de Lafayette. What one feels at work in *La Princesse de Clèves*, as in *La Princesse de Montpensier* or *La Contesse de Tende*, is a constant suspicion of love. This is already visible in her language, where it really seems as if certain words burn her mouth: 'What Madame de Clèves had said of his portrait had restored him to life by making him realize that it was he whom she did not hate.' But the characters, in their own way, also convince us that this healthy suspicion is valid. They are strange heroes who all die of emotion, and who seek out mortal illnesses in thwarted passions. Even the minor characters die through impulses of the soul: 'He received his pardon when he was expecting only the death blow, but fear had so seized him that he was out of his mind and died a few days later.' The most audacious of our Romantics never dared attribute so much power to passion. And it is easy to understand that, faced with these ravages of feeling, Madame de Lafayette should take as mainspring of her plot an extraordinary theory of marriage considered as a lesser evil: it is better to be unhappily married than suffer from passion. It is here that we recognize the deep-seated idea whose obstinate repetition gives the work its meaning. It is an idea of order.

Long before Goethe, in fact, Madame de Lafayette balanced the injustice of an unhappy condition against the disorder of the passions; and long before him, by an amazing upsurge of pessimism, she chose injustice, which disturbs nothing. The only difference is that the order with which she is concerned is less that of a society than that of a system of ideas and of a soul. And far

6. In Russian novels, for example, or in experiments like those of Joyce.

Intelligence and the Scaffold

from wishing to make the passions of the heart the slave to social prejudices, she uses these prejudices to provide a remedy for the disorderly impulses which terrify her. She is not interested in defending institutions, which do not concern her; but she does wish to protect the core of her being, whose only enemy she knows. Love is nothing but madness and confusion. It is not hard to guess what burning memories surge beneath these disinterested phrases, and it is this, far more than an illusory composition, which offers us a great lesson in art. For there is no art where there is nothing to be overcome, and we realize that the monotony of this ceremonious harmony is as much the result of a clear-sighted calculation as of an anguished passion. If there is only one feeling present, this is because it has eaten up everything else, and if it always speaks in the same rather formal tone, this is because it is not allowed to shout. This objectivity is a victory. Other writers, who can offer lessons but who achieve no victories, have tried to be objective. But this was because they were capable of nothing else. This is why the novelists who are called naturalists or realists, who have written so many novels and many good ones, have not written a single great one. They could not go beyond description. The greatness of this lofty art lies, on the contrary, in the fact that in Madame de Lafayette we feel that these limits have been put there *on purpose*. They thus immediately disappear, and the whole work echoes far around. This stems from a concerted art which owes everything to intelligence and its concern for discipline. But it is quite obvious that this art is, at the same time, born of an infinite possibility of suffering, and of a firm decision to master this suffering by means of language. Nothing expresses this disciplined distress, this powerful light with which intelligence transfigures pain, better than an admirable sentence from *La Princesse de Clèves*: 'I told him that so long as his suffering had had limits, I had approved of it and shared it; but that I should pity him no longer if he gave way to despair and lost his reason.' This tone is magnificent. It assumes that there is a certain strength of soul which can impose limits on misery by censuring its expression. It brings art into life by giving man, in his struggle against his destiny, the powers of language. And we thus see that if this literature is a school for life, it is *precisely because* it is a school of art. To be more accurate, we should say that the lesson of these lives and these works of art is no longer simply one of art, but one of style. We learn from them to give our behaviour a certain form. And this permanent truth which Madame de Lafayette never stops repeating, which she expresses in this sentence in unforgettable form, takes on its full significance and illuminates what I mean when we see that it is the same man (the Prince de Clèves) who says this and who will nevertheless himself die of despair.

It would be easy to find in Sade, in Stendhal, in Proust and in a few of our contemporaries a similar lesson in style and life, very different in each case, but always made up of a choice, a calculated independence and a clarity of aim. Perseverance in sin which has become legitimate in Sade,[7] the litanies of energy in Stendhal,[8] the heroic effort of Proust to remould human suffering into a wholly privileged existence, all say one thing and nothing else. Each of them uses a single feeling which has invaded them for ever in order to make a work whose faces are both different and monotonous.

Of course, all I am doing here is giving certain indications. They will perhaps be enough to show that the rigour, the purity and the concentrated force of French classical fiction do not stem from its purely formal qualities (in any case, such a term has no meaning in art). What does matter is the stubborn perseverance in a certain tone, a certain constancy of soul, a human and literary knowledge of sacrifice. Such a classicism stems from deliberate choices[9] (*partis pris*). This cult of effective intelligence creates

7. 'He invented cruelties that he never practised himself, and which he would have had no desire to practise, in order to enter into contact with the great problems' (Otto Flake). The great problem of Sade is the irresponsibility of man without God.

8. The remark by the Prince de Clèves can be placed by the side of this notation in Stendhal's *Journal*: 'As often happens to men who have concentrated their energy on one or two vital points, he looked lazy and untidy.'

9. This is why *Le Parti pris des choses* of Francis Ponge is one of the few contemporary classical works.

not only an art but also a civilization and a way of life. It is of course possible that such an attitude is not without certain limitations. But these are perhaps necessary limitations. We tend nowadays to undervalue this lucid effort. And we are very proud of the universality of our taste. But this universality perhaps diminishes our inner strength. If anyone asked him how he had managed to construct his theory, Newton could reply: 'By thinking about it all the time.' There is no greatness without a little obstinacy.

In any case, this is how I explain the very strong feeling which I have when I read our great novels. They bear witness to the powers of human creativity. They convince you that the work of art is a human thing, never human enough, and that the creator can dispense with dictates from above. They are born not of flashes of inspiration but of a daily fidelity. And one of the secrets of the French novel is its ability to show at one and the same time a harmonious sense of fatality and an art which springs wholly from individual liberty – to present, in short, the perfect domain in which the forces of destiny clash with human decisions. This art is a revenge, a means of overcoming a difficult fate by imposing a form upon it. They teach us the mathematics of destiny, which are a means of freeing ourselves from it. And if the Prince de Clèves shows that he is, in spite of everything, superior to this quivering sensitivity which will cause his death, it is precisely because he is capable of forming that admirable sentence which refuses to depict madness and despair. None of our great novelists has turned his face away from the sufferings of men, but we can also say that none of them has given way to it, and that by an inspiring patience they have all mastered it through artistic rules. The concept of virility offered to the modern Frenchman (and naturally this has nothing to do with beating the big drum) is perhaps something which he owes to this succession of dry and burning works where, to the very foot of the gallows, the mind unfalteringly pursues its highest efforts until it reaches victory.

Article entitled 'Problèmes du roman' published in a special number of the review *Confluences* in July 1943

LECTURE GIVEN IN ATHENS ON THE FUTURE OF TRAGEDY

AN oriental sage always included in his prayers the request that the Gods would spare him from living in an interesting age. Our age is extremely interesting, that is to say it is tragic. Do we at least have, to purge us of our miseries, the theatre suited to our age or can we hope to have it? In other words, is modern tragedy possible? This is the question I would like to ask myself today. But is it a reasonable question? Is it not of the same type as 'Shall we have a good government?' or 'Will our authors become modest?', or again 'Will the rich soon share their fortunes with the poor?', interesting questions without a doubt, but which make us dream rather than think.

I do not think so. I believe, on the contrary, and this for two reasons, that we can legitimately raise the question of modern tragedy. The first reason is that great periods of tragic art occur, in history, in centuries of crucial change, at moments when the life of nations is heavy both with glory and with threats, when the future is uncertain and the present dramatic. After all, Aeschylus fought in two wars, and Shakespeare lived through quite a remarkable succession of horrors. Moreover, they both stand at a kind of dangerous turning in the history of their civilization.

It can in fact be noted that in the thirty centuries of Western history, from the Dorians to the atomic bomb, there have been only two periods of tragic art, both of which are narrowly defined in both time and space. The first is Greek. It presents a remarkable unity, and lasts a century, from Aeschylus to Euripides. The second lasts very little longer, and flourishes in the countries bordering on the very edge of Western Europe. It has, in fact, been insufficiently noted that the magnificent explosion of the Elizabethan theatre, the Spanish theatre of the Golden Age, and French

The Future of Tragedy

seventeenth-century tragedy, are practically contemporary with one another. When Shakespeare died, Lope de Vega was 54 and had already had a large number of his plays performed; Calderón and Corneille were alive. And, finally, there is no more distance in time between Shakespeare and Racine than between Aeschylus and Euripides. Historically, at least, we can consider ourselves in the presence, although with differing aesthetics, of a single magnificent flowering, that of the Renaissance, born in the inspired disorder of the Elizabethan stage and ending in formal perfection in French tragedy.

Between these two tragic moments lie almost twenty centuries. During these twenty centuries, there was nothing at all, nothing, except Christian mystery plays, which can be dramatic but which, for reasons I shall explain, cannot be tragic. We can therefore say that we are dealing with very exceptional times, which should by their very peculiarity tell us something about the conditions for tragic expression. This is, in my view, a fascinating subject for study, and one that should be pursued with thoroughness and patience by true historians. But I am not competent to deal with it and I should simply like to mention what I think about it as a man of the theatre. If you look at the movement of ideas both in these two periods and in the tragic works that were written in them, you will find one constantly recurring factor. Both periods mark, in fact, a transition between forms of cosmic thought, each impregnated with the notion of divinity and holiness, and the other forms which, on the contrary, are inspired by individualistic and rationalist concepts. The movement from Aeschylus to Euripides is, roughly speaking, the movement which goes from the great pre-Socratic thinkers to Socrates himself (Socrates, who despised tragedy, made an exception for Euripides). Similarly, from Shakespeare to Corneille, we go from the world of dark and mysterious forces, which is still that of the Middle Ages, to the universe of individual values affirmed and maintained by the human will and by reason (almost all the sacrifices in Racine are motivated by reason). It is the same movement, in short, which leads from the passionate theologies of the Middle Ages to Descartes. Although this evolution is more clearly visible in Greece, because it is simpler and limited to one place, it is the same in both cases. Each time, in the history of ideas, the individual frees himself little by little from a corpus of sacred concepts and stands face to face with the ancient world of terror and devotion. Each time, in the works, we move from ritual tragedy and from almost religious festivals, to psychological tragedy. And each time the final triumph of individual reason, in the fourth century in Greece and in the eighteenth century in Europe, dries up tragic production for centuries.

What, as far as we are concerned, can we draw from these observations? First of all the very general remark that the tragic age always seems to coincide with an evolution in which man, consciously or not, frees himself from an older form of civilization and finds that he has broken away from it without having found a new form which satisfies him. It seems to me that we, in 1955, have reached this stage, and can therefore ask whether this inner anguish will find a tragic expression in our world. However, the twenty centuries separating Euripides from Shakespeare should encourage us to be prudent. After all, tragedy is one of the rarest of flowers, and there is only the slimmest chance that we shall see it bloom in our own day. But there is another reason which encourages us to wonder about this chance. It involves this time a very particular phenomenon that we have been able to observe in France for some thirty years now, and which began with the reform carried out by Jacques Copeau. This phenomenon is the use of the stage by writers, a stage which up to then had been colonized by theatrical merchants and manufacturers. This intervention by writers thus leads to the resurrection of tragic forms, which tend to put dramatic art back in its rightful place, at the summit of the literary arts. Before Copeau (except for Claudel, whom nobody performed) the privileged place for theatrical sacrifices was, in France, the double bed. When the play was particularly successful, the sacrifices were multiplied, and the beds as well. In short, a business, like so many others, in which the price of everything was marked – with, if I may say so, the mark of the beast. This, moreover, was what Copeau said about it:

The Future of Tragedy

... If we are asked what feelings inspire us, what passion urges us forward, compels us, forces us, and which finally overwhelms us, it is this: *indignation*.

A frantic industrialization which, more cynically every day, degrades the French stage and makes the educated public turn away from it; the monopolization of most of our theatres by a handful of entertainers hired by shameless merchants; everywhere, and even in places where great traditions ought to preserve some modesty, the same spirit of ham acting and commercial speculation, the same vulgarity; everywhere, bluff and all conceivable kinds of exaggeration and exhibitionism live like parasites on a dying art, itself now no longer even mentioned; everywhere the same flabbiness, disorder, indiscipline, ignorance and stupidity, the same contempt for the creator, the same hatred for beauty; an ever more vain and stupid output of plays, ever more indulgent critics, and ever more misguided public taste: that is what inspires our indignation and revolt.

Since this magnificent protest, followed by the creation of the Vieux-Colombier, the theatre in France, and this is our inexhaustible debt to Copeau, has gradually recovered its claim to nobility, that is to say, it has found a style. Gide, Martin du Gard, Giraudoux, Montherlant, Claudel and so many others have restored a glory and ambitions that had disappeared a century ago. At the same time a movement of ideas and reflections on the theatre, whose most significant product is the fine book of Antonin Artaud, *Le Théâtre et son double*, the influence of foreign theoreticians such as Gordon Craig and Appia, have put tragic themes back at the centre of our preoccupations.

Thus I can, by bringing all these observations together, clearly define the problem which I should like to discuss in your presence. Our time coincides with a drama in civilization which could today, as it did in the past, favour tragic modes of expression. At the same time many writers, in France and elsewhere, are concerned with providing our times with its tragedy. Is this a reasonable dream, is this enterprise possible, and what conditions must be fulfilled? This, for me, is the question which matters today for all those whom the theatre excites as would a second life. Of course, no one today is in a position to give a definite reply to this question and say: 'Favourable conditions. Tragedy following.' I shall thus limit myself to a few suggestions concerning this great hope which inspires men of culture in the West.

*

First of all, what is a tragedy? The problem of defining 'the tragic' has greatly occupied both literary historians and writers themselves, although no formula has ever received universal agreement. Without claiming to solve a problem which makes so many thinkers hesitate, we can nevertheless adopt a comparative method and try to define how, for example, tragedy differs from drama or melodrama. This is what seems to me to be the difference: the forces confronting each other in tragedy are equally legitimate, equally justified. In melodramas or dramas, on the contrary, only one force is legitimate. In other words, tragedy is ambiguous and drama simple-minded. In the former each force is at one and the same time both good and bad. In the latter one is good and the other bad (which is why, in our day and age, propaganda plays are nothing but the resurrection of melodrama). Antigone is right, but Creon is not wrong. Similarly, Prometheus is both just and unjust, and Zeus, who pitilessly oppresses him, also has right on his side. Melodrama could thus be summed up by saying: 'Only one is just and justifiable', while the perfect tragic formula would be: 'All can be justified, no one is just.' This is why the advice given by the chorus of classical tragedies is mainly one of prudence. For the chorus knows that up to a certain limit everyone is right and that the person who, through blindness or passion, oversteps this limit is heading for catastrophe if he persists in his desire to assert a right which he thinks he alone possesses. The constant theme of classical tragedy is thus that of the limit which must not be transgressed. On either side of this limit stand equally legitimate forces locked in quivering and unending combat. The man who makes a mistake about this limit, who tries to destroy this balance, is heading for his ruin. This idea of the limit which no one should overstep, and beyond which lies death or disaster, also recurs in *Macbeth* and *Phèdre*, though in a less pure form than in Greek tragedy. Finally, this explains why the ideal drama, like the Romantic drama, is first and foremost

The Future of Tragedy

movement and action, since what it represents is the struggle between good and evil and the different incidents in this struggle. The ideal tragedy, on the other hand, and especially Greek tragedy, is first and foremost tension, since it is the conflict, in a frenzied immobility, between two powers, each of which wears the double mask of good and evil. It is of course true that between these two extreme types of tragedy and melodrama, dramatic literature offers all possible intermediaries.

But if we restrict ourselves to the pure forms, what are the two forces which, in Greek classical tragedy for example, enter into conflict? If we take *Prometheus Bound* as typical of this kind of tragedy, we can say that there is, on the one hand, man and his desire for power, and on the other the divine principle reflected by the world. Tragedy occurs when man, through pride (or even through stupidity, as in the case of Ajax) enters into conflict with the divine order, personified by a god or incarnated in society. The more justified this revolt, and the more necessary this order, then the greater the tragedy which stems from the conflict.

Consequently everything which, within a tragedy, tries to destroy this balance destroys the tragedy itself. If the divine order cannot be called into question and admits only sin and repentance, there is no tragedy. There can be only mysteries or parables, or again what the Spaniards call acts of faith or sacramental acts, that is to say spectacles in which the one truth that exists is solemnly proclaimed. It is thus possible to have religious drama but not religious tragedy. This explains the silence of tragedy up to the Renaissance. Christianity plunges the whole of the universe, man and the world, into the divine order. There is thus no tension between the world and the religious principle, but, at the most, ignorance, together with the difficulty of freeing man from the flesh, of renouncing our passions in order to embrace spiritual truth. Perhaps there has been only one Christian tragedy in history. It was celebrated on Golgotha during one imperceptible instant, at the moment of the 'My God, my God, why hast thou forsaken me?' This fleeting doubt, and this doubt alone, consecrated the ambiguity of a tragic situation. Afterwards the divinity of Christ was never again called in doubt. The mass, which gives a daily consecration to this divinity, is the real form which religious theatre takes in the West. It is not invention, but repetition.

On the other hand, everything which frees the individual and makes the universe submit to his wholly human law, especially by the denial of the mystery of existence, once again destroys tragedy. Atheistic or rationalist tragedy is thus equally impossible. If all is mystery, there is no tragedy. If all is reason, the same thing happens. Tragedy is born between light and shade, and from the struggle between them. And this is understandable. In both religious and atheistic drama the problem has in fact already been solved. In the ideal tragedy, on the contrary, it has not been solved. The hero rebels and rejects the order which oppresses him, while the divine power, by its oppression, affirms itself exactly to the same extent as it is denied. In other words, revolt is not enough to make a tragedy. Neither is the affirmation of the divine order. Both a revolt and an order are necessary, the first pushing against the second, and each reinforcing the other with its own strength. No Oedipus without the destiny summed up by the oracle. But the destiny would not have all its fatality if Oedipus did not refuse it.

And if tragedy ends in death or punishment, it is important to note that what is punished is not the crime itself but the blindness of the hero who has denied balance and tension. I am talking, of course, of the ideal tragic situation. Aeschylus, for example, who remains close to the religious and Dionysiac origins of tragedy, granted Prometheus forgiveness in the last section of the trilogy; the Furies were replaced by the Kindly Ones. But in Sophocles the balance is for most of the time scrupulously observed, and it is in this respect that he is the greatest tragedian of all time. Euripides, on the other hand, will upset the tragic balance by concentrating on the individual and on psychology. He is thus a forerunner of individualistic drama, that is to say of the decadence of tragedy. Similarly, the great Shakespearean tragedies are still rooted in a kind of vast cosmic mystery which puts up an obscure resistance against the undertakings of its

The Future of Tragedy

passionate individuals, while Corneille ensures the triumph of the individual ethic, and by his very perfection announces the end of the genre.

People have thus said that tragedy swings between the two poles of extreme nihilism and unlimited hope. For me nothing is more true. The hero denies the order which strikes him down, and the divine order strikes because it is denied. Both thus affirm that they exist at the very moment when this existence is called into question. The chorus draws the lesson, which is that there is an order, that this order can be painful, but that it is still worse not to recognize that it exists. The only purification lies in denying and excluding nothing, in thus accepting the mystery of existence, the limitations of man, in short the order where men know without knowing. Oedipus then says 'All is well', when his eyes have been torn out. Henceforth he knows, though he never sees again. His darkness is filled with light, and this face with its dead eyes shines with the highest lesson of the tragic universe.

What can be drawn from these observations? A suggestion and a working hypothesis, nothing more. It seems in fact that tragedy is born in the West each time that the pendulum of civilization is halfway between a sacred society and a society built around man. On two occasions, twenty centuries apart, we find a struggle between a world that is still interpreted in a sacred context and men who are already committed to their individuality, that is to say, armed with the power to question. In both cases, the individual increasingly asserts himself, the balance is gradually destroyed, and the tragic spirit finally falls silent. When Nietzsche accuses Socrates of having dug the grave of classical Greek tragedy, he is right up to a certain point – exactly to the same extent that it is true to say of Descartes that he marks the end of the tragic movement born of the Renaissance. At the time of the Renaissance, in fact, the traditional Christian universe is called into question by the Reformation, the discovery of the world and the flowering of the scientific spirit. Gradually, the individual stands up against the sacred order of things and against destiny. Shakespeare then throws his passionate creatures against the simultaneously evil and just order of the world. Death and pity invade the stage and once again the final words of tragedy ring out: 'A higher life is born of my despair.' Then the pendulum moves increasingly in the opposite direction. Racine and French tragedy carry the tragic movement to its conclusion in the perfection of chamber music. Armed by Descartes and the scientific spirit, triumphant reason then proclaims the rights of the individual and empties the stage: tragedy will go down into the street on the bloody boards of revolution. Romanticism will thus write no tragedies but simply dramas, and among them only those of Kleist or Schiller reach true greatness. Man is alone, and he is thus confronted with nothing but himself. He ceases to be a tragic character and becomes an adventurer. Dramas and novels will depict him better than any other art. The spirit of tragedy consequently disappears until our own day, when the most monstrous wars have not inspired a single tragic poet.

What then could bring about a renaissance of tragedy among us? If my hypothesis is valid, our only reason for hope lies in the visible transformation of individualism, and in the slow recognition by the individual, under the pressure of history, that he does have limits. The world which the individual of the eighteenth century thought he could conquer and transform by reason and science has in fact taken shape, but this is a monstrous one. Rational and excessive at one and the same time, it is the world of history. But at this degree of *hubris*, history has put on the mask of destiny. Man doubts whether he can conquer history, all he can do is struggle within it. By a curious fatality, humanity has refashioned itself a hostile destiny with the very same weapons that it used to reject fatality. After having deified the human reign, man is once more turning against this god. He is struggling, at the same time both a warrior and a refugee, torn between absolute hope and final doubt. Thus he lives in a tragic climate. Perhaps this explains why tragedy is seeking to be reborn. Today, man is proclaiming his revolt while knowing that this revolt has limits, is demanding liberty and undergoing necessity, and this contradictory man, torn apart, conscious henceforth of human and historical ambiguity, is the essentially tragic man. He is per-

The Future of Tragedy

haps striding towards the formulation of his own tragedy, which will be reached on the day when *All is well*.

*

And what, in fact, the French dramatic renaissance offers us today are the first tentative movements in this direction. Our dramatic writers are seeking for a tragic language because no tragedy can exist without a language, and because this language is all the more difficult to formulate when it must reflect the contradictions of the tragic situation. It must be, at one and the same time, both hieratic and familiar, barbarous and learned, mysterious and clear, haughty and pitiful. Our authors, in quest of this language, have thus gone instinctively back to its sources, that is to say to the tragic epochs which I have mentioned. We have thus seen a rebirth of Greek tragedy in our country, but in the only forms possible to highly individualistic minds. These are either derision, or highly mannered literary transposition. That is to say, in short, humour and fantasy, comedy alone belonging to the realm of the individual. Two good examples of this attitude are provided by Gide's *Oedipe* or Giraudoux's *La Guerre de Troie*.

Extract

What is also visible in France is an effort to reintroduce the language of religion on to the stage. A logical thing to do. But this had to be done by classical religious images, while the problem of modern tragedy lies precisely in the need to recreate new sacred images. We have thus witnessed either a kind of pastiche, in both style and sentiment, as in Montherlant's *Port-Royal* which is at the moment triumphing in Paris.

Extract

or the resurrection of authentic Christian sentiments as in the admirable *Partage de midi*.

Extract

But here we can see just how the religious theatre is not tragic: it is not a theatre in which the creature and creation are pitted one against the other, but a theatre in which men abandon the love they had for other human beings. In a way, the works of Claudel before his conversion, such as *Tête d'Or* or *La Ville*, are more significant in our immediate context. But, however that may be, religious theatre always precedes tragedy. In a way, it foreshadows it. It is thus not surprising that the dramatic work in which the style, if not the situation, is already perceptibly tragic should be Henry de Montherlant's *Le Maître de Santiago*, from which I should now like to read the two principal scenes:

Extract

For me, a work like this already contains an authentic tension, although a slightly rhetorical and, above all, a highly individualistic one. But I feel that tragic language is taking shape in it and that this language gives us more than does the play itself. In any case, if the attempts and researches that I have tried to present to you through some of their most outstanding examples do not give you the certainty that a dramatic renaissance is possible, they do at least leave us with the hope that it may happen one day. The path still to be travelled must first of all be followed by our Society itself, in search of a synthesis between liberty and necessity, and by each one of us, who need to keep alive in ourselves our power of revolt without yielding to our ability for negation. If we can pay this price, the tragic sensibility which is taking shape in our time will flourish and find its expression. This amounts to saying that the real modern tragedy is the one that I am not going to read you, because it does not yet exist. To be born, it needs our patience and a genius.

My only aim has been to make you feel that there does exist in modern French dramatic art a kind of tragic nebula within which various nuclei are beginning to coagulate. A cosmic storm may, of course, sweep the nebula away, and with it the future planets. But if this movement continues in spite of the storms of time, these promises will bear their fruit and the West will perhaps experience a rebirth of the tragic theatre. It is certainly in preparation everywhere. Nevertheless, and I say this without nationalism (I love my country too much to be nationalistic), it is in France that the first signs of such a renaissance are visible. In France, of course, but I have surely said enough to make you share my conviction that the model, and the inexhaustible inspiration, remains for us the genius of Greece. To express to you both this hope and a double gratitude, first of all the one which French writers have towards Greece, their common fatherland, and secondly my own gratitude for the welcome you have given us, I can find no better way of ending this lecture than by reading you an extract from the magnificent and learnedly barbarous transposition that Paul Claudel has made of Aeschylus's *Agamemnon*, in which our two languages are mutually transfigured in one wondrous and inimitable tongue.

Extract

1955

PART THREE
CAMUS ON *THE OUTSIDER* AND *THE PLAGUE*

PREFACE TO THE AMERICAN
UNIVERSITY EDITION OF *THE OUTSIDER*

'Avant Propos', by Albert Camus in 'L'Étranger' by Albert Camus, edited by Germaine Brée and Carlos Lynes, Jr. Copyright © 1955 by Appleton-Century-Crofts, Inc. 'Avant Propos' was written especially for the Brée and Lynes edition by Albert Camus and is reprinted by permission of Appleton-Century-Crofts, Division of Meredith Publishing Company.

I SUMMED up *The Outsider* a long time ago by a remark which I agree was highly paradoxical: 'In our society any man who does not weep at his mother's funeral runs the risk of being sentenced to death.' All I meant was that the hero of my book is condemned because he does not stick to the rules. In this respect he is foreign to the society in which he lives, he wanders about on the fringe, in the suburbs of private, solitary, sensual life. And this is why readers have been tempted to look upon him as a piece of social wreckage. A much more accurate idea of the character, or at least one much closer to the author's intentions, will emerge if it is asked just how Meursault refuses to conform. The reply is a simple one: he refuses to lie. To lie is not only to say what is not the case. It also, above all, means saying more than is the case, and, as far as the human heart is concerned, more than we feel. It is what we all do, every day, to simplify life. Meursault, contrary to appearances, does not want to simplify life. He says what he is, he refuses to exaggerate his feelings, and immediately society feels itself threatened. He is asked, for example, to say that he regrets his crime in the approved manner. He replies that what he feels is not so much true regret as a certain boredom. And this shade of meaning condemns him.

Meursault, for me, is thus not a piece of social wreckage, but a man who is naked and poor, in love with the sun that leaves no shadows. Far from being empty of all feelings, he is inspired by a passion which is deep because it is stubborn, a passion for the absolute and for truth. This truth is still a negative one, the truth of what we are and what we feel, but without it no conquest of ourselves or of the world will ever be possible.

One would therefore not be much mistaken in reading *The Outsider* as the story of a man who, with no heroics, accepts to die for truth. I have also happened to say, still paradoxically, that I had tried to present in my character the only Christ whom we deserve. It will be understood after my explanations that I said this with no blasphemous intent, and solely with the slightly ironic affection which an artist has the right to feel for the characters he has created.

THE RECEPTION OF *THE OUTSIDER*

From the entries made in *Notebook IV* for 1942

To J.T. on *The Outsider*

It is a very carefully planned book, and the tone ... is deliberate. It rises four or five times, it is true, but this is to avoid monotony and to provide a structure. With the prison chaplain my Outsider does not try to justify himself. He flies into a rage, which is very different. Then it is I who am explaining, you may say. Yes, and I have thought a lot about that. I decided to do so because I wanted my character to be brought face to face with the one great problem by way of everyday and natural events. This great moment had to be underlined. Notice moreover that there is no sudden change in Meursault here. In this chapter as in the rest of the book he restricts himself to *replying to questions*. Previously, the questions were those which the world asks us every day – now, they are those that the chaplain asks him. Thus I define my character negatively.

All this, of course, concerns the artistic means, not the end. The meaning of the book lies precisely in the parallelism of the two parts. Conclusion: society needs people who weep at their mother's funeral; or, you are never condemned for the crime you think. Besides, I can see ten other possible conclusions.

*

Criticisms of *The Outsider*. The air is ringing with high moral principles. Fools who think that denial means giving up when in fact it is a choice. (The author of *The Plague* shows the heroic aspect of denial.) No other life is possible for a man deprived of God – and all men are. People who imagine that virility consists of leaping prophetically up and down, that greatness lies in spiritual affectation! But this struggle through poetry and its obscurities, this apparent rebellion of the mind is *the cheapest*. It has no effect and tyrants are very well aware of this.

*

No tomorrow

'What do I contemplate which is greater than I and which I feel without being able to define it? A kind of difficult march towards a sainthood of negation – a heroism without God – pure man in fact. All the human virtues, including solitude with respect to God.

'What is it that gives Christianity its superiority *as an example* (the only one it has)? Christ and his saints – the quest for a *style of life*. This work will include as many forms as there are stages on the way towards a perfection that offers no reward. The Outsider marks absolute zero. As does The Myth. *The Plague* marks a progress, not from zero towards infinity, but towards a deeper complexity that awaits definition. The last stage will be the saint, but he will have his arithmetical value – measurable as man is.'

*

On criticism

Three years to write a book, five lines to make fun of it – and wrong quotations.

Letter to A.R., literary critic (letter not intended to be sent).

One sentence in your article particularly struck me: 'I will not take into account ...' How can an experienced critic, knowing how deliberately planned any work of art is, refuse to take into account in the depiction of a character the *sole moment* when this character talks about himself and entrusts something of his secret to the reader? And how could you not have felt that this end was also a drawing together of the different themes, a privileged place in which the very disjointed character whom I described finally took on some form of unity?

... You credit me with the ambition to write realistically. Realism is an empty word (*Madame Bovary* and *The Possessed*

Reception of The Outsider

are realist novels and have nothing in common). This was never my concern. If I did have to describe my ambition, I should on the contrary speak of a symbol. And you did feel this. But you give this symbol a meaning which it does not have, and you have, in short, quite gratuitously credited me with a ridiculous philosophy. There is in fact nothing in this book which allows you to state that I believe in natural man, that I identify a human being with a vegetable creature, that human nature has nothing to do with morality, etc. The central character in my book never takes the initiative. You did not notice that he always restricts himself to *replying to questions*, those of life or those of men. Thus he never affirms anything. And I have given only the negative of a snapshot of him. Nothing could enable you to prejudge his deepest attitude except precisely the last chapter. But you 'will not take it into account'.

The reasons for this desire to 'say as little as possible' would take up too much time. But I can at least regret that a superficial study of my book should have led you to credit me with a commercialized philosophy that I am not prepared to accept. You will perhaps understand me better if I tell you that the only quotation you give in your article is incorrect (give it and correct it) and that the conclusions it justifies are therefore invalid. There perhaps was another philosophy and you touched upon it by writing the word 'inhumanity'. But what is the good of proving this?

You may perhaps think that this is a lot of fuss over a small book by an unknown writer. But I think that this affair goes beyond me personally. For you have taken up a moral attitude which prevents you from judging with the clear-sightedness and talent which you were acknowledged to possess. This position is indefensible, as you know better than anyone. There is a very vague boundary between your criticisms and those which could soon be made under a literature controlled by the state (and which were made not so very long ago) concerning the moral character of such and such a work. I am quite without anger when I tell you that this is abominable. Neither you nor anyone else is qualified to judge whether a work can serve or harm the nation, either now or ever. In any case, I refuse to submit to such jurisdiction and this is why I am writing to you. I should be grateful if you would in fact believe that I would have quite calmly accepted graver criticisms made in a less intolerant spirit.

In any case, I should not like this letter to give rise to any further misunderstanding. These remarks do not come from a discontented author and I would ask you not to make any part of this letter available for publication. You will not have seen my name very frequently in the reviews published nowadays, which are nevertheless of fairly easy access. The reason is that, having nothing to say in them, I do not want to make any sacrifices to publicity. The only reason why I am now publishing books which have taken me years of work is that they are finished and I am preparing those which follow them. I expect them to bring me neither material advantage nor reputation. I was merely hoping that they would win me the attention and patience normally accorded to any sincere enterprise. I must now believe that this itself was an exaggerated demand. I am, nevertheless, yours sincerely ...

*

Three people entered into the making of *The Outsider*: two men (of whom one was myself) and one woman.

*

The Outsider and the critics: Impassibility, they say. Wrong word. Benevolence would be better.

THE COMPOSITION OF *THE OUTSIDER*

From the entries in *Notebooks I, II* and *IV*
between 1937 and 1940

June 1937
The condemned man visited by the priest every day. Because the neck is sliced off, because the knees give way, because the lips would like to form a name, because the body thrusts itself madly towards the earth to hide itself in a 'My God, My God!'

And every time the resistance in the man who doesn't want this easy way out, and who wants to chew over and taste all his fear. He dies without a word, his eyes full of tears.

*

December 1937
The man who showed all kinds of promise and who is now working in an office. He does nothing apart from this, simply going back home, lying down and smoking until dinner-time, going back to bed again and sleeping until the next morning. On Sundays he gets up very late and stands at the window, watching the sun or the rain, the passers-by or the silent street. The whole year round. He is waiting. He is waiting for death. What good are promises anyway, since in any case ...

*

May 1938
The old woman who dies in the old people's home. Her friend, the friend she has made over a period of three years, weeps 'because she has nothing left'. The caretaker of the little mortuary

who is a Parisian and lives there with his wife. 'Who could have told them that at seventy-four he would finish up at an old people's home at Marengo?' His son has a good job. They left Paris. The daughter-in-law didn't want them. Scenes. The old man finally 'raised his hand to him'. His son put them in an old people's home. The grave-digger who was one of the dead woman's friends. They often went to the village together in the evening. The little old man who insisted on following the procession to the church and then to the cemetery (two kilometres). Since he is an invalid, he cannot keep up and walks twenty yards behind. But he knows the country and takes short cuts that enable him to catch up with the procession several times until he falls behind again.

The Arab nurse who nails down the coffin has a cyst on her nose and wears a permanent bandage.

The dead woman's friends: little old people ridden with fancies. Everything was wonderful in the past. One of them to a neighbour: 'Hasn't your daughter written to you?' 'No.' 'She might remember that she does have a mother.'

The other has died – as a sign and a warning to them all.

*

Belcourt
Story of R. 'I knew a woman ... you might say she was my mistress ... I realized there was something funny going on.' Story of the lottery tickets ('Did you buy one for me?'). Story of the two-piece suit and her sister. Story of the bracelets and the pawn ticket.

Worked out on the basis of 1,300 francs. That doesn't give her enough: 'Why don't you work half-days? You'd help me a lot for all these little things. I bought you the two-piece, I give you 20 francs a day, I pay the rent for you, and you spend the afternoon drinking coffee with your friends. You give them the coffee and sugar. I give you the money. I've been good to you, and you're doing me wrong.'

He wants some advice. He still 'likes to have it now and then'.

Composition of The Outsider

He wants a letter with 'nasty things in it' and 'things to make her feel sorry'.

Ex., 'You just want to have a good time with it, that's all.' And then: 'I'd thought that...' etc.

'You don't see that people are jealous of all the happiness I'm giving you.'

'I knocked her about, but nicely as you might say. She yelled, I closed the shutters.'

The same thing with her friend.

He wants it to be her who comes back. There is something tragic about him in this liking to humiliate her. He is going to take her into an hotel and call the vice squad.

Story of his friends and of the beer. 'You lot, you say you're in the underworld.' 'They told me that if I wanted they would carve her up.'

Story of the overcoat. Story of the matches.

'One day, you'll realize how happy I made you.'

She is an Arab.

*

Old people's home (the old man cutting across the fields). Burial. The sun melts the tar of the roads – people's feet sink down into it and leave the black flesh gaping open. You notice a resemblance between this black mud and the driver's boiled leather hat. And all these shades of black, the sticky black of the open tar, the dull black of the clothes, the shiny black of the hearse – the sun, the smell of leather and horse dirt, of varnish and incense. Tiredness. And the other man, cutting across the fields.

He is going to the burial because she is his only friend. At the home they used to say: 'She's your fiancée,' as if they were children. And he used to laugh. And he was happy.

*

2 P. Today mother died. Or it might have been yesterday. I don't know. I had a telegram from the Home: 'Mother died. Funeral tomorrow. Yours faithfully.' It doesn't mean anything. It might have been yesterday.

As the concierge said: 'It's hot in the plain. You bury them more quickly, especially here.' He told me he came from Paris and had found it hard to get used to things. Because in Paris you can stay with the body for two, sometimes three days. Here you don't have the time. You've only just got used to the idea that they're dead when you have to start running after the hearse.

... But the procession was going too fast as well. And the sun was beating down like a great bully. And as the assistant nurse very rightly said: 'If you go too slowly, you risk getting sunstroke. And if you go too fast, you're covered in perspiration and then you catch a chill in the church.' She was right. There was no way out.

The undertaker's assistant said something to me that I didn't quite catch. He was lifting his hat up from time to time and using his handkerchief to wipe his head. 'What?' I said to him. 'Hot,' he replied, pointing to the sky. 'Yes,' I said. Shortly afterwards he asked me: 'That your mother?' 'Yes.' 'Was she old?' 'So-so,' I replied, since I didn't know exactly. Then he fell silent.

*

On the Absurd?
There is only one case in which despair is pure: that of the man sentenced to death. (May I be allowed a short illustration?) A man driven to despair by love might be asked if he wanted to be guillotined on the next day and would refuse. Because of the horror of the punishment? Yes. But here, the horror springs from the complete certainty of what is going to happen – or rather, from the mathematical element which creates this certainty. Here, the absurd is perfectly clear. It is the opposite of anything irrational. It is the plain and simple truth. What is and would be irrational is the fleeting hope, itself already near to death, that it is all going to stop and that this death can be avoided. But the absurd cannot. The truth of the matter is that they are going to chop his head off while he knows what is happening – when in fact his whole mind is concentrated on the fact that his head is going to be chopped off.

Composition of The Outsider

Kirilov is right. To commit suicide is to prove that one is free. And there is a simple solution to the problem of liberty. Men have the illusion that they are free. But when they are sentenced to death they lose it. The whole problem lies in whether or not the illusion is real in the first place.

Before: 'This heart, this little sound that has been with me for so long, how can I imagine that it will ever cease beating, how can I imagine this at the very moment when...'

'Oh, prison, prison, the paradise of prison.'

(The mother: 'And now they are giving him back to me.... This is what they have done with him ... they are giving him back to me in two pieces.')

'Eventually I slept only a little during the day, and waited patiently at night for dawn to break, bringing with it the truth of another day. For the whole of that uncertain hour when I knew that *they* usually came.... Then I became like an animal. ... Afterwards I had one more day.

'I worked it out. I tried to control myself. There was my appeal. I always assumed the worst. It was rejected. Well then, I would die. Perhaps sooner than others. But how often had not the idea of dying made me see life as absurd? Since we are going to die anyway, it doesn't matter how and when. Therefore I must accept. Then, at that moment, *I had the right* to consider the other possibility. I was pardoned. I tried to tame the upsurge in my body and blood which made my eyes smart with an insane hope. I tried to make this cry less intense, so as to make my resignation more plausible if my first assumption were correct. But what was the use? The dawns came, and with them the uncertain hour...

'But here they are. Yet it's still very dark. They've come earlier. I've been robbed, I tell you I've been robbed...

'Run away. Wreck everything. No, I'll stay. Cigarette? Why not. Time. But at the same time, he's cutting my shirt collar away. At the same time. I haven't gained any time at all. I tell you I'm being robbed.

'... How long this corridor is, but how quickly these people are walking.... As long as there are a lot of them, as long as they greet me with cries of hatred. As long as there are a lot of them, and I am not alone...

'... I'm cold. How cold it is. Why have they left me in my shirt-sleeves? It's true that it doesn't matter any more. No more illnesses for me. I've lost the paradise of suffering, I'm losing it, as I'm losing the joy of spitting out my lungs, of being eaten away by a cancer under the gaze of someone I love.

'... And this starless sky, these black windows, and this busy street and this man in the front row, and the foot of this man who...'

END

*

Tolba and his brawls. (1939)
'I'm not a bad bloke, but I'm very touchy. I hops from right to left. The other bloke says to me: "If you're a man, get down off the tram." I says to him: "Go on, keep your hair on." So he says: "You're not a man." So I gets off and says to him. "Now then, that's enough, or I'll square you off." "You and who else?" So I bonks him. Down he goes. I go to help him up. And he tries to kick me. So I shoves my knee in his face and slaps him a couple of times. There's blood all over his face. So I says: "Had enough?" "Yes," he says.

*

Tailors like Marie-Christine are 'not only fashionable but always up to date'. Laxatives are 'only a temporary remedy. The roots of constipation remain untouched.'

*

Characters.
The old man and his dog. Eight years hatred.
The other man, and his verbal mannerism: 'He was charming, and, moreover, very pleasant.'

Composition of The Outsider

'It's eternal, and, moreover, human.'
'A deafening noise, and, moreover, one that made you jump.'
A.T.R.

*

May 1940
The Outsider is finished.

LETTER TO ROLAND BARTHES ON
THE PLAGUE

Paris, 11 January 1955

My dear Barthes,

However attractive it may appear, I find it difficult to share your point of view on *The Plague*. Of course, all comments are justifiable, within an honest critical appraisal, and it is both possible and significant to venture as far as you do. But it seems to me that every work contains a number of obvious factors to which the author is justified in calling attention if only to indicate how far the commentary can go. To say, for example, that *The Plague* teaches men to ignore history and abstain from politics involves, in my view, exposing oneself to a number of contradictions, and, above all, involves going beyond a certain number of obvious facts which I shall briefly summarize here:

1. *The Plague*, which I wanted to be read on a number of levels, nevertheless has as its obvious content the struggle of the European resistance movements against Nazism. The proof is that although this enemy is nowhere named, everyone in every European country recognized him. I will add that a long extract from *The Plague* appeared under the Occupation, in a collection of resistance texts, and that this fact alone would justify the transposition that I have made. *The Plague* is, in a sense, more than a chronicle of the resistance. But it is certainly not anything less.

2. Compared to *The Outsider*, *The Plague* does represent, beyond any possible discussion, the movement from an attitude of solitary revolt to the recognition of a community whose struggles must be shared. If there is an evolution from *The Outsider* to *The Plague*, it is towards solidarity and participation.

3. The theme of separation, whose importance in the book you

Letter to Roland Barthes on The Plague

bring out very well, throws a good deal of light on this point. Rambert, who embodies this theme, does in fact give up private life in order to take his place in the common struggle. I should point out, in parenthesis, that this character shows how artificial the contrast is between the friend and the militant. For one virtue is common to them both, and this is active fraternity, with which no history, in the last resort, has learned to dispense.

4. *The Plague* ends, moreover, on the announcement and acceptance of further struggles. It bears witness for 'all that had had to be done, and that [men] would doubtless have to do again against terror and its tireless weapons, whatever might be their personal anguish...'

I could develop my point of view further. But even if I do find it possible to consider the ethic at work in *The Plague* inadequate (and it must then be said what more complete ethic is being used as criterion), and legitimate to criticize its aesthetic (many of your remarks are clarified by the very simple fact that I do not believe in realism in art), I find it, on the contrary, very difficult to agree with you when you say in your conclusion that its author refuses to participate in our present history. It is difficult and, let me say this in all friendship, a little depressing.

In any case, the question which you ask, 'What would the fighters against the plague do when confronted with the overhuman face of the scourge?' is unjust in this respect: it ought to have been couched in the past tense, and it would then have received its reply, which is a positive one. What these fighters, whose experience I have to some extent translated, did do, they did in fact against men, and at a cost which you know. They will do it again, no doubt, when any terror confronts them, whatever face it may take on, for terror has several faces. This, once again, justifies me for not having named any particular one, in order better to strike at them all. It is doubtless the fact that *The Plague* can apply to every form of resistance against all and every tyranny which explains the reproaches directed against me. But it is not legitimate to reproach me or, above all, accuse me of refusing history – unless it is proclaimed that the only way of taking part in history is to legitimize tyranny. This is not what you do, I know; as far as I am concerned, I am perverse enough to believe that resigning oneself to such an idea would amount to accepting human solitude. And, far from feeling installed in a career of solitude, I have, on the contrary, the feeling that I am living by and for a community which nothing in history has so far been able to touch.

Here, too briefly expressed, is what I wanted to tell you. I should merely like to assure you in conclusion that this friendly discussion alters nothing of the high opinion which I have of you as a writer and a person.

Albert Camus
Letter published in *Club*, the review of
the *Club du meilleur livre*, February 1955

THE COMPOSITION OF *THE PLAGUE*

From the entries in *Notebooks II, III* and *IV*

December 1938

It is to Jeanne that some of my purest joys are linked. She often used to say to me: 'You're silly.' It was her expression, the one she used when she laughed, but she always said it when she loved me most. We both came from poor families. She lived a few streets away from me, in the rue de Centre. Neither of us ever went out of our own neighbourhood, for everything brought us back to it. And in both our homes we found the same sadness and the same sordid life. Our meetings were a way of escaping from all this. Yet today, when I look back over so many years and see her face, like a tired child's, I realize that we were not really escaping from it, and that what is now priceless in our love stemmed from the very shadow which this poverty cast over us.

I think that I really did suffer when I lost her, but I had no feelings of rebellion. This is because I have never felt very much at ease in ownership. Regret has always seemed much more natural to me. And although I can see my feelingss quite clearly, I have never been able to stop thinking that Jeanne is much more a part of me at a moment like today than she was when she stood a little on tip-toe to put her arms around my neck. I can't remember how I met her. But I know that I used to go and visit her at her home. And that her father and mother laughed. Her father worked on the railway, and when he was at home he always sat in a corner, looking thoughtfully out of the window, his enormous hands flat on his thighs. Her mother was always doing housework. So was Jeanne, but in such a light and carefree manner that she never looked as if she were really working. She wasn't very small, but she seemed so to me. And I felt she was so light and tiny that I always had a twinge of sadness when I saw her dart across the road in front of the lorries. I can see now that she was probably not very intelligent. But at the time I never thought about it. She had her own particular way of playing at being cross that almost made me cry with delight. And this heart, now closed to so much, can still be touched by the memory of the secret gesture she would make when she turned round and threw herself into my arms when I begged her for forgiveness. I can't remember now whether I wanted her physically or not. I know that everything was mixed up, and that all my feelings melted into tenderness. If I did want her, I forgot about it the first day that, in the corridor of her flat, she kissed me to thank me for a little brooch that I had given her. With her hair drawn back, her uneven mouth with its rather large teeth, her clear eyes and straight nose, she looked that evening like a child that I had brought into the world for the sake of its love and tenderness. Helped by Jeanne herself, who always called me her 'big friend', I kept that impression for a long time.

There was a strange quality to the joys we shared together. When we got engaged, she was eighteen and I twenty-two. But what filled our hearts with grave and joyful love was the official character that it now had. And for Jeanne to come home with me, for mother to kiss her and call her 'my girl', were all opportunities for rather ridiculous moments of joy that we made no attempts to hide. But Jeanne's memory is linked in my mind with an impression that I now feel can never be expressed. I can still recognize it, however, and I only need to be sad, and see a few moments later a woman whose face touches me, and a brilliantly lit shop-front, to find Jeanne with me again, her face turned towards me as she says 'How lovely', and be hurt by the truth of the memory. It was at Christmas time, and the local shops made a great show with lights and decorations. We would stop in front of the confectioners' windows. The chocolate models, the imitation rockwork of gold and silver paper, the snowflakes of cotton wool, the gilded plates and rainbow-coloured cakes, all sent us into raptures. I felt a little ashamed. But I could not hold

Composition of The Plague

back the upsurge of joy that filled my whole being and brought tears to Jeanne's eyes.

If today I try to analyse this strange feeling, I can find many different things in it. Certainly this joy came first and foremost from Jeanne – from her scent and the way she used to hold tightly on to my wrist, or pout her lips. But there was also the sudden brightness of the shops in a neighbourhood that was normally so dark, the hurried air of the passers-by, laden with parcels, the delight of the children in the streets, which all helped to tear us from our world of loneliness. The silver paper round the chocolates was the sign that a confused but noisy and golden period was beginning for the simple-hearted, and Jeanne and I snuggled closer together. Perhaps we were vaguely aware of the particular happiness that a man feels when his life falls into harmony with what he is himself. Normally, we carried the magic desert of our love through a world from which love had disappeared. And on days like these it seemed that the flame which rose in us when we held hands was the same one which we saw dancing in the shop windows, in the hearts of the workmen who had turned round to look at their children, and in the depths of the pure and icy December sky.

*

The liberating plague (April 1941)

Happy town. People live according to different systems. The plague: abolishes all systems. But they die all the same. Doubly useless. A philosopher there is writing an 'anthology of insignificant actions'. He will keep a diary of the plague, from this point of view. (Another diary, this time from the point of view of the suffering involved. A classics master. He realizes that he had not understood Thucydides and Lucretius until then. His favourite phrase: 'In all probability.' 'The tram company had only 760 workers available instead of 2,130. In all probability this is due to the plague.')

A young priest loses his faith at the sight of the black pus flowing from the wounds. He takes his holy oil away again. 'If I get out alive ...' But he does not. Everything must be paid for.

The bodies are taken away in trams. Whole strings of carriages, filled with flowers and dead bodies, drive along the cliffs. They immediately sack all the conductors: the passengers no longer pay.

The agency 'Ransdoc–S.V.P.' (information please) gives all information on the telephone. 'Two hundred victims today. A charge of two francs will be added to your telephone account.' 'Impossible, I'm afraid, no more coffins for four days. Consult the Transport Authority. A charge ...' The agency advertises itself on the radio. 'Do you want to know the daily, weekly, or monthly number of plague victims? Phone "Information Please" – six lines: 253–91 to 253–96.'

The town gates are closed. People die in over-crowded isolation. One gentleman, however, keeps his habits. He continues to dress for dinner. One by one, the members of his family disappear from the table. He dies with his meal in front of him, still dressed for dinner. As the maid said: 'Well, there's something to be said for it. We don't need to get him ready for the funeral.' They stop burying the dead, and throw them into the sea. But there are too many of them. It's like a monstrous foam on the blue sea.

A man loves a woman and reads the signs of the plague on her face. Never has he loved her so much, and never has he been so disgusted by her. He is divided against himself. But it is always the body that wins. Disgust prevails. He takes her by the hand, drags her from the bed, into the room, the hall, the corridor of the block of flats, through two small streets into the main road. He leaves her near a sewer. 'After all there are other women.'

At the end, the most insignificant character decides to speak: 'In a way,' he says, 'it's a disaster.'

*

Plague. Second version (December 1942)
Bible: Deuteronomy, xxviii, 21; xxxii, 24. Leviticus, xxvi, 25. Amos, iv, 10. Exodus, ix, 4; ix, 15; xii, 29. Jeremiah, xxiv, 10; xiv, 12; vi, 19; xxi, 7 and 9. Ezekiel, v, 12; vi, 12; vii, 15.

'Each man seeks his desert, and as soon as he is there finds it too harsh. It shall not be said that I cannot bear my own.'

Composition of The Plague

Originally, the first three parts made up of diaries – note-books – notes – sermons – treatises – and of objective accounts which were to suggest, catch the attention, and open up the depths of the book. The last part, made up entirely of events, was to bring out the general meaning through them and through them alone.

Each part was also to draw the links between the characters a little closer together – and was also to make the reader feel this by the gradual fusion of the different diaries into one, and complete this in the scenes in part IV.

Second version.
The Plague picturesque and descriptive – little passages of documentation and a dissertation on plagues and scourges.

Stephan – chapter 2: He curses ths love which has deprived him of everything else.

Impersonal style throughout (sermons – diaries, etc.) and monotonous relief by descriptions of the plague?

It must definitely be an account, a chronicle. But what a lot of problems this creates.

Perhaps: revise Stephan completely by missing out the love theme. Stephan lacks development. The continuation suggested something fuller.

Carry on with the theme of separation right to the end.

Have a general report writtten on the plague at O.?

Those who find a flea on themselves.

A chapter on poverty.

For the sermon: 'Have you noticed, brethren, how monotonous Jeremiah is?'

Additional character: a man who is separated, an exile, who does everything to get out of the town and who does not succeed. The official steps he takes: he wants to obtain a safe-conduct under the pretext that he 'is not from here'. If he dies, show that he suffers first of all from not having found the other person again, and from so many things left in suspense. This is touching the very depths of the plague.

Be careful: asthma does not justify so many visits.

Introduce the atmosphere of Oran.

Nothing 'grimacing', stick to what is ordinary.

Civil heroism.

Develop social criticism and revolt. That they are lacking in imagination. They settle down to an epic as they would to a picnic. They don't think on the right scale for plagues. And the remedies they think up are barely suitable for a cold in the nose. They will die (develop).

A chapter on illness. 'They noticed once again that physical suffering never came to them alone but was always accompanied by mental sufferings (family – frustrated loves) which gave it its depth. They thus realized – and contrary to popular belief – that if one of the atrocious privileges of the human condition was to die alone, an equally true and no less true image of this condition was that man could never die really alone.'

Moral of the plague: it has served nothing and nobody. Only those whom death has touched personally or through their family have learned anything. But the truth they have thus achieved concerns only themselves. It has no future.

The events and chronicles should give the social meaning of the plague. The characters give the deeper meaning. But all this broadly.

Social criticism. The encounter between the administration, which is an abstract entity, and the plague, which is the most concrete of all forces, can give only comic and scandalous results.

The man separated from his loved one escapes because *he cannot wait until she has grown old*.

A chapter on relatives isolated *in the camps*.

End of part I. The increase in the cases of plague must be based on the increase in the number of rats. Expand. Expand.

The phoney plague?

Part I is concerned with exposition and should all be over very quickly – even in the diaries.

Composition of The Plague

One of the possible themes: struggle between medicine and religion: the powers of what is relative (and how relative!) against those of the absolute. It is the relative which wins or, more exactly, does not lose.

'Of course, we know that the plague has advantages, that it opens people's eyes, makes them think. From this point of view it is like all the evils of this world and like the world itself. But what is also true of the evils of this world and of the world itself is also true of the plague. Whatever greatness individuals may draw from it we must, when we look at the wretchedness of our brothers, be mad, criminal or cowardly to accept the plague, and in face of it the only watchword for a man is revolt.'

All seek peace. Underline this.

? Describe Cottard *backwards*: describe his behaviour and reveal *at the end* that he was afraid of being arrested.

The papers have nothing else to talk about except the plague. People say: there's nothing in the paper.

They bring doctors in from outside.

What seems to me most characteristic of this period is *separation*. All were separated from the rest of the world, from those they loved or from their habits. And, in this retreat, those who could were forced to meditate, and the others to live the life of a hunted animal. In short, there was no middle way.

At the end the exile catches the plague, runs to a high place and calls loudly to his wife over the walls of the city, the countryside, three villages and a river.

? A preface by the narrator with considerations on objectivity and on bearing witness.

At the end of the plague, all the inhabitants look like emigrants.

Add details, 'epidemic'.

Tarrou is the man who can understand everything – and who suffers from this. He can judge nothing.

What is the ideal of the man exposed to the plague? – I am really going to make you laugh: it's honesty.

Cross out: 'at the beginning – in fact – in reality – the first days – at about the same time' etc.

? Show throughout the book that Rieux is the narrator by a series of clues. At the beginning: the smell of a cigarette.

Hostility and need for warmth at one and the same time. Reconciled in the cinema, where people are packed together without knowing one another.

Little islands of light in the darkened town towards which a people of shadows converge like a heliotropically governed swarm of paramecia.

For the exile: evenings in cafés where they save electricity by waiting as long as possible before putting on the lights, where dusk flows in like grey water and the last sunlight glimmers faintly in the window panes, while a pale sheen forms on the marble-topped tables and chairbacks: it is then that he feels forsaken.

The Separated part 2: 'They were struck by the number of little things which counted a great deal for them and which had no existence for other people. They thus discovered personal life.' 'They knew perfectly well that they had to get it over with – or at least that they ought to long for the end – and consequently they did desire it, but without the flame of the beginning – and only with the very clear reasons which they had to desire it. All that was left of the great initial upsurge was a bleak despondency which made them forget the very reason for this dismay. They had the outward air of sadness and misfortune but no longer felt their real bite. And basically their misfortune lay precisely in this. Before, they were simply stricken with despair. It was thus that many of them were not faithful. For all that they had kept of their suffering from love was the taste and the need for love, and as they progressively grew away from the person who had brought these to birth, they had felt weaker and had finally given way to the first promise of tenderness. They were thus unfaithful through love.' 'Seen from a distance, their lives now seemed to them to form a whole. It was then that they clung to this life with a new strength. Thus the plague gave them back their unity. We must therefore conclude that these men did not know how to live with their unity, although they did possess it – or rather that they were capable of experiencing it only when it had been taken

Composition of The Plague

from them.' – 'Sometimes, when they thought of one day showing something to a friend who was no longer there, they realized that they had still not passed beyond the first stage. They still had hope. The second phase really began when they could think only in plague terms.' – 'But sometimes in the middle of the night their wound opened up again. And suddenly awoken, they would touch its angry lips, finding their suffering still quite fresh, and with it the distressed face of their love.'

I want to express by means of the plague the suffocation from which we all suffered and the atmosphere of threat and exile in which we lived. At the same time, I want to extend this interpretation to the notion of existence in general. The plague will give the image of those whose share in this war has been that of reflection, silence – and moral suffering.

*

Plague. Second version. The separated have difficulties with weekdays. With Sunday naturally. With Saturday afternoon. And with certain days formerly devoted to certain rites.

Id. A chapter on the Terror: 'People that were fetched away in the middle of the night...'

In the chapter on the isolation camps: relatives are already separated from the dead person – then for reasons of hygiene children are separated from their parents and men from women. So much so that *separation becomes general*. All are brought face to face again with loneliness.

Thus make separation into the main theme of the novel. 'They had asked nothing of the plague. At the heart of an incomprehensible world, they had patiently built up a private, totally human universe in which their days were divided between tenderness and habit. And now it was doubtless not enough to be separated from the world itself; the plague also had to separate them from their modest daily creations. After having blinded their minds, it tore out their hearts.' In practice: *the novel contains only solitary men.*

*

Plague. Second version.

We seek for peace and go towards people expecting them to give it to us. But what they can give to begin with is only madness and confusion. We must then seek peace elsewhere, but the heavens are silent. And it is then, and only then, that we can go back to people since they can give you, if not peace, at least sleep.

*

Plague. Second version.
It is good that there should be terraces above the plague.
All are right, says Rieux.
Tarrou (or Rieux) forgives the plague.

*

Grace? (1944)
We should serve justice because our condition is unjust, increase happiness and joy because this world is unhappy. Similarly, we should sentence no one to death, since we have been sentenced to death ourselves.

The doctor, God's enemy: he fights against death.

*

Plague. Rieux said that he was God's enemy since he was fighting against death and that it was even his job to be God's enemy. He also said that by trying to save Paneloux he was showing him at the same time that he was wrong and that by accepting to be saved Paneloux was accepting the possibility of not being right. All that Paneloux said to him was that he would be right in the end since he doubtless would die and Rieux replied that the essential thing was not to accept and to fight to the very end.

*

Meaning of my work: So many men lack grace. How can one live without grace? We must really get down to it and do what Christianity has never done: concern ourselves with the damned.

PART FOUR
SKETCHES FOR A SELF-PORTRAIT

NOTEBOOK I
May 1935–September 1937

May 1935
What I mean is this: that one can, with no romanticism, feel nostalgic for lost poverty. A certain number of years lived without money are enough to create a whole sensibility. In this particular case, the strange feeling which the son has for his mother constitutes *his whole sensibility*. The latent material memory which he has of his childhood (a glue that sticks to the soul) explains why this way of feeling shows itself in the most widely differing fields.

Whoever notices this in himself feels gratitude and therefore a guilty conscience. If he has moved into a different class, the comparison also gives him the feeling that he has lost great wealth. For rich people, the sky is just an extra, a gift of nature. The poor, on the other hand, can see it as it really is: an infinite grace.

A guilty conscience needs to confess. A work of art is a confession, and I must bear witness. When I see things clearly, I have only one thing to say. It is in this life of poverty, among these vain or humble people, that I have most certainly touched what I feel is the true meaning of life. Works of art will never be enough. Art is not everything for me. Let it at least be a means.

What also count are the small acts of cowardice, the times one is ashamed, the way one thinks of the other world, the world of money, without being aware of doing so. I think that the world of the poor is one of the few, if not the only one, which is wholly turned in upon itself, which is an island in society. It is quite cheap to go there and play at being Robinson Crusoe. But someone who has dived down right into it has to say 'over there' when talking about the doctor's house next door.

All this must be expressed through a study of the mother and the son.

What I have just written applies to things in general. When one comes down to particular instances, everything becomes more complicated.

1. A setting. A neighbourhood and its inhabitants.
2. The mother and what she does.
3. The relationship between the son and his mother.

What is the solution? The mother? End with a chapter describing how her symbolic value comes into being through the son's nostalgia???

*

The theme of comedy is also important. What saves us from our worst suffering is the feeling that we are abandoned and alone, and yet not sufficiently alone for 'other people' to stop 'sympathizing with us' in our unhappiness. It is in this sense that our moments of happiness are often those when we are filled and lifted up into an endless sadness by the feeling that everyone has forsaken us. Also in this sense that happiness is often only the self-pitying awareness of our unhappiness.

Striking among the poor – God put self-pity by the side of despair like the cure by the side of the disease.

*

January 1936
Beyond the window there is a garden, but I can see only its walls. And a few branches flowing with light. A little higher, I see more branches, and higher still the sun. And of all the jubilation of the air that can be felt outdoors, or all that joy spread out over the world, I can see only shadows of branches playing on white curtains. There are also five rays of sunlight patiently pouring into the room the golden scent of dried grass. A breeze, and the shadows on the curtains come to life. If a cloud covers up the sun and then lets it through again, the bright yellow

of the vase of mimosas leaps out of the shade. The birth of this single flash of brightness is enough to fill me with a confused and whirling joy.

A prisoner in the cave, I lie alone before the shadow of the world. A January afternoon. But the heart of the air is full of cold. Everywhere a thin film of sunlight that you could split with a touch of your fingernail, but which clothes everything in an eternal smile. Who am I and what can I do – except enter into the movement of the branches and the light, be this ray of sunlight in which my cigarette smoulders away, this soft and gentle passion breathing in the air? If I try to reach myself, it is at the heart of this light that I am to be found. And if I try to taste and understand this delicate flavour that contains the secret of the world, it is myself that I find at the heart of the universe. Myself, that is to say this intense emotion which frees me from my surroundings. Soon my attention will be filled again with other things and with the world of men. But let me cut out this moment from the cloth of time as other men leave a flower in the pages of a book. In it they enclose the memory of a walk in which they were touched by love. I also walk through the world, but am caressed by a god. Life is short, and it is a sin to waste one's time. I waste my time all day long, while other people say that I am very active. Today is a resting place, and my heart goes out to meet itself.

If I still feel a grain of anxiety, it is at the thought of this unseizable moment slipping through my fingers like a ball of quick-silver. Let those who want to stand aside from the world. I no longer feel sorry for myself, for now I see myself being born. I am happy in this world for my kingdom is of this world. A cloud passes and a moment grows pale. I die to myself. The book opens at a well-loved page – how tasteless it is when compared to the book of the world. Is it true that I have suffered, is it not true that I am suffering? And that I am drunk with this suffering because it is made up of that sun and these shadows, of this warmth and that coldness which can be felt afar off, at the very heart of the air? Why wonder at death and human suffering, when everything is written on this window where the sky pours forth its fullness? I can say, and in a moment I shall say, that what counts is to be true, and then everything fits in, both humanity and simplicity. And when am I truer and more transparent than when I *am* the world?

Moment of adorable silence. Men have fallen silent. But the song of the world rises and I, a prisoner chained deep in the cave, am filled with delight before I have had time to desire. Eternity is here while I was waiting for it. Now I can speak. I do not know what I could wish for rather than this contained presence of self with self. What I want now is not happiness but awareness. You think you have cut yourself off from the world, but it is enough to see an olive tree upright in the golden dust, or beaches glistening in the morning sun, to feel this resistance melt away. Thus with me. I become aware of the possibilities for which I am responsible. Every minute of life carries with it its miraculous value, and its face of eternal youth.

*

In the Balearic Isles. Last summer
What gives value to travel is fear. It is the fact that, at a certain moment, when we are so far from our own country (a French newspaper acquires incalculable value. And those evenings when in cafés you try to get close to other men just to touch them with your elbow), we are seized by a vague fear, and an instinctive desire to go back to the protection of old habits. This is the most obvious benefit of travel. At that moment we are febrile but also porous. The slightest touch makes us quiver to the depths of our being. We come across a cascade of light, and there is eternity. This is why we should not say that we travel for pleasure. There is no pleasure in travelling. It is more an occasion for spiritual testing. If we understand by culture the exercise of our most intimate sense – that of eternity – then we travel for culture. Pleasure takes us away from ourselves in the same way as distraction, in Pascal's use of the word, takes us away from God. Travel, which is like a greater and a graver science, brings us back to ourselves.

*

Seek contacts. All contacts. If I want to write about men, should I stop talking about the countryside? If the sky or light attract me, shall I forget the eyes or voices of those I love? Each time I am given the elements of a friendship, the fragments of an emotion, never the emotion or the friendship itself.

You go to see an older friend to tell him everything. Or, at least, something which is stifling you. But he is in a hurry. You talk about everything and about nothing at all. Time passes. And here I am, more alone and emptier than before. How a careless word from a friend escaping from my presence will lay waste this feeble wisdom that I am trying to construct! 'Non ridere, non lugere' ... and doubts about myself and about other people.

*

March
A day of sunshine and clouds. The cold spangled with yellow. I ought to keep a diary of each day's weather. The fine transparent sunshine yesterday. The bay trembling with light – like a moist lip. And I have worked all day.

*

Yesterday. The sun on the quays, the Arab acrobats, and the port leaping with light. It is as if for the last winter that I shall spend here this country were lavishing all its riches upon me. This unique winter, glistening with cold and sunlight. Blue cold.

Lucid ecstasy and smiling destitution – the despair which we see in the virile acceptance reflected in Greek *stelae*. Why do I need to write or create, to love or suffer? The part of my life which is now lost is not, basically, the most important. Everything becomes pointless.

Neither despair nor joy seems justified before this sky and the shining suffocating heat pouring down from it.

*

16 May
A long walk. Hills with the sea in the background. And the delicate sun. White eglantines in all the bushes. Heavy, syrupy flowers

with violet-coloured petals. Also the return home, gentleness and friendship of women. Grave and smiling faces of young women. Smiles, jokes and plans. One goes back into the game. And, without believing in them, everyone smiles at appearances and pretends to accept them. No false notes. I am linked to the world by everything I do, to men by all the gratitude I feel. From the hilltop we could see the mists left by the recent rains being pressed down and brought back to life by the sun. Even as I came down through the woods, sinking into this cotton wool, I sensed the sun above me with the trees standing out one by one in this miraculous day. Trust and friendship, sun and white houses, scarcely grasped shades of meaning – oh, my untouched moments of happiness, already drifting away and offering no more help in the sadness of the evening than a young woman's smile or the intelligent glance of a friendship which knows that it is understood.

*

August 1937
Every day he would disappear into the mountains and come back speechless, his hair full of grass, and his body covered with the scratches of a whole day's rambling. And each time it was the same conquest without seduction. He was gradually wearing down the resistance of this hostile country, managing to make himself like the round white clouds behind the solitary pine tree standing out on the crest of a hill, like the fields of pinkish willowherb, rowan trees and bell-flowers. He was becoming part of this fragrant, rocky world. When he reached the distant summit and saw the immense countryside suddenly stretching out before him, he felt not the calm peace of love but a kind of inner pact which he was signing with this alien nature, a truce concluded between two hard and savage faces, the intimacy of two enemies rather than the harmony between two friends.

*

September
If you say: 'I don't understand Christianity, I want to live without consolation', then you are narrow minded and prejudiced. But

if, living without consolation, you say: 'I understand and admire the Christian position', you are a shallow dilettante. I am beginning to grow out of being concerned by what people think.

NOTEBOOK II

September 1937–April 1939

30 September
I always end up by seeing every aspect there is of a person. It's a question of time. There always comes a moment when I feel the break. What is interesting is that this always happens when I feel this person lacking in curiosity about something.

*

4 October
'I lived until the last few days with the idea that I had to do something in life, and, more exactly, that because I was poor, I had to earn a living, get a job, settle down. I must accept the fact that the roots of this idea, which I still dare not call a prejudice, went very deep, since it lived on in spite of all my irony and "last words on the subject". And then, once appointed at Bel-Abbès, faced with all the permanence that being established there implied, everything suddenly ebbed away. I rejected it, doubtless because I saw security as unimportant compared to my opportunities for real life. I recoiled before the dull, stifling routine of such an existence. If I had got through the first few days, I should certainly have accepted. But that was the danger. I was afraid, afraid of being lonely and of being permanently fixed. Today I don't know whether it was strength or weakness to have rejected this life, to have shut the door of what people call "a future" in my own face, and to remain instead poor and insecure. But at least I know that if there is a conflict, it is for something worth while. Unless, later on. ... No. What made me run away was doubtless not so much the fear of settling down, but of settling down permanently in something ugly.

'Am I now capable of what other people call "a serious attitude to life"? Am I lazy? I don't think so, and have given myself proof to the contrary. But have we the right to refuse difficulties under the pretext that we don't like them? I think that only people lacking in character go to pieces through laziness. If I lacked character, there would be only one solution left for me.'

*

10 October

To be worth something or nothing. To create or not to create. In the first case everything is justified. Everything, without exception. In the second, absolute absurdity. The only choice then to be made is the most aesthetically satisfying form of suicide: marriage, and a forty-hour week; or a revolver.

*

On the road to La Madeleine. Once again, in presence of such great natural beauty, the desire to be stripped bare of everything.

*

20 October

The demand for happiness and the patient quest for it. We need not banish our melancholy, but we must destroy our taste for difficult and fatal things. Be happy with our friends, in harmony with the world, and earn our happiness by following a path which nevertheless leads to death.

'You will tremble before death.'

'Yes, but I shall have left nothing unfulfilled in my mission, which is to live.' Don't give way to conformity and to office hours. Don't give up. Never give up – always demand more. But stay lucid, even during office hours. As soon as we are alone in its presence, strive after the nakedness into which the world rejects us. But above all, in order to be, never try to seem.

*

21 October

You need a good deal more energy to travel with very little money than to play at 'the hunted traveller'. Travelling steerage, arriving tired out and with a feeling of emptiness, going long distances third class, often eating only once a day, counting your money and being constantly afraid of having an already very difficult journey interrupted by an unexpected accident – all this requires a courage and will-power that make it impossible to take sermons about 'the need to uproot oneself' very seriously. It is neither amusing nor easy to travel. If you are young and penniless, you need a liking for difficulties and a love for the unknown if you are to transform your dreams of travel into reality. But, after all, this does save you from dilettantism – although I wouldn't go as far as to say that what is lacking in Gide and Montherlant is the fact that they have never travelled on a cheap ticket which compelled them to spend six days in the same town. But I am perfectly certain that basically I can never see things as Gide or Montherlant do – because of the cheap tickets.

*

February 1938
The spirit of revolution lies wholly in man's protest against the human condition. Under the different forms which it assumes, it is in this respect the only eternal theme of art and religion. A revolution is always carried out against the Gods – from that of Prometheus onwards. It is a protest which man makes against his destiny, and both tyrants and bourgeois puppets are nothing but pretexts.

This spirit can certainly be grasped in its historical manifestations, but you need all Malraux's emotion not to give way to the desire to prove. It is simpler to discover it in its essence and destiny. From this point of view a work of art that retraced the conquest of happiness would be a revolutionary one.

*

Find an excess in moderation.

*

April 1938
What sordid misery there is in the condition of a man who works and in a civilization based on men who work.

But we must hang on and not let go. The natural reaction is always to scatter one's talents outside work, to make people admire you the easy way, to create an audience and an excuse for cowardice and play-acting (most marriages are organized on this basis). Another inevitable reaction is to try to be clever about it. Besides, the two things fit in very well together, if you let yourself go physically, neglect your body, and let your will-power slacken.

The first thing to do is to keep silent – abolish audiences and learn to be your own judge. Keep a balance between an active concern for the body and an attentive awareness of being alive. Give up all feeling that the world owes you a living and devote yourself to achieving two kinds of freedom: freedom from money, and freedom from your own vanities and cowardice. Have rules and stick to them. Two years is not too long a time to spend thinking about one single point. You must wipe out all earlier stages, and concentrate all your strength first of all on forgetting nothing, and then on learning patiently.

If this price is paid, then there is one chance in ten of escaping from the most sordid and miserable of conditions: that of the man who works.

*

I can still remember the despair that seized me when my mother told me that 'Now I was old enough, and would get useful presents at New Year'. Even today I can't stop myself from wincing secretly whenever I receive this type of present. And certainly I knew that it was the voice of love – but why must love sometimes take on such derisory tones?

*

An essay on the forty-hour week.
In my family: ten hours' work followed by sleep. On Sunday and Monday – unemployment: the man weeps. His greatest misery is that he should both weep and wish for what humiliates him (competition).

*

People talk a lot nowadays about the dignity of work, and about the need for it. Monsieur Gignoux, in particular, has very definite ideas on the subject.

But it's a fraud. There is dignity in work only when it is work freely accepted. Only idleness has a moral value because it can give a standard by which to judge men. It is fatal only to the second rate. That is its lesson and its greatness. Work, on the other hand, crushes everyone down to the same level. It provides no basis for judging men. It brings into action a metaphysic of humiliation. Under the form of slavery which the supporters of the establishment now give it, the best men cannot survive its effects ...

I suggest that we stand the usual expression on its head and make work a fruit of laziness. There is a 'dignity of labour' in the little barrels which men make for themselves on Sundays. Here work and play come together again, and play linked with technique attains the dignity of a work of art and of creation itself.

Then there are some people who are indignant or go off into raptures. 'What, I tell you, some of my workmen earn 40 francs a day.'

*

End of the month, when the mother says with an encouraging smile: 'This evening, we'll have *café au lait*. It's a change from time to time.'

But at least they might make love ...

*

The only fraternity which is now possible, which is offered or allowed to us, is the sordid and sticky fraternity in face of death in battle.

*

June
In the cinema, the little woman from Oran sitting next to her husband, the tears streaming down her face at the misfortunes

of the hero. Her husband begs her to stop. In the middle of her tears she says: 'But let me make the most of it.'

*

Artist and work of art. The true work of art is the one which says least. There is a certain relationship between the global experience of an artist, his thought + his life (his system, in one sense – leaving out anything systematic which this word implies), and the work reflecting this experience. This relationship is wrong when the work gives the whole of this experience surrounded by a fringe of literature. It is right when the work of art is a section cut out of his experience, the facet of a diamond in which the gem's inner lustre is reflected but not exhausted. In the first case there is exaggeration, and literature. In the second a work which is fruitful because of a whole implied content of experience whose wealth is not directly expressed.

The problem is to acquire that knowledge of life (or rather to have lived) which goes beyond the mere ability to write. So that in the last analysis the great artist is first and foremost a man who has lived greatly (it being understood that in this case living also implies thinking about life – that living is in fact precisely this subtle relationship between experience and our awareness of it).

*

At the meeting. The old railwayman, clean, well-shaven, his shoes shining, his plaid-lined overcoat carefully folded inside out and carried over one arm, who asks me 'if it's here' that the meeting is going to take place, and tells me how worried he is when he thinks about what the working man is going to be like in the future.

*

At the hospital. The tubercular patient who is told by the doctor that he has five days to live. He anticipates and cuts his throat with a razor. Obviously, he can't wait five days.

One of the male nurses tells the journalists: 'Don't talk about it in your papers. He's suffered enough already.'

*

The man who loves *on this earth* and the woman who loves him with the certainty of finding him again in the hereafter. Their loves are not on the same scale.

*

Death and a writer's work. Just before dying he has his last work read over to him. He still hasn't said what he had to say. He orders it to be burnt. And he dies with nothing to console him – and with something snapping in his heart like a broken chord.

*

Sunday
The wind in the mountain holding us back, gagging us, shouting in our ears. The whole forest twisted from top to bottom. Above the valleys, the red ferns flying from one mountain to the next. And this beautiful orange-coloured bird.

*

Mobilization
The eldest son is leaving. He's sitting in front of his mother and saying: 'It won't come to anything.' The mother says nothing. She has picked up a newspaper that was lying on the table. She folds it into two, then into four, then into eight.

*

At the station the crowd seeing people off. Men packed into the carriages. A woman crying. 'But I never thought it would be like this, that it would hurt as much.' Another: 'It's funny, people rushing off like that to get killed.' A girl cries in her fiancé's arms. He looks grave and says nothing. Smoke, shouts and jolts. The train leaves.

From Notebook II

Women's faces, delights of the sun and sea – that is what is being murdered. And if we don't accept murder, then we have to hang on. We're living right in the middle of a contradiction, the whole of our century is stifling and living up to its neck in this contradiction, without a single tear to relieve its anguish.

Not only is there no solution, but there aren't even any problems.

NOTEBOOK III

April 1939–February 1942

August

1. Oedipus puts an end to the Sphinx, and, if he casts out mystery, it is by his knowledge of man. The whole universe of the Greeks is clear.

2. But it is the same man who is savagely destroyed by destiny, by the implacable destiny of blind logic. The unshadowed light of tragic and mortal things.

*

See Epicurus (essay).

The grotto of Aglauros in the Acropolis. Minerva's statue, stripped bare of its clothes once a year. Probable that all statues were similarly clothed. Naked Greek statues are our invention.

*

The war has broken out. But where is it? Where does this absurd event show itself, except in the news-bulletins we have to believe and the notices we have to read? It's not in the blue sky over the blue sea, in the chirring of the grass-hoppers, in the cypress trees on the hills. It isn't in the way the light leaps youthfully in the streets of Algiers.

We want to believe in it. We look for its face, and it hides itself away. The world alone is king with the magnificent countenance it shows us.

We had lived hating this beast. Now it stands before us and we can't recognize it. So few things have changed. Later on, certainly, there will be mud and blood and an immense feeling of nausea. But today we find that the beginning of a war is like the first days of peace: neither the world nor our hearts know they are there.

*

... Remember the first days of what will probably be a highly disastrous war as days of immense happiness – a strange and instinctive destiny ... I am seeking reasons for my revolt which nothing real has so far justified ...

*

There are those made for living love and those who are made for loving.

*

We always exaggerate the importance of an individual life. So many people don't know what to do with their own that it is not completely immoral to take it from them. On the other hand, everything takes on a new value. But this has already been said. The essential absurdity of this catastrophe does not alter the fact that it exists. It generalizes the slightly more essential absurdity of life itself. It makes it more immediate and more relevant. If this war can have an effect on man, it will be to confirm the idea which he has of his own existence and the way he judges it. As soon as this war 'is', any judgement which can take it into account is false. A reflective man generally spends his time adapting his own idea of things to the alterations imposed by new facts. It is in this process of bending and adjusting thought, in this conscious elimination of error, that truth – that is to say, what life can teach us – is to be found. This is why, however vile this war may be, no one can stand aside from it. I myself first of all, naturally, since I can have no fear in risking my life by wagering on death. And then all the nameless and resigned who go off to this unpardonable slaughter – and who, I feel, are all with me as brothers.

*

They are all traitors, those who preached resistance and those who talked of peace. There they are, all as docile and guilty as one another. And never before has the individual stood so alone before the lie-making machine. He can still feel contempt and use it as a weapon. And if he has no right to stand on one side and feel scorn, he still has the right to judge. Humanity in general, the crowd, can offer nothing. It was treason to believe the opposite. We die alone. They are all going to die alone. Let the man who is alone at least keep his scorn, and the ability to pick out from this terrible ordeal what serves his own greatness.

Accept the ordeal and everything which it entails. But swear, in the least noble of tasks, to perform only the noblest of actions. And real nobility (that of the heart) is based on scorn, courage and profound indifference.

*

7 September
We used to wonder where war lived, what it was that made it so vile. And now we realize that we know where it lives, that it is inside ourselves. For most people it's the embarrassment, the need to make a choice, the choice which makes them go but feel remorse for not having been brave enough to stay at home, or which makes them stay at home but regret that they can't share the way the others are going to die.

It's there, that's where it really is, and we were looking for it in the blue sky and the world's indifference. It is in this terrible loneliness both of the combatants and of the non-combatants, in this humiliated despair that we all feel, in the baseness that we feel growing on every face as the days go by. The reign of beasts has begun.

*

The hatred and violence that you can already feel rising up in people. Nothing pure left in them. Nothing unique. They think together. You meet only beasts, bestial European faces. The world makes us feel sick, like this universal flood of cowardice, this mockery of courage, this parody of greatness and this withering away of honour.

*

'But this lad's very ill,' said the lieutenant. 'We can't take him.'
I'm twenty-six, I have my life, and know what I want.

*

Letter to a man in despair.

You write that you are overwhelmed by the war, that you would agree to die, but that what you cannot bear is this universal stupidity, this bloodthirsty cowardice and this criminal simple-mindedness which still believes that human problems can be solved by the shedding of blood.

I read and understand you. And what I understand most clearly is this choice and the contrast which you make between your own readiness to die and your revulsion at the idea of other people's death. This proves a man's quality, and classes him as someone you can talk to. How, in fact, can we avoid falling into despairs? Those we love have often been in danger before. Illness, death or madness, but we still had ourselves and the things we believed in. Often the values which made our life have almost collapsed. But never before have these values and those we love been threatened all together and all at the same time. Never before have we been so completely handed over to destruction.

I can understand you, but I cease to agree when you try to base your life on this despair, maintain that everything is equally pointless, and withdraw behind your disgust. For despair is a feeling, and not a permanent condition. You cannot live on despair. And this feeling must give way to a clear view of things.

You say: 'Besides, what is to be done? And what can I do?' But the question doesn't start by presenting itself like that. You still believe in the individual, since you do feel what is worth while both in those around you and in you yourself. But these individuals can do nothing, and so you despair of society. But remember: you had already rejected this society a long time before the catastrophe took place; you and I knew that it was destined to end in war, we both denounced this state of affairs, and both felt that there was nothing in common between this society and ourselves. It is the same society today. It has reached its normal end. And, when you look at things dispassionately, you have no more reasons to despair now than you had in 1928. In fact, you have exactly as many, no more and no less.

And, when you really think about it, the men who fought in 1914 had more reasons to despair, since they understood things less clearly than we do. You may say that knowing there were as many reasons to despair back in 1928 as there are now in 1939 doesn't get us any further. This is only apparently true. For you didn't despair completely in 1928, whereas today you find everything completely pointless. If circumstances are the same, then it must be your judgement which is wrong. This happens every time that instead of seeing a truth as reason presents it to us we see it in the flesh. You had foreseen the war, but thought you could prevent it. And this kept you from falling completely into despair. Today you think you can no longer prevent anything at all. That is the crux of the argument.

But first of all you must ask yourself if you really did do everything necessary to prevent this war. If so, then you could look on it as inevitable, and you could consider that there is nothing more to be done. But I am not convinced that you yourself, any more than any one of us, did do all you should have done. You couldn't prevent it? No, that is not true. This war, as you know, was not inevitable. It would have been enough for the Treaty of Versailles to have been revised in time. This was not done. That is all there is to it, and you see that things could have been different. But there is still time to revise this treaty, or any other cause. We can still make it unnecessary for Hitler to stick to his word. There is still time to reject those acts of injustice that have led to other similar acts, and thereby make these unnecessary as well. There is still something useful to be done. You assume that the role you can play as an individual is practically non-existent. But I will reverse my earlier argument and tell you that it is neither greater nor smaller than it was in 1928. Besides, I know that you are not very sure about this idea of uselessness. For you do not, to my knowledge, support conscientious objection. And this is not because you lack courage or the ability to admire, but because you don't think that it does any good. Thus you already have some notion of what is useful and what is not which enables you to follow what I am saying.

There is something for you to do, have no doubt about it. Every man has at his disposal a certain zone of influence, which he owes as much to his defects as to his qualities. But whichever is the case, this zone is there, and can be immediately used. Push no one to rebel. We must be sparing of other people's blood and liberty. But you can convince ten, twenty or thirty men that this war is not and was not inevitable, that there are ways of preventing it that have not yet been tried, and that we must say this, writing it when we can and shouting it if we must. These ten or thirty men will in turn tell it to ten others, who will repeat what the first have said. If laziness prevents them, so much the worse, start again with others. And when you have done what you can in your own zone, in your own field, then you can call a halt and despair as much as you like. Understand this: we can despair of the meaning of life *in general*, but not of the particular forms that it takes; we can despair of existence, for we have no power over it, but not of history, where the individual can do everything. It is individuals who are killing us today. Why should not individuals manage to give the world peace? We must simply begin without thinking of such grandiose aims. You must realize that men make war as much with the enthusiasm of those who want it as with the despair of those who reject it with all their soul.

•

Paris. March 1940

What is hateful in Paris: tenderness, feelings, a hideous sentimentality that sees everything beautiful as pretty and everything pretty as beautiful. The tenderness and despair that accompany these murky skies, the shining roofs and this endless rain.

What is inspiring: the terrible loneliness. As a remedy to life in society, I would suggest the big city. Nowadays, it is the only desert within our means. Here the body loses its prestige. It is covered over, and hidden under shapeless skins. The only thing left is the soul, the soul with all its sloppy overflow of drunken sentimentality, its whining emotions and everything else. But the soul also with its one greatness: silent solitude. When you look at Paris from the Butte Montmartre, seeing it like a monstrous cloud of steam beneath the rain, a grey and shapeless swelling on the surface of the earth, and then turn to look at the Calvary of Saint-Pierre de Montmartre, you can feel the kinship between a country, an art and a religion. Every line of these stones, and every one of these scourged or crucified bodies is quivering with the same wanton and defiled emotion as the town itself, and is pouring it into men's hearts.

But, on the other hand, the soul is never right, and here less than elsewhere. For the most splendid expressions which it has given to this soul-obsessed religion have been hewn out of stone in imitation of bodily forms. And if this God touches you, it is because his face is that of a man. It is a strange limitation of the human condition that it should be unable to escape from humanity, and that it should have to clothe in bodies those of its symbols which try to deny the body. They do deny it, but it gives them its titles to greatness. Only the body is generous. And we feel that this Roman legionary is alive because of his extraordinary nose or hunched back, this Pilate because of the expression of ostentatious boredom that stone has preserved for him over the centuries.

From this point of view Christianity has understood. And if it has made so deep an impact on us, it is by its God who was made man. But its truth and greatness come to an end on the cross, at the moment when this man cries out that he has been forsaken. Tear out the last pages of the New Testament, and we are offered a religion of loneliness and human grandeur. Certainly its bitterness makes it unbearable. But that is its truth, and all the rest is a lie.

Hence the fact that being able to live alone in a cheap room for a year in Paris teaches a man more than a hundred literary *salons* and forty years' experience of 'Parisian life'. It is a hard, terrible and sometimes agonizing experience, and always on the verge of madness. But, by being close to such a fate, a man's quality

From Notebook III

must either become hardened and tempered – or perish. And if it perishes, then it is because it was not strong enough to live.

*

Eisenstein and Mexican death festivals.

Ghoulish masks to amuse the children, sugar skulls that they nibble at with delight. The children laugh with death, finding it funny, finding it sweet and sugary. Likewise the 'little dead ones'. Everything leads up to 'Our friend Death'.

*

Paris

The woman from the floor above has killed herself by jumping into the courtyard of the hotel. She was thirty-one, said one of the tenants. Old enough to live, and, if she has lived a little, to die. The shadow of the drama still lingers on in the hotel. She sometimes used to come down and ask the owner's wife to let her stay for supper. She suddenly used to kiss her – from a need to feel another person's warmth and presence. It ended with a three-inch split in her forehead. Before she died she said: 'At last.'

*

Paris

The black trees against the grey sky, and the grey pigeons matching it. The statues on the grass, and this melancholy elegance.

The pigeons fly away with a sound like clothes flapping on a line. You hear them cooing in the green grass.

*

Paris. The little cafés at five in the morning – their windows steamed over – boiling hot coffee – the people who work in the markets and who bring in the food – the little morning glass of liqueur, and Beaujolais later on.

La Chapelle. Mists – airy paths and candelabra.

*

The little Spanish soldier in the restaurant. Not a word of French and this desire for human warmth when he talks to me. A peasant from Estremadura, fought on the Republican side, was in Argelès concentration camp, joined the French Army. When he says the word 'Spain', the whole sky of his native country leaps into his eyes. Has a week's leave. Has come to Paris, which has reduced him to pulp in a few hours. Getting lost in the métro, not speaking a word of French, a foreigner, foreign to everything that is not his own country, his joy would be to find the friends from his own regiment again. So that even if he is to die under low clouds, in thick mud, it will at least be by the side of men from his own country.

*

An artist who goes to Port-Cros in order to paint. And everything is so beautiful that he buys a house, puts his paintings away, and never touches them again.

*

At *Paris-Soir* you feel the whole heart of Paris and its despicable shop-girl values. Mimi's garret has become a sky-scraper, but her heart is still the same. Rotten with sentimentality, prettiness, self-indulgence, all the sticky refuges which man uses to defend himself in so harsh a town.

*

You would not write so much about loneliness if you knew how to get the most out of it.

*

'I', he said, 'am an olfactive type. And there is no art that addresses itself to the sense of smell. Only life.'

*

Short story. A priest, happy with his lot in a country parish in

Provence. By accident, has to succour a man sentenced to death just before his execution. Loses his faith because of it.

*

An overwhelming impulse to cast ourselves away and reject everything, to become like nothing at all, utterly destroying what makes us what we are, offering the present only solitude and nothingness, and returning to the only platform where our destinies can always be renewed. The temptation is a permanent one. Should we resist or give way? Is it possible to live a monotonous, repetitive life while perpetually haunted by the thought of a work to be created, or should we adjust our life to this work, follow the lightning flash? Beauty, like liberty, my gravest concern.

*

Contradiction in the modern world. In Athens the people could really exercise their power only because they spent most of their time on politics, while slaves spent all day doing the work which remained. Once slavery is abolished, everyone has to work. And it is when European man has reached the furthest extreme of proletarianization that the idea of popular sovereignty is at its strongest: this is impossible.

*

In Athens men concerned themselves with the dead only during the period of the Anthesterias. Once these were ended: 'Depart, souls, the Anthesterias are over.'

Originally, in Greek religion, everyone is in Hades. There are neither rewards nor punishments – similarly in Jewish religion. It is social considerations which give rise to the idea of rewards.

*

404. Athens having signed the armistice with Lysander, the end of the Peloponnesian war was marked by Lysander's attack on the walls of Athens to the sound of flutes.

*

The striking story of Timoleon, tyrant of Syracuse (he had his father imprisoned in order to kill him as a traitor).

*

In certain Greek cities in the fourth century the following oath was taken by the oligarchs: 'I will always be an enemy of the people, and will advise it to do what I know will be most harmful to its interests.'

The flight of Darius pursued by Alexander (293–4).

The nuptials at Susa: Alexander with 10,000 soldiers, 80 generals take Persian wives.

Demetrius Poliorcetes – sometimes on the throne, at the height of power, sometimes wandering from village to village.

Antisthenes: 'It is a regal thing to do good and hear evil spoken of oneself.'

Cf. Marcus Aurelius: 'Wherever it is possible to live, it is possible to live well.'

'What prevents a work from being completed becomes the work itself.'

What bars our way makes us travel along it.

Ended February 1942

NOTEBOOK IV

January 1942–July 1945

For a generous psychology.
We help a person more by giving him a favourable image of himself than by constantly confronting him with his faults. Everyone normally tries to be like the best image of himself. Can be extended to education, history, philosophy and politics. We, for example, are the result of twenty centuries of Christian imagery. For 2,000 years man has been presented with a humiliated image of himself. We can see the result. Who, in any case, can say what we would have become if these twenty centuries had seen the continuation of the classical ideal with its admirable image of man?

*

A man who has reached the absurd and tries to live consistently with his views always discovers that the most difficult thing in the world to maintain is awareness. Circumstances almost always stand in his way. He has to live lucidly in a world where dispersion is the rule.

He thus realizes that the real problem, *even without God*, is the problem of psychological unity (the only problem which living out the absurd really poses is that of the metaphysical unity between the world and the mind) and inner peace. He also realizes that this peace is not possible without a discipline which is difficult to reconcile with the world. *Here lies the problem*, for it must be reconciled with the world. What we must do is *live in the world, but observe a Rule*.

The obstacle lies in the *part of life already lived* (profession, marriage, previous opinions), what has already happened. Elude no element of this problem.

*

Secret of my universe: To imagine God without human immortality.

*

Calypso offers Ulysses the choice between immortality and the land of his fathers. He rejects immortality. This is perhaps the whole meaning of the Odyssey. In Book XI Ulysses and the dead before the trench filled with blood – and Agamemnon tells him: 'Never be too gentle with your wife, nor show her all that is in your mind.'

*

The modern mind is in complete disarray. Knowledge has stretched itself to the point where neither the world nor our intelligence can find any foothold. It is a fact that we are suffering from nihilism. But what is most amazing are the 'back to' sermons. Back to the Middle Ages, back to primitive mentality, back to the land, back to religion, back to the arsenal of old solutions. To give these soothing potions the slightest efficacy we should have to behave as if we had forgotten all our knowledge – as if we had learnt nothing – pretend, in fact, to wipe out what is indelible. With one stroke of the pen we should have to cross out the achievement of several centuries, together with the undeniable gains of a mind which (this is its latest progress) recreates chaos for its own sake. This is impossible. Any cure must come to terms with this lucidity and clear-sightedness. We must take into account the knowledge of our exile which we have suddenly acquired. The mind is not in disarray because our knowledge has turned the world upside down, but because it cannot come to terms with this upheaval. It 'hasn't got used to the idea'. Once it gets used to it, the disarray will be at an end. All that will remain is the confusion and the clear awareness which our mind has of it. We have to recreate a whole civilization.

*

Panelier. Before daybreak above the high hills the fir-trees cannot be distinguished from the folds in the hills where they grow. Then the sun, from behind and afar-off, gilds the tree tops. Against the still sombre back-cloth of the sky what looks like an army of feathered savages comes surging up from behind the hill. As the sun rises and the sky grows lighter, the fir-trees grow and the barbarian army seems to advance and mass in a tumult of feathers before the invasion. Then, when the sun is high enough, it suddenly lights up the fir-trees which rush down the mountain side. And it looks like a fierce rush down to the valley, the start of a brief and tragic struggle in which the barbarians of the day will drive off the fragile army of the thoughts of night.

*

An essay written on France a long time hence would not be complete without a reference to the present day. This idea came to me in a little local train as I saw going past me, massed in tiny stations, these shapes and faces of French people that I shall find it hard to forget: old peasant couples, her face as wrinkled as parchment, his smooth face lit up by two clear eyes and a white moustache – their bodies twisted by two winters of privation, clad in shiny and much mended clothes. Elegance has fled from this poverty-stricken people. The suitcases in the trains look worn out, tied together with string and mended with bits of cardboard. All the French look like emigrants.

Id. In the industrial towns – the old workman whom I noticed at his window, wearing his glasses as he uses the last glimmer of daylight to read by, sensibly holding his book flat open on his two out-stretched hands.

At the station a whole hurried people unprotestingly absorbs abominable food and then goes out into the unlit town, rubs shoulders without making contact, and then returns to hotels, to rooms, etc. A life of silence and despair that the whole of France endures while waiting for something to happen.

Round about the tenth, eleventh and twelfth of the month everyone smokes. On the eighteenth you can't get a light in the street. People in the trains talk about the drought. It is less spectacular here than in Algeria but no less tragic. An old workman describes his poverty. He has two rooms an hour from Saint-Étienne. Two hours travelling, eight hours work – nothing to eat at home – too poor to use the black market. A young woman takes in washing because she has two children and her husband has come back from the war with a stomach ulcer. 'He's supposed to have white meat, well grilled. Now where can you find that? They've given him a diet certificate. So he gets a pint and a half of milk but they've taken away his fats ration. How can you feed a man on milk?' Sometimes the clothes she has taken in to wash are stolen and she has to pay for them.

Meanwhile the rain drowns the squalid landscape of an industrial valley – the acrid smell of this poverty – the atrocious distress of these lives. And other people make speeches.

Saint-Étienne in the morning fog as the sirens call men to work in the midst of a jumble of towers, buildings and thick chimneys which raise their crown of slag towards an overcast sky like a monstrous sacrificial cake.

*

Panelier. The first September rain with a light wind mingling the yellow leaves with the downpour. They hover a moment and then the weight of water they are carrying slaps them suddenly down on the earth. When, as here, nature is banal, one is more aware of the changing seasons.

*

A poor childhood. The raincoat several sizes too big – the siesta. The bottle of Vinga beer – Sundays at the aunt's house. Books – the town library. Coming home on Christmas night and the dead body in front of the restaurant. Games in the cellar (Jeanne, Joseph and Max). Jeanne picks up all the buttons, 'that's how you get rich'. The brother's violin and the singing lessons – Galoufa.

*

As when we are attracted towards certain towns (almost always those where we have already lived) or to certain lives, by sexual images – and then we are disappointed. For even the least spiritual among us never base our lives on sex, or at least there are too many things in everyday life which have nothing to do with it. The result is that after having painfully and occasionally incarnated one of these images, or brought closer one of these memories, life is over-laden with long stretches of empty time as with dead skin. And then we have to long for other towns.

*

Wuthering Heights is one of the greatest love novels because it finishes in failure and revolt – I mean in death without hope. The main character is the devil. Such a love can be maintained only by the final failure which is death. It can be continued only in hell.

*

October
The tall woods red under the rain, the meadows strewn with yellow leaves, the smell of drying mushrooms, wood fires (fir-cones reduced to embers glow like the diamonds of hell), the wind moaning round the house – where could one find so conventional an autumn? The peasants now lean slightly forward as they walk – against the wind and rain.

In the autumn forest the beeches form stains of yellow gold or stand alone at the edge of the woods like great nests running with golden honey.

*

Sexuality leads to nothing. It is not immoral but it is unproductive. You can devote yourself to it for as long as you do not wish to produce. But only chastity is linked to a personal progress.

There is a time when sexuality is a victory – when we free it from moral imperatives. But it then quickly becomes defeat – and the only victory is the one which we then wrest from it: chastity.

*

Think about the commentary for Molière's *Don Juan*.

*

November 1942

In autumn this landscape blossoms with leaves – the cherry trees turn red, the maples yellow, the beeches clothe themselves in bronze. The plateau is covered by the thousand flames of a second spring.

*

Giving up youth. It is not I who give up people and things (I could not) but people and things that give me up. My youth is fleeing from me: that is what being ill means.

*

In the mornings everything is covered with hoar frost, the sky shines behind the garlands and streamers of an immaculate fairground. At ten, when the sun begins to warm up, the whole landscape is filled with the crystal-clear music of thawing air: slight cracklings as if the trees were sighing, frost sliding down to the ground with the sound of white insects thrown on top of one another, late leaves ceaselessly falling under the weight of the ice, and scarcely bouncing, like gossamer bones, as they reach the ground. All around hills and valleys fade away in smoke. If you look at it for a certain time, you realize that by losing all its colours this landscape has suddenly aged. It is a very old country that in the course of one morning is returning to us across thousands of years. ... This spur of land covered with trees and ferns juts into the junction of the two rivers like the prow of a ship. When the first rays of sunlight free it from the frost, it remains the only living thing in the midst of a landscape white as eternity. Here at least the mingled voices of the two streams join forces against the limitless silence which surrounds them. But little by little the song of the waters blends itself into the countryside. Without the slightest fall in tone it nevertheless fades into silence. And it needs the infrequent passage of three smoke-coloured crows to restore any sign of life to the sky.

Seated high on this prow I sail motionlessly through this country of indifference. Not less than the whole of nature and this white peace which winter brings to over-warm hearts – to calm this heart devoured by a bitter love. I watch this swelling light which denies the portents of death as it widens in the sky. At last a sign of the future, above me to whom everything now speaks of the past. Be silent, lungs. Devour this wan and icy air which is your food. Keep quiet. And let me cease hearing your slow decay – that I may finally turn to ...

*

Saint Étienne
I know what Sunday means for a poor man who works. Above all, I know what Sunday evening means, and if I could give meaning and form to what I know, I could make a poor man's Sunday into a work of humanity.

*

Excessive use of Eurydice in the literature of the forties. Because there have never been so many separated lovers.

*

The whole art of Kafka lies in making us *read him again*. The way his books end – or the way they don't in fact end – suggests explanations which are never clearly stated and which compel us to read the story again from a different point of view to find a basis for them. Sometimes the book can be interpreted in two or three different ways, and therefore has to be read two or three times. But it would be wrong to try to interpret everything in detail in Kafka. A symbol always remains on the general plane and an artist gives a rough translation of it. Word for word translations don't exist. Only the general movement is restored. As far as the rest is concerned we must take into account the role of chance, which is great in every creator.

In this country where winter has abolished every colour since everything has turned white, the slightest sound since the snow stifles it, all fragrance since it is overladen with cold, the first whiff of spring grass must be like a call to joy, the bursting trumpet of sensation.

*

A poor childhood. Essential difference when I went to see my uncle. At home objects didn't have a name. We said: the soup plates, the pot on the mantelpiece, etc. At his house: the Vosges glazed earthenware, the Quimper service ... etc. I awoke to the idea of choice.

*

Because the sky is blue, the snow-covered trees on the river bank which cast their white branches very low over the frozen water look like almond trees in flower. This country offers the eye a constant confusion between spring and winter.

I am having an affair with this country, that is to say that I have reasons to love and reasons to hate it. For Algeria, on the contrary, I feel a boundless passion and give myself over completely to the delights of love. Question: can one love a country as one loves a woman?

*

What lights up the world and makes it bearable is the feeling which we usually have of our links with it – and more particularly of what joins us to other people. Human relations always help us to carry on because they always presuppose further developments, a future – and also because we live as if our only task were precisely to have relationships with other people. But on the days when we become aware that this is not our only task, above all when we realize that it is only our will that keeps these people attached to us – stop writing or talking, cut yourself off and you will see them melt away – when we realize that most of them have their backs to us (not that they wish us ill but simply because they don't care) and that the others are *always* able to be interested in something else, when we thus imagine how contingent and accidental everything in what we call a love or a friendship is, then the world goes back to darkness and we to that great cold from which human tenderness had for a moment rescued us.

*

From Notebook IV

What troubles me in my thinking or in the discipline necessary to a work of art is my imagination. I have a disordered, immoderate, slightly monstrous imagination. Difficult to know what an enormous part it has played in my life. And yet I noticed this personal peculiarity only when I was thirty.

Occasionally time drags in the train or bus and I stop myself wandering off into a series of images or constructions that I find sterile. When I tire of constantly correcting the slope of my thoughts, of bringing them back to what I need them to feed on, a moment comes when I let myself go, or, to be more accurate, let myself flow. Time passes in a flash and I am there without realizing it.

*

Philosophers in the ancient world (and with good reason) thought much more than they read. That is why they stuck so closely to concrete cases. Printing has changed that. People read more than they think. We don't have philosophies but merely commentaries. This is what Gilson says in arguing that the age of philosophers concerned with philosophy has been followed by the age of professors of philosophy concerned with philosophers. This attitude contains both modesty and impotence. And a thinker who began his book with the words: 'Let us take things from the beginning' would raise some smiles. We have reached the point where a book of philosophy published nowadays that did not rely on any authority, quotation, commentary, etc. would not be taken seriously. And yet...

*

For *The Plague*: There are in men more things to admire than to despise.

*

When one chooses renunciation in spite of the certainty that 'Everything is permitted', something nevertheless remains: we no longer judge other people.

What attracts many people to the novel is that it is apparently a *genre* which has no style. In fact it demands the most difficult style, the one which subordinates itself completely to its subject. One can thus imagine an author writing each of his novels in a different style.

*

The sensation of death which from now on is familiar to me: it lacks the help of pain. Pain hooks us to the present, requires a struggle which *fills our mind*. But to have a foreboding of death simply at the sight of a pocket-handkerchief filled with blood is to be effortlessly plunged back into time in the most breath-taking manner: it is the terror of becoming.

*

The thickness of the clouds diminished. As soon as the sun could come out, the ploughed fields began to steam.

*

Saint-Étienne and its suburbs. A sight like this is a condemnation of the civilization which gave it birth. A world in which there is no more room for human beings, for joy, for active leisure, is a world that should die. No people can live outside beauty. It can survive itself for a time and that is all. And this Europe which here offers one of its most permanent faces is ceaselessly moving away from beauty. This is why it is in such convulsions, and why it will die if peace does not mean for it a return to beauty and the restoration of love to its rightful place.

*

20 *May*
For the first time: curious feeling of satisfaction and fullness. A question I asked myself, lying in the grass, in the warm heavy evening: 'If these days were my last ...' Reply: a quiet smile within me. Nevertheless nothing that I can be proud of: nothing is decided, even my behaviour is not very certain. Is it the hardening which ends an experience, or the gentleness of evening, or

on the contrary the beginning of a wisdom that no longer denies anything?

*

June. Luxembourg.
A Sunday morning full of wind and sun. The wind scatters the water from the fountain around the main pond, the tiny yachts over the wrinkled water, and the swallows around the tall trees. Two young men discussing: 'You who believe in human dignity'.

*

Prologue: – Love...
– Knowledge...
– It's the same word.

While in the daytime birds always look as if they are flying about aimlessly, in the evening they always seem to find a destination again. They fly towards something. Also perhaps in the evening of life...
Is there an evening of life?

*

Those who love truth should seek for love in marriage, that is to say for love without illusions.

*

For my 'creation against God'. It is a Catholic critic (Stanislas Fumet) who says that art, *whatever its aim*, always sets up a guilty rivalry with God. Similarly Roger Secrétain, *Cahiers du Sud*, August–September 1943. Again Péguy: 'There is even a poetry which draws its brilliance from the absence of God, which aims at no salvation, which relies on nothing but itself, a human effort, rewarded on this earth, to fill the void of space.'

There is no compromise between the literature of apologetics and the literature of rivalry.

*

On justice – the man who ceases to believe in it from the moment he is beaten up.

Id. What I hold against Christianity is that it is a doctrine of injustice.

My thirtieth birthday
The primary faculty of man is forgetfulness. But it is fair to say that he forgets even the good things he has done.

*

On naturalness in art. Impossible in its absolute form. Because reality is impossible (bad taste, vulgarity, unable to satisfy man's deepest demand). This is why human creation, based on the world, always finally turns against the world. Serial stories are bad because for the most part they are true (either because reality has come to resemble them, or because the world is conventional). It is art and the artist who remake the world, but always with an underlying protest.

*

I have spent ten years winning something which I find priceless: a heart free of bitterness. And, as often happens, once I had gone beyond bitterness, I enclosed it between the covers of one or two books. So I shall always be judged on that bitterness which no longer means anything to me. But this is just. It is the price that has to be paid.

*

There is no objection to the totalitarian attitude other than the religious or moral one. If this world has no meaning, they are right. I cannot accept their being right. So ...

It is our task to create God. He is not the creator. This is the whole history of Christianity. For we have only one way to create God, which is to become God.

*

Creation Corrected

The tank that overturns and struggles like a centipede. Bob in the summer meadows in Normandy. His helmet covered with wall flowers and weeds.

Cf. the reports of the English atrocity commission in *The Times*.

The Spanish journalist Suzy told me about (ask for his text) (children laugh as they show him the corpses).

Like an hour's cold shower in my heart.

All day they talk about the possibility of there being a milk soup in the evening because it makes you piss several times during the night. That the lavatories are a hundred yards from the block, that it is cold, etc.

– Women who had been deported coming into Switzerland and bursting out laughing at the sight of a funeral: 'That is how they treat corpses here.'

– Jacqueline.

– The two young Poles who at the age of fourteen are made to burn down their house with their parents in it. From fourteen to seventeen, Buchenwald.

– The concierge of the Gestapo, who took over two floors of a building in the rue de la Pompe. In the morning she cleans up with tortured bodies all around. 'I never worry about what my tenants do.'

Jacqueline going back from Koenigsberg to Ravensbruck – 100 kilometres on foot. In a large tent divided into four by a frame. So many women that they can sleep on the ground only by fitting in like pieces of a jigsaw puzzle. Dysentry. The lavatories a hundred yards away. But you have to step over bodies and trample on them. They relieve themselves where they are.

– World wide aspect in the dialogue between politics and morality. In face of this conglomeration of gigantic forces: Sintès.

X., a woman who has been deported, liberated with a tattoo mark on her skin: served a year at the S.S. camp of ...

30 July 1945

At thirty a man should know himself like the palm of his hand, know the exact number of his defects and qualities, know how far he can go, foretell his failures – be what he is. And above all accept these things. Things are real now. Everything to do and everything to give up. Settle down in day-to-day life, but keep one's mask. I have experienced enough to be able to give up almost everything. There remains an immense, daily, obstinate effort. An effort pursued in secret, with neither hope nor bitterness. No longer deny anything since everything can be asserted. Above the anguish of being torn apart.

NOTEBOOK V
September 1945–April 1948

The aesthetic of revolt. If classicism can be defined as the bringing of passions under control, then a classical period is one where art finds the form and phrases that express the passions of its members. Today, when collective passions have taken precedence over individual ones, it is no longer love which art has to dominate, but politics, in the strictest sense of the word. Man has conceived a passion, either a hopeful or a destructive one, for his condition.

But how much more difficult our task is: (1) because, if we have to live through our passions before formulating them, collective passion takes up all the artist's time; (2) because the chances of dying are greater – and one could even say that the way of living through collective passion authentically is to accept to die for it. Here then the greatest chance of authenticity is also the greatest chance of a defeat for art. Thus classicism is perhaps impossible. But if it were, then the history of human rebellion does have a meaning, which is to reach this limit. Hegel would be right, and we could imagine the end of human history, but only as failure. And here Hegel would be wrong. But if, as we seem to think, this classicism is possible, at least we see that it can be the work only of a whole generation – and no longer of one single man. In other words, the chances of failure which I am talking about can be counter-balanced only by numerical chance, that is to say by the chance that out of ten authentic artists, one will survive and succeed in finding in his life the time for passion and the time for creation. The artist can no longer stand alone. Or, if he does, it is in the triumph which he owes to a whole generation.

November – 32 years old

Man's most natural bent is to ruin himself and everyone else with him. What immense efforts simply to be normal! And what an even greater effort is needed by the man whose ambition is to dominate himself and to dominate the mind. By himself man is nothing. He is only an infinite chance. But he is the person infinitely responsible for this chance. Man's own tendency is to water himself down. But if his will, his confidence, his spirit of adventure carry the day, the chance he represents starts to grow. No one can say that he has gone as far as man can go. The last five years that we have lived through have taught me that. From beasts to martyrs, from the spirit of evil to hopeless sacrifice, every piece of evidence has been overwhelming. Each of us has the task of exploiting within ourselves man's greatest chance, his final virtue. On the day when it means something to talk about human limits, then we shall be faced with the problem of God. But not before, never until we have lived man's potentialities through to the very end. There is only one possible aim for great actions and that is the fruit which man can bear. *But first of all we must achieve mastery over ourselves.*

*

It is by a continual effort that I can create. My tendency is to roll to a stop. My deepest, most certain leaning is towards silence and everyday activity. It has taken me years of perseverence to escape from distractions and the fascination of purely mechanical action. But I know that I remain only through this very effort, and that if I stopped believing in it for one single moment I should roll down the precipice. This is how I keep myself from falling ill and from giving up, holding my head up with all my strength so as to breathe and conquer. It is how I despair and how I cure myself of despair.

*

What right has a communist or a Christian (to take only respectable forms of modern thought) to reproach me with being

From Notebook V

pessimistic? It was not I who invented man's wretched sinfulness or the terrible curses of divine wrath. It was not I who said that man could not save himself by his own efforts and that from the depths of his lowliness he could find certain hope only in divine grace. And as to the famous Marxist optimism, it just makes me laugh. Few men have mistrusted their fellows more completely. Marxists do not believe in persuasion or in dialogue. A bourgeois cannot be made into a worker, and in their world economic conditions represent a more terrible form of fatality than the whims of God.

As for M. Herriot and the readers of *Annales!*

Communists and Christians will tell me that their optimism has a longer range, that it is on a higher plane and that God or history, as the case may be, are satisfying conclusions to their dialectic. I can put forward the same argument. If Christianity is pessimistic about man, it is optimistic about human destiny. Marxism, pessimistic about human destiny and human nature, is optimistic about the march of history (its contradiction!). I would say myself that, pessimistic about the human condition, I am optimistic about man.

How can they fail to see that no one has ever uttered such a cry of confidence in man? I believe in dialogues, in sincerity. I believe that they point the way to an unparalleled psychological revolution; etc., etc.

*

Origins of this modern lunacy. It was Christianity that turned man away from the *world*. It reduced him to himself and to his history. Communism is the logical consequence of Christianity. It's a Christian kind of business.

Id. After two thousand years of Christianity, the revolt of the body. It has taken two thousand years for us once again to be able to show it naked on the beaches. Hence the excess. And it has recovered its place in our customs. What we now have to do is to put it back in philosophy and metaphysics. This is one of the meanings of the modern convulsion.

Death of an old actor.

A morning in Paris full of snow and mud. The oldest and gloomiest part of the town, the district where they have put La Santé, Sainte-Anne and Cochin. Along these black and icy streets live the mad, the sick, the poor and the condemned. As to Cochin: a barracks for poverty and sickness whose walls ooze with the filthy damp of sorrow.

It was there that he died. At the end of his life he was still doing utility parts (stage people have these funny terms) changing his one increasingly threadbare suit, fading from black to yellow, for the more or less sumptuous costumes that small parts do after all have to be given. He had to give up his work. He could now drink nothing but milk and in any case there wasn't any milk. They took him to Cochin and he told his friends that he was going to have an operation and that then it would all be over (I remember a phrase from his part 'when I was a little boy', and, when he was told how to say something 'Ah,' he used to say, 'I don't feel it like that.') They did not operate on him and sent him out telling him he was cured. He even went back to playing the small part – a grotesque character – that he had been acting up to then. But he had got thinner. It has always surprised me to notice how a certain loss of weight, a certain way of letting one's cheek bones stand out and of baring one's gums, are the obvious sign that it will be all over soon. It is only the person who is losing weight who never seems to 'realize'. Or, if he does 'realize', it is perhaps only fleetingly, and naturally I can't know this. All that I can know is what I see and what I saw in fact was that Liesse was going to die.

He did in fact die. He stopped work again. He went back to Cochin. They still didn't operate on him, but he died without that – one night without anyone noticing. And in the morning his wife came to visit him as usual. No one had told her at the desk because no one knew. It was the people in the neighbouring beds who told her. 'You know,' they said, 'it happened last night.'

And this morning he is there, in the little mortuary that looks

From Notebook V

out on to the rue de la Santé. Two or three of his old friends are there with his widow and with his widow's daughter who is not his child. When I arrived, the chief undertaker (why was he wearing a tricolour sash like a mayor?) told me that we could still have a look at him. I didn't want to, this stubborn, leprous morning lay heavy on my stomach and I couldn't swallow it down. But I went. You could only see his head, since what was being used as a winding sheet was pulled right up to the chin. He was even thinner. – I didn't believe that this could have been possible for him. But he nevertheless managed it and you then noticed the size of his bones and realized that this heavy, knotted head was built to carry a heavy weight of flesh. The flesh not being there, his teeth stuck out and looked terrible. But why describe this? A corpse is a corpse, everyone knows that, and you must let the dead bury the dead. What a pity, though, what an atrocious pity.

The men who stood at his head, their hands on the edge of the coffin as if they were introducing him to the visitor, then went into action. Went into action is certainly the word, for these clumsy robots, ill at ease in their coarse clothes, suddenly threw themselves at full speed on the winding sheet, the lid and a screwdriver. In a moment the lid was down and two men were turning the screws, leaning on them terribly with a brutal movement of the forearm. Ah, they seemed to be saying, you won't get out of that! These living men wanted to get it over, you could see that straight away. He was moved out. We followed. The widow and daughter went into the hearse at the same time as the corpse. We piled into a car that followed. Not a flower, nothing but black.

We were going to the cemetery of Thiais. The widow thought it was a long way, but the authorities had insisted. We left by the Porte d'Italie. I had never felt the sky hanging so low over the Paris suburbs. Bits of sheds, stakes, black and sparse vegetation stuck out from piles of snow and mud. Six kilometres through this countryside and we arrived at the monumental gates of the most hideous cemetery in the world. An attendant with a flushed, red face came and stopped the procession at the gate and demanded the entrance certificate. 'In you go,' he said, once in possession of his treasure. We went on for a good ten minutes through piles of mud and snow. Then we stopped behind another procession. A bank of snow stood between us and the burial ground. Two crosses had been stuck sideways in the snow, one, as I read, was for Liesse, and the other for a little girl of eleven. The procession in front of us was for the little girl. But the family were getting back into the hearse. This set off and we could move a few yards forward. We got out. Tall men in blue, wearing sewermen's boots, left the shovels they had been holding as they watched the scene. They came forward and started to pull the coffin out of the hearse. At that moment a kind of postman dressed in red and blue, a battered peaked cap on his head, loomed up carrying a book of counterfoils with carbon paper slipped between the pages. The sewermen then read out the number carved on the coffin: 3237 C. The postman followed the lines on his list with the point of his pencil and said 'Right' as he ticked off a number. Then they let the coffin through. We went into the burial ground. Our feet sank into an oily and slightly springy clay. The hole had been dug between four other graves, one on each side. The sewermen slid the box in quite quickly. But we were all a very long way from the hole because the graves stopped us from going forward and the narrow path that lay between them was cluttered up with tools and earth. When the coffin reached the bottom, there was a moment's silence. We all looked at one another. There was no priest, no flowers, and not a word of peace or regret was uttered. And we all felt that this moment ought to be more solemn – that we ought to have marked it, and no one knew how. Then a sewerman said: 'If the ladies and gentlemen would like to throw in a little earth.' The widow nodded. He took some earth up on a shovel, brought a scraper from his pocket and put a little earth on it. The widow reached forward over a block of earth. She took the scraper and threw the earth towards the hole, without really aiming. We heard the hollow sound of the box. But the daughter missed. The earth flew over the hole. She made a sign which meant 'too bad'.

The bill: 'And he was put in clay for an exorbitant price.'

You know, here it's the burial ground for people who have been condemned to death.

Laval is a little further on.

*

Novel. Poor childhood. I was ashamed of my poverty and of my family. (But they are monsters!). And if today I can talk about it with simplicity it is because I am no longer ashamed of this shame and no longer despise myself for having felt it. I experienced this shame only when I was sent to the lycée. Before then everyone was like me and poverty was as natural as the air we breathed. At the lycée I learnt how to compare.

A child is nothing by himself. It is his relatives who represent him. And, once you have become a man, you have much less merit in not having these ugly feelings. For you are then judged on what you are and you even go to the point of judging your relatives by what you yourself have become. I now realize that I should have needed a heart of exceptional and heroic purity not to suffer from the days when I saw on the face of a richer friend the surprise which he could not manage to hide at the sight of the house where I lived.

Yes, I did bear the world a grudge, as is common. And if, up to the age of twenty-five, I always felt fury and shame at the memory of this grudge, it was because I refused to be common. While nowadays I know that I am common and, finding this neither good nor bad, I think about something else ...

I loved my mother with despair. I have always loved her with despair.

*

I like men who take sides more than literatures that do. Courage in one's life and talent in one's work is already quite good. And then the writer takes sides when he wants to. His merit lies in his instinctive reaction. And if this is imposed by law, professional obligation or terror, where does the merit then lie?

It would appear that to write a poem about spring would

nowadays be serving capitalism. I am not a poet, but I should have no second thoughts about being delighted by such a poem if it were beautiful. One either serves the whole of man or one does not serve him at all. And if man needs bread and justice, and if we have to do everything essential to serve this need, he also needs pure beauty, which is the bread of his heart. Nothing else matters.

Yes, I should like them to take sides less in their books and a little more in their everyday life.

*

Existentialism has kept the fundamental mistake of Hegelianism which lies in reducing man to history. But it has not followed out the consequences of this, which is in fact to deny him all liberty.

*

29 October. Koestler – Sartre – Malraux – Sperber and myself. Between Piero della Francesca and Dubuffet.

K. – Need to define a basic political morality. Thus begin by freeing ourselves of a certain number of false scruples ('fallacies', he calls them) (a) that what we say can serve causes that we cannot serve. (b) Examine our consciences. The order of injustices. 'When the interviewer asked me if I hated Russia, there was something inside me that stopped dead. And I made an effort. I said that I hated the Stalinist régime as much as I hated the Hitlerite régime and for the same reasons. But then there was something in me that seemed to come unstuck.' 'So many years spent struggling together. I lied for them ... and now like this pal who banged his head against the walls of my room and, blood all over his face, turned to me and said: "There's no more hope, no more hope." – Means of action, etc.'

M. Temporary impossibility of reaching the proletariat. Is the proletariat the highest historical value?

C. Utopia. Today, a utopia will cost them less than a war. War is the opposite of a utopia. On the one hand. And on the other: 'Don't you think that we are all responsible for the absence of values? And that if all of us who are the descendants of Nietzscheanism, of nihilism or of historical realism were to proclaim publicly that we were wrong and that there are moral values and that from now on we would do everything necessary to found and illustrate them, don't you think it would be the beginning of a hope?'

S. 'I can't turn my moral values solely against the U.S.S.R. For it is true that the deportation of several million men is more serious than the lynching of a Negro. But the lynching of a Negro is the result of a situation that has been going on for over a hundred years and which in the final analysis represents over the years the unhappiness of as many Negroes as there were people deported from the southern Caucasus.'

K. We must say that as writers we are traitors in the eyes of history if we do not denounce what should be denounced. A conspiracy of silence will condemn us in the eyes of those who come after us.

S. – Yes, etc., etc.

And all the time it is impossible to say exactly how much fear and how much truth enters into what each one says.

*

If we believe in moral values, we believe in morality right up to and including sexual morality. The reform is a total one.

*

Panelier. 17 June 1947

Marvellous day. A gleaming and tender light foaming above and around the tall beech trees. It seems secreted by every branch. The clusters of leaves that move slowly in this bluish gold, like a thousand many-lipped mouths tasting this airy, golden, sugared juice all day long – or, again, a thousand tiny and twisted fountain mouths of green bronze ceaselessly irrigating the sky with a blue and shining water – or again . . . but that's enough.

*

I have read through all these *cahiers* – from the first one. What leaped to my eyes is that landscapes disappear, little by little. The modern cancer is eating me away too.

*

Merleau-Ponty. Learn how to read. He complains that people have misread – and misunderstood him. This is the type of complaint that I would have tended to make in the past. Now I know that it is unjustified. There are no mistakes.

Libertines with virtuous principles. True men. But from a practical point of view, and for the moment, I prefer a debauchee who kills no one to a puritan who kills everyone. And what above all I have never been able to stand is a debauchee who wants to kill everybody.

M.P. or the typical contemporary man: someone who keeps the score. He explains that no one is ever right and that it isn't as simple as all that (I hope that he doesn't give himself the trouble of proving this for my sake). But a little further on he proclaims that Hitler is a criminal against whom any resistance will always be justified. If nobody is right, then we must not judge. It is because *today* you must be against Hitler. The score has been totted up. On we go.

*

Leysin. Snow and clouds filling the valley to the summits. Flights of jackdaws skim like black seagulls across this dead calm and fleecy sea, taking the spray from the snow on their wings.

*

NOTEBOOK VI

April 1948–March 1951

London. I remember London as a city of gardens where the birds woke me in the mornings. London is the opposite, and yet my memory is correct. The barrows of flowers in the streets. The docks, tremendous.

N. Gallery. Marvellous Piero and Velasquez.

Oxford. The well-groomed studfarm. The silence of Oxford. What business would the world have there?

*

Dawn on the Scottish coast. Edinburgh: swans on the canals. The city round a false acropolis, mysterious and covered with haze. The Athens of the north is all at sea. Chinese and Malays in Princes Street. It is a port.

*

End of the novel – 'Man is a religious animal,' he said. And on the cruel earth there fell an inexorable rain.

*

Creation corrected: He is the only representative of that religion as old as man himself and he is hunted everywhere.

*

I have tried with all my strength, knowing my weakness, to be a moral person. Morality kills.

Hell is a special favour reserved to those who have much requested it.

*

We must judge a man, according to Beyle, neither by what he says, nor by what he writes. I add: nor by what he does.

*

Bad reputations are easier to bear than good ones, for good ones are heavy to drag about, you must live up to them, and any lapse is held against you as a crime. With bad reputations, allowances are made for your lapses.

*

Dinner with Gide. Letters from young writers who ask him if they should carry on. Gide replies: 'What? You can stop yourself writing and you hesitate?'

*

Algiers after ten years. The faces I recognize, after a certain hesitation, and which have aged. It is the soirée at the Princesse de Guermantes. But on the scale of a town where I feel lost. There is no turning back upon myself. I am with this immense crowd which is marching with no respite towards a pit into which they will all fall, one after the other, pushed by a new crowd, behind them, which, itself ...

*

Programme for February–June.
(1) *The Rope*.
(2) *The Rebel*.
Finish preparing the three volumes of essays:

(1) Literary essays. *Preface* – The Minotaur + Prometheus in the underworld + Helen's exile + Cities of Algeria + ...

(2) Critical essays. *Preface* – Chamfort + Intelligence and the scaffold + Agrippa d'Aubigné + Preface to the *Chroniques italiennes*: Commentaries on Molière's *Don Juan* + Jean Grenier.

(3) Political essays. *Preface* + 10 editorials + Intelligence and

courage + Neither victims nor hangman + Replies to d'Astier + Why Spain + The Artist and freedom.

February 18–28: Finish first version of Rope.
March–April: Finish first version of The Rebel.
May: Essays.
June: Revise version of Rope and The Rebel.
Get up early. Shower *before* breakfast.
No cigarettes before midday.
Obstinacy in work. It overcomes weaknesses.

*

Portraits. From behind her little veil, she watches with wide and beautiful eyes. Calm, slightly milkmaidy beauty. Suddenly she starts talking and her mouth is clenched in a parallelogram. She is ugly. A society lady.

*

You are talking to him. He is replying. Suddenly he continues his sentence, but his eyes are somewhere else, still on you through necessity, but already drifting off. Womanizer.

*

First cycle. From my first books (*Nuptials*) through to *Rope* and *The Rebel*, my whole effort has been in fact to depersonalize myself (each time in a different tone). Afterwards I shall be able to speak in my own name.

*

The sole effort of my life, everything else having been given to me, and generously (except money, which I don't care about), has been to live the life of a normal man. I did not want to be a man of abysses. This immense effort has been of no avail. Little by little, instead of being more and more successful in my undertaking, I can see the abyss drawing nearer.

*

End October 1949. Relapse

An invalid must be clean to make people forget about him, forgive him. And even then. Even his cleanliness has something odd about it. It is suspect – like the extra-large decorations that confidence tricksters wear in their buttonholes.

*

After so long a certainty of being cured, this recurrence ought to overwhelm me. It does in fact. But since I have been so uninterruptedly overwhelmed of late, it makes me want to laugh. At last I am free. Madness is a liberation as well.

*

Novel (end). He remembered the time when he would devour biographies of famous men, tearing through the pages towards the moment of their death. What he was then trying to discover was what protection genius, greatness and sensitivity offer against death. But he now knew that this frenzy was pointless and that great lives held no lessons for him. Genius does not know how to die. Poor women do.

*

The mistral has scraped the sky until it shows a new skin, as blue and brilliant as the sea. From everywhere the songs of birds burst forth, with a strength, a jubilation, a joyful discord, an infinite delight. The day shimmers and shines.

*

The world in which I am most *at ease*: Greek myth.

*

The heart is not everything. It *must exist*, for without it. ... But it should be mastered and transfigured.

*

The whole of my work is ironic.

*

From Notebook VI

My constant temptation, the one against which I have never ceased to wage an exhausting struggle: cynicism.

*

Paganism for oneself, Christianity for other people, is everyone's instinctive desire.

Not the difficulty, but the impossibility of being.

Love is injustice, but justice is not enough.

*

There is always a part of man that refuses love. It is the part that *wants* to die. It is the part which needs to be forgiven.

*

A.'s suicide. Overwhelmed because I was very fond of him, of course, but also because I suddenly realized that I wanted to follow his example.

Claudel. This greedy old man rushing to the Lord's Table to gulp down honours.... What wretchedness!

*

The girl who hangs around in bars. 'Letters, ah, no thanks. I don't want a lot of bother.'

*

The nineteenth century is the century of revolt. Why? Because it was born from a revolution that failed and where the only thing that was killed was belief in God.

*

My work during the first two cycles: people without lies, consequently not real. They are not of this world. This is why up to now I have doubtless not been a novelist in the usual meaning of the word. But rather an artist who creates myths on the scale of his passion and anguish. This is why also the people who have exalted me in this world have always been those who had the strength and exclusivity of these myths.

*

With them I have felt neither poverty, nor deprivation nor humiliation. Why not say it: I have felt and still feel my nobility. When I am with my mother, I feel that I am of a noble race: one that envies nothing.

*

Faulkner. To the question: What do you think of the young generation of writers, he replies: it will leave nothing worthwhile. It has nothing more to say. To write, you must have let the great primary truths take root in you and have directed your work towards one of them or towards them all at the same time. Those who do not know how to speak of pride, honour, pain are writers of no consequence and their work will die with them or before them. Goethe and Shakespeare have stood up to everything because they believed in the human heart. Balzac and Flaubert as well. They are eternal.
– What is the reason for this nihilism that has invaded literature?
– Fear. On the day men stop being afraid, then they will write masterpieces again, that is to say works that endure.

*

Those who have not demanded the absolute virginity of human beings and of the world, and howled with nostalgia and impotence in the face of its impossibility, those who have destroyed themselves by trying to love, without ever reaching it, a face that cannot invent love and only repeats it, such men will never understand the reality of revolt and its destructive fury.

*

Paris. The wind and the rain have cast the autumn leaves down on to the avenues. You walk on a damp tawny fur.

*

A taxi-driver, a Negro, of an unaccustomed courtesy in this Paris of 1950, says to me as we drive past the Théâtre-Français surrounded by numerous cars: 'The Maison de Molière is playing to a full house this evening.'

*

For 2,000 years, we have been witnessing the constant and persevering calumny of Greek values. In this respect Marxism has carried on after Christianity. And for 2,000 years Greek values have been resisting to such an extent that beneath its ideologies the twentieth century is more Greek and pagan than Christian or Russian.

*

It is because France is a military nation that Communism has its opportunities there.

*

7 March 1951
Completed the first version of *The Rebel*. This book brings to an end the first two cycles. Thirty-seven years old. And now, can creation be free?

*

Every achievement is a servitude. It compels us to a higher achievement.

NOTES

NOTES

NOTES TO PART ONE

Betwixt and Between (L'Envers et l'endroit)

As Camus says in his 1958 preface, this volume of essays was published in Algiers in 1937, and remained virtually unobtainable until it was republished in Paris by Gallimard in 1958. Camus's first publisher was a bookseller in Algiers called Charlot, who also published a 'Review of Mediterranean culture' called *Rivages*, to which Camus contributed. According to Roger Quilliot, who has had access to all Camus's manuscripts, the themes treated in these essays first appear in note form as early as 1934, and the first volume of Camus's *Notebooks* shows that certain sections from 'Between Yes and No' were written in January 1936.[1] What is perhaps more significant is that in May 1937 Camus seemed to anticipate the ideas which he did not finally express until his 1958 preface was published when he wrote in a 'projected preface': 'In their present state most of these essays will appear rather formless. This does not spring from a convenient disregard for form, but simply from an insufficient maturity.'[2] In the essays themselves Camus is both using and transposing his own personal experiences: the phrase 'He's in the moon' ('Il est dans la lune'), applied in the essay *Betwixt and Between* to an unnamed old man, was in fact occasionally used by Camus's mother when speaking about her own mother, Marie Sintès.[3] His loneliness in Prague seems to be based directly on a visit which he made in 1936, but also appears to have been chosen for personal reasons not developed in the essay: Roger Quilliot notes that he visited Eastern Europe with his first wife, Simone Hié, and a friend called Bourgeois, and left them because his

---

1. *Carnets*, Gallimard 1962, pp. 20–21, Hamish Hamilton translation, 1963, pp. 4–5. Unless otherwise stated, all quotations of the *Carnets* (*Notebooks*) in English are from the translations of the two volumes, published by Hamish Hamilton, London, in 1963 and 1966 respectively.

2. *Carnets*, Gallimard, 1962, p. 48; translation 1963, p. 19.

3. *Essais*, Pléiade edition, Gallimard, 1965, p. 1176.

marriage was breaking up.[4] The description of the mother in *Betwixt and Between* fits everything at the moment known about Camus's own mother, Catherine Camus, *née* Sintès, while Camus's father is the obvious model for the narrator's father in *Betwixt and Between*: he too was killed in the first battle of the Marne in 1914. Camus's attitude towards his maternal grandmother's family can perhaps be inferred from the fact that he gave the name Sintès to the rather shady character, Raymond, whose intrigues eventually place Meursault in the position where he commits the murder for which he is executed. The name Sintès also occurs immediately after some notes on life in the Nazi concentration camps (see p. 273, of this translation). The one character who never seems to appear in any of Camus's works is his elder brother Lucien, born in 1909.

In 1949 Camus again took up some of the themes that he was to use in his preface to *L'Envers et l'endroit* in 1958, noting that he felt 'artistic resistances as others feel moral or religious ones'.[5] Roger Quilliot states that the preface was completed in its present form by 1954, but offers no explanation of the four years delay in its publication.[6]

Page 17. Brice Parain. In 1944 Camus published a long review of two of his recent works: *Essai sur le logos platonicien* and *Recherches sur la nature et les fonctions du langage*. This article, entitled 'Sur une philosophie de l'expression' ('On a Philosophy of Expression'), appeared in the review *Poésie* and was translated into English in the volume of essays entitled *Lyrical and Critical* (Hamish Hamilton, 1967). It can be found in French in The Pléiade edition, II, pp. 1671–82.

Page 19. Jean Grenier, born in 1898, was Camus's philosophy teacher at the Lycée d'Alger and later at the University of Algiers. It was under his direction that Camus undertook research for his *Diplôme d'Études Supérieures*, which he successfully completed in 1936, on *Métaphysique chrétienne et néoplatonisme*.

Page 30. 'Wretchedness of man in God'. The French 'misère de l'homme en Dieu' is an ironic echo of Pascal's famous 'misère de l'homme sans Dieu' ('wretchedness of man without God').

Page 62. 'Bewtixt and Between'. Roger Quillot notes that the

4. ibid,. p. 1178. 'La rupture avec sa femme va se consommer.'
5. *Carnets II*, Gallimard 1964, p. 296, translation p. 153.
6. Pléiade edition, II, p. 1180.

incidents described in this essay are based on reality. He quotes Lucien Camus as giving a certain Marie Burg as the person who told Camus the story, which was based on her own employer. Roger Quilliot also states that it was Marie Burg who died at an old person's home at Marengo, and whose funeral is described in *The Outsider*.[7]

Nuptials (Noces)

Although certain passages in these essays appear in Camus's *Notebooks* as early as 1937 (the description of the cloister of the dead in the Santissima Annuziatia, for example, was noted down in September after Camus's visit to Italy[8]), the volume itself did not appear until May 1939. It was then published by Charlot in Algiers, and republished in 1945, again by Charlot, but this time also in Paris. A further edition appeared in Paris and Algiers in 1947, when *Nuptials* was included as the thirty-ninth volume in the Gallimard series *Les Essais*. Camus's note to the 1950 Paris edition is thus not quite accurate, and had in fact also appeared in the 1945 edition. Roger Quilliot argues that the two-year gap between *Betwixt and Between* and *Nuptials* corresponds to two fairly separate phases in Camus's early life: in the first, from 1935 to 1937, the pessimism that dominates in *Betwixt and Between* is linked to the failure of his marriage to Simone Hié, to his increasing disillusionment with the Communist Party, and to the poor health which prevented him from taking the *Agrégation de Philosophie* in 1937; in the second the more optimistic tone reflects his success in earning his living as a journalist on *Alger-Républicain*, and his realization that he has managed to elaborate a valid personal philosophy.[9] This difference of tone does not quite explain why Camus should have narrowed the gap between the publication of the two volumes of essays, stating that *Nuptials* was published in 1938 when it did not in fact appear until the middle of 1939. One possible explanation is that he wished to avoid providing evidence for a biographical interpretation of his early work. However, as will be seen, most of the essays were completed in 1938.

Page 69. Tipasa is a village on the Mediterranean coast, about forty-

7. Pléiade edition, II, p. 1178.
8. *Carnets I*, Gallimard, 1962, pp. 70–72, translation, pp. 29–30. See pp. 96–7 of the present volume.
9. Pléiade edition, II, p. 1334.

five miles to the West of Algiers. Camus went there frequently in 1935 and 1936.

Roger Quilliot argues from the state of the manuscripts he has been able to consult that the essay actually entitled *Nuptials* was virtually completed by the end of summer 1937.

Page 75. 'The Wind at Djemila' seems to have been written between 1936 and 1938. In Spring 1936 Camus flew to Djemila in a plane chartered by some of his friends.

Page 81. 'Summer in Algiers' appears to have been written between 1937 and 1938. One section, about the mint pastilles passed round in the cinema, appeared in *Rivages* in February 1939, and another, the description of the fight, in the *Revue Algérienne* in the same month.

Jacques Heurgon was in 1939 professor at the Faculté des Lettres in Algiers, and editor of the review *Rivages*.

Page 91. Musette was the pseudonym of Auguste Robinet, who invented a character called Cagayous who was supposed to incarnate the traditional features of the Algerian working class. Gabriel Audisio, a friend of Camus's, published a collection of Musette's stories in 1931.

Page 9. The essay 'The Desert' was probably not finished until late in 1938 or early in 1939. *Carnets I* (p. 140, translation p. 65) contains alternative versions for the last sentence. The ideas it contains, however, were set down in the *Notebooks* in 1937, after Camus's trip to Italy.[10]

Page 93. In his notes to the Pléiade edition (p. 1361), Louis Faucon points out that these ideas on art were also expressed by André Malraux in an article on Piero della Francesca published in a review entitled *Verve* in 1937–8, before being more fully developed in *Les Voix du silence* (*The Voices of Silence*).

Summer (*L'Été*)

The essays published together in this volume in 1954 cover a much wider period than those included either in *Betwixt and Between* or *Nuptials*. As Camus's own note to p. 105 indicates, he began writing 'The Minotaur or the Halt at Oran' as early as 1939, and 'The Almond-Trees' was first published on 25 January 1941 in *La Tunisie Française* under the title of 'Pour préparer le fruit'. The theme of *The Sea Close By*, on the other hand, first appears in note form in October 1949 in *Carnets II* (p. 290, translation p. 149), and was not published

10. See *Carnets I*, pp. 70–72, translation pp. 29–30.

in review form until 1954. The idea of publishing a third volume of lyrical essays is mentioned by Camus in February 1950, when he noted down the alternative titles of *Summer*: *Midday* or *The Festival* (*Midi*; *La Fête*) for what he called 'essais solaires' (*Carnets II*, p. 311, translation p. 160). Roger Quilliot gives the following 'Prière d'insérer', a note which Camus prepared for insertion in the 1954 edition:

> This book contains several essays written between 1939 and 1953. They are all obviously inspired by the same theme. Each of them treats, although from a different standpoint, a theme that can be called 'solar', and which was already treated in one of the first of the author's works, *Nuptials*, published in 1938.
> Twenty years later, these new *Nuptials* thus bear witness, in their own way, to a long fidelity. (Pléiade edition, II, p. 1829)

Page 105. *The Minotaur or the Halt at Oran*. Oran was a town that Camus knew very well. In the first volume of his *Notebooks* he refers to two visits that he made there in 1939, and it was the birthplace of his second wife, Francine Faure, whom he married in 1940. *The Plague* (*La Peste*) is set in Oran, and the contrast between the ordinary, down-to-earth atmosphere of the city and the events that take place there is an important theme in the novel.

The meaning of the title is not wholly clear, in spite of the description on p. 111 of the Oranais walking round in their city and finally accepting to be eaten alive by the monster of boredom. Roger Quilliot points out[11] that Camus had orginally intended to preface the essay with a quotation from André Gide's *Un esprit non prévenu* which he had noted down in *Notebooks II* in 1942: 'I can imagine him at the Court of King Minos, anxious to discover what kind of unspeakable monster the Minotaur might be; whether it is terrible as all that, or whether it might not perhaps be charming.'[12] Perhaps the implication is that Theseus, or anyone charged with a dangerous mission, can find a temporary refuge and resting place in boredom.

The date, 1939, does not correspond to any actual publication. This text first appeared in February 1946 in the review *L'Arche*. It was first published in book form by the Éditions Charlot in 1950.

Page 125. 'The Almond Trees'. Camus first noted down the remark by Napoleon in his *Notebooks* in 1939, and sketched out a description

---

11. Pléiade edition, II, p. 1819.
12. *Carnets II*, p. 13, translation p. 3. The quotation is from p. 77 of the Kra edition of *Un esprit non prévenu*.

of the almond-trees later in the same year (see *Carnets I*, pp. 186, 196; translation pp. 87, 93).

Page 126. The quotation from D. H. Lawrence is taken from a letter written to A. W. McLeod on 6 October 1912 : 'I hate Bennett's resignation. Tragedy ought to be a great kick at misfortune.' Camus first noted it down in 1939 (*Carnets I*, p. 183; translation p. 86).

Page 128. 'Prometheus in the Underworld'. This essay was first published by Palimugre in 1947.

Page 136. 'Helen's Exile'. First published in *Les Cahiers du Sud* in August 1948. The poet René Char, to whom it was originally dedicated, was a close personal friend of Camus's. The ideas which this essay expresses form the basis for many of the political and philosophical arguments developed in *The Rebel* (*L'Homme révolté*) in 1951.

Page 141. 'The Enigma'. This essay was published for the first time in the volume, *Summer*, though a slightly different version did appear in English in *The Atlantic Monthly* in June 1953 under the title 'What a Writer Seeks'. According to Camus it was composed in 1950, and Roger Quilliot notes that there is a manuscript copy dedicated to René Char.[13] As the essay shows, Camus suffered a great deal from the reluctance of critics to recognize that his attitude had evolved since the days when he devoted *The Outsider* and *The Myth of Sisyphus* to a discussion of the problems of the absurd. Later on, even before the publication of *The Rebel* had led to violent public quarrels with André Breton and Jean-Paul Sartre in 1951 and 1952, Camus became increasingly pessimistic about his relationship with his public and with his literary colleagues. Thus in *Carnets II* (p. 321, translation p. 165) he wrote :

Paris begins by serving a work and advances it. But once it has been established, then the pleasure begins. What matters now is to destroy it. Thus there are in Paris, as there are in certain rivers in Brazil, thousands of tiny fish whose task lies in doing this. They are minute, but innumerable. Their whole mind, if I may say so, is on their teeth. And they strip a man of his flesh, completely, in less than five minutes, leaving only the bare bones. Then they depart, have a short sleep, and start again.

Page 155. 'The Sea Close By'. This essay first appeared in the *Nouvelle Nouvelle Revue Française* in 1954.

13. Pléiade edition, II, p. 1827.

NOTES TO PART TWO
La Nausée (Nausea)

Page 167. When Camus wrote this review of Sartre's first novel (alternative English titles: *The Diary of Antoine Roquentin, Nausea*) and the following one of the volume of short stories published in English under the title of *Intimacy*, the two men had never met.

Herman Melville

Page 179. Camus probably read *Moby Dick* in the French translation by Lucien Jacques, Joan Smith and Jean Giono, published by Gallimard in 1941. If this is the case, then the page numbers refer more or less to the following episodes (page references to the Everyman edition):

120 – end Chapter XXX. Ahab's leg. E. p. 114.
121 – beginning Chapter XXXI. E. p. 115.
123 – E. p. 117. Whether a whale be a fish.
139 – E. pp. 122–3. Black Fish – Narwhal.
173–7 – Chapter XLI. The Whiteness of the Whale. E. pp. 163–7.
203 – E. p. 192. 'Now the advent of these outlandish strangers ...'
209 – E. p. 197. Queequeg as the standard bearer 'hopelessly holding up hope in the midst of despair'.
241 – Chapter LIII. The *Town-Ho's* story of how the mate Radney was eaten by Moby Dick. E. p. 227.
310 – E. p. 290. The Right Whale's Head.
313 – end of Chapter LXXIV – resolution in facing death.
339 – end of Chapter LXXXII, beginning of Chapter LXXXIII. E. pp. 317–18.
373 – Chapter XC. E. p. 350 – the smell of the *Rosebud*.
415 – Chapter CIII. E. pp. 393–4.
452 – Chapter CXXII. E. p. 420 – the tempering of the harpoon.
457 – E. p. 425. The meeting with the *Bachelor*.
460 – E. p. 248. Beginning of Chapter CXVI.
472 – E. pp. 438–9. Chapter CXX.
485 – E. p. 451. End of Chapter CXXV.
499 – E. p. 463. Beginning of Chapter CXXXI – *The Symphony* – Ahab weeps into the sea.
503 – E. p. 480 – Moby Dick breaks Ahab's ivory leg.
520 – end of Chapter CXXXIII.
522 – E. p. 482 – 'I meet thee, this third time, Moby Dick.'

It should be noted that there is a difference in the chapter numberings between the French translation and the Everyman edition referred to here. Thus the French edition is consistently one chapter number ahead – so that Chapter CXXXIV in the Everyman edition is Chapter CXXXV in the French edition. The chapter headings here refer to the Everyman edition.

On Faulkner

Page 183. Camus's adaptation of *Requiem for a Nun* was produced in September 1956 at the Théâtre des Mathurins-Marcel Herrand.

Intelligence and the Scaffold

Page 185. The initial notes for this essay appear in *Carnets II*, pp. 60–61 (translation pp. 28–9). Since at the time Camus was planning the first version of *The Plague*, it is perhaps useful to bear in mind the ideas he expresses in this essay when discussing the construction of that novel. *The Rebel* also contains a long discussion of the Marquis de Sade and Proust.

Page 190. Francis Ponge (born 1899) is known for his minute descriptions of individual physical objects. A long letter from Camus to Ponge, in which he describes 'Le Parti pris des choses' as 'an absurd work in the purest sense of the term' was published in the *Nouvelle Nouvelle Revue Française* in September 1956. It was written in 1943 in reply to a letter from Ponge to Camus, and is reprinted in the Pléiade II edition, pp. 1662–6.

On the Future of Tragedy

Page 192. Like his early association with the Théâtre de l'Équipe when he lived in Algiers, and his later adaptations of Dostoyevsky's *The Possessed* and Faulkner's *Requiem for a Nun*, this lecture demonstrates the continuity of Camus's interest in the theatre. He pointed out on a number of occasions that his own ambition was to write a modern tragedy.

Page 194. Jacques Copeau (1878–1949) was one of the outstanding theatrical directors of the twentieth century. After an initial association with Antoine and the realism of the Théâtre Libre, he founded his own theatre, the Vieux Colombier, in 1913. There he was able to put into practice his idea that the staging of a play should be subordinated to the meaning of the text and not to the ambition of the famous actor playing the main part. His conception of drama as involving the active participation of his audience as well as the combined efforts of the actors, the director and the designer is already visible in Camus's work in 1936 in the play entitled *Révolte dans les Asturies*.

Page 195. Antonin Artaud's *Le Théâtre et son Double* (*The Theatre and Its Double*) was published in 1938. Artaud puts forward the view that the Western theatre is wrong to attempt an imitation of life. The true aim of the theatre, he argues, should be to shock the spectator into an awareness of the violence which lies beneath the veneer of civilization, and into a recognition of the importance of man's more primitive instincts. Artaud began his career as a member of the surrealist movement, and his views have recently found a possibly accidental echo in the plays of Jean Genet – see Robert Brustein: *The Theatre of Revolt* (Boston and Toronto, Little, Brown and Co., 1962). In her study of Camus's work Professor Germaine Brée also discusses a possible influence of Artaud's ideas on *The Plague* (see *Camus*, Rutgers University Press, 1959, p. 116).

Page 195. Arthur Gordon Craig (1872–1966). Son of Ellen Terry, and a famous theatrical designer and director. In 1908 he founded *The Mask*, in Florence, and ran a school of acting. Like Copeau he tended to increase the importance of the director at the expense of the 'star' performer and like Artaud was very interested in Oriental forms of drama.

NOTES TO PART THREE
Camus on The Outsider

Page 207. This preface was written in 1955 for the edition of *The Outsider* which Germaine Brée and Carlos Lynes published in America and England in 1956. It is clearly aimed at those critics who, like Wyndham Lewis, or Nathan A. Scott, consider Meursault to have been a 'moron' or a 'forlorn, dispirited *isolato*', or who, like Robert de Luppé or Aimé Patri, think that the book represents 'our miserable, automatic life', or describes the case-history of a schizophrenic.[14] An opposite,

14. See Wyndham Lewis, *The Writer and the Absolute*, Methuen, 1952, p. 87; Nathan A. Scott, *Camus*, Bowes & Bowes, 1962, p. 37; Robert de Luppé, *Albert Camus*, Presses Universitaires, 1951, p. 67; Aimé Patri, *L'Arche*, No. 15, 1944, pp. 115–17.

more favourable view of Meursault's character is taken by critics such as Robert Champigny, who maintain that Meursault is, in H. A. Mason's phrase, 'a worthy representative of a valid attitude towards life', or who share Cyril Connolly's opinion that he represents a number of pagan values.[15] Here Camus seems to be lending support to this more positive view, though it is interesting to see how much more definite he was in 1955 than in 1943, when he noted down his reactions to the reception of *The Outsider* in his *Notebooks*, or in 1946, when he limited himself to telling an interviewer in *Le Littéraire*:

What I see as most important in my novel is the physical presence, the bodily experience which the critics have not noticed: a land, a sky, a man fashioned by that land and that sky. Men in Algeria live like my hero, quite simply. Naturally you can understand Meursault, but an Algerian will enter much more deeply and much more easily into an understanding of him.[16]

Page 209. *The Outsider* was published in May 1942. I have not been able to discover who 'J.T.' was, or who the critics were who gave vent to 'high moral principles' when reviewing the book. No reviews were published in the periodicals where blatantly high moral principles were most in evidence in France in 1942: *Le Temps, L'Action Française, Candide* or *France-Révolution*.

The unsent letter on criticism seems to have been inspired by the review of *The Outsider* published by the well-known Catholic critic André Rousseaux (A.R.) in *Le Figaro Littéraire* on 17 July 1942. While praising Camus's talent as a narrator, Rousseaux commented that 'the reality which he seeks to unveil is indeed a poor one', and made a general comparison between the way in which French poetry was revealing 'the strength and hopes' of France, while the novel was still describing its moral decadence.

The phrase which especially annoyed Camus runs as follows: 'In order to explain this character, I shall neglect the episode – a dialogue with the prison chaplain – in which the "outsider" expresses his refusal of God.' André Rousseaux goes on to write that what he finds more characteristic and more serious is the fact that Camus has

15. See H. A. Mason, *Scrutiny*, December 1946, pp. 82-9; Robert Champigny, *Sur un heros paien*, Gallimard, Les Essais, 1959; Cyril Connolly, preface to English translation of *The Outsider*, Hamish Hamilton, 1946. See Penguin translation p. 6: '*The Outsider* is not at all a morbid book, it is a violent affirmation of health and sanity.'

16. *Le Littéraire*, 10 August 1946.

Notes to Part Two

created a man 'without humanity, without human value, and even, in spite of the ambition to be realistic which provides the sole framework to the book, without any kind of human truth'. Similar presentations of 'man stripped of everything which gives value to mankind' could, in Rousseaux's view, show 'a disquieting tendency of present-day literature if it marked a readiness to accept a lowering of man's value beneath the catastrophe which is overwhelming humanity'.

The wrong quotation which Camus notes in this review concerns the conversation between Meursault and his lawyer. Meursault is asked whether it would be in order for him to say at the trial that, on the day of his mother's funeral, Meursault had 'kept his feelings under control' (Pléiade edition, p. 1170, Penguin, p. 69). He refuses to allow this excuse to be made because, as he says, it was not true, and his reaction is one of the signs of the extreme moral honesty which makes him incapable of playing society's game. André Rousseaux writes:

> The poor fellow states that he has never 'kept his feelings under control'. And if he is condemned by a court of law and a jury it is because they find in his attitude on the occasion of his mother's death the sign of this amoral 'nature' which cuts him off from social life.

All this would only be true in Rousseaux's view if 'man's nature was rigorously comparable to that of plants or tiny animals', and he accuses Camus of thinking that man's nature is foreign to morality.

Other critics also gave rather a pessimistic interpretation of the character of Meursault when the novel was first published. Thus J. M. A. Paratoud, writing in *Confluences* in October 1942, pp. 209-10, spoke of 'the tasteless existence of this man who lacks both will and passion', and Fieschi, reviewing the novel in the *Nouvelle Revue Française* for October 1942, pp. 368-9, saw it as primarily a novel of social revolt aimed at denouncing a society which deprived Meursault of the means of looking after his mother adequately himself. The only critic who seems to have understood the philosophical implications of *The Outsider* as soon as it was published, and without having had the opportunity of reading *The Myth of Sisyphus*, was Henri Hell, whose review in *Fontaine* in July 1942, pp. 353-5, insisted on the similarity between Camus's ideas and those of Sartre, Malraux and Kierkegaard. Camus certainly read this review, for he noted later that one critic's use of the word 'impassibility' – it occurs three times in Hell's review – was not justified.

Page 213. The entry in June 1937 is clearly first draft of some of the ideas developed in *The Outsider*. Meursault's terror is not analysed in such detail, but is clearly there in the novel.

The man who showed all kinds of promise – an entry made in December 1937 – applies both to Meursault, the hero of *The Outsider*, and to Meursault, the hero of the unpublished novel *La Mort heureuse* which Camus wrote in the late 1930s. As the ending of *The Outsider* makes clear, it is his awareness of the inevitability of death that has made Meursault realize the absurdity of all normal ambitions. Meursault's Sunday – see Pléiade edition, I, pp. 1137–40. Penguin pp. 29–32 – follows the same pattern as that described in the extract.

Page 213. The entry for May 1938 is a more obvious sketch for *The Outsider*. The 'little old man' becomes Pérez, and a number of other details also recur in the final version of the novel.

Belcourt – the name of the working-class district in Algiers where Camus was brought up. These notes form the basis for the incidents which lead Meursault to be involved with his neighbour, Raymond Sintès – see Penguin edition, pp. 37–8, Pléiade edition I, pp. 1144–5. The next entry, describing the different shades of black, is also incorporated into the final version of the novel – Pléiade edition, I, p. 1134. Penguin, p. 26.

Page 215. 2P. What subsequently became the opening sentences in *The Outsider* were written straight out into the original notebook, without any corrections. The note 2P (second part?), when taken in combination with a plan for *La Mort heureuse* which Camus sketched out elsewhere in the first volume of the *Notebooks*[17] gives the impression that originally Camus may have intended to describe what kind of a person Meursault was before the discovery of the absurd.

Page 216. 'On the Absurd?' This is the first draft of an idea which links *The Outsider* to the philosophical views more fully developed in *The Myth of Sisyphus*. The character of Kirilov, from Dostoyevsky's *The Possessed*, is studied on pp. 142–52 of *The Myth of Sisyphus* (Hamish Hamilton translation, pp. 85–91).

Page 218. 'Tolba and his brawls'. As can be seen on p. 91, Camus took great interest in the local speech habits of people in Algiers, and seems to have had a knack of reproducing what he heard. This particular incident is repeated in *The Outsider* (Penguin p. 36, Pléiade edition, I, pp. 1143–4).

Page 218. 'Tailors', etc. Meursault also likes to cut out advertise-

17. See Gallimard edition, pages 65–6, translation 26–7.

ments for laxatives – see Penguin p. 29. Pléiade edition, I, p. 1138. The phrase 'not only fashionable but up to date' is in English in the text. These two characters both figure in *The Outsider*, as Salamano and Raymond's friend Masson respectively.

Camus on The Plague

Page 220. In an article in the review *Club* in February 1955 Roland Barthes had argued that *The Plague* was an inadequate transposition of the problems of the Resistance movement because Camus had replaced a struggle against men by a struggle against the impersonal microbes of the plague. This is a fairly common criticism of *The Plague*, and it could be argued that Camus also neglected an important aspect of the Resistance Movement when he made no reference to the moral problem created by the German habit of executing innocent hostages. The Resistance fighter risked having on his conscience the death of fifteen or twenty people executed as a direct result of his act of sabotage; no such possibility threatened the member of Tarrou's *équipes sanitaires* who helped Rieux fight against the plague.

Page 223. 'It is to Jeanne', etc. This is the first fragment in Camus's *Notebooks* later to be used in *The Plague*. Grand, an insignificant clerk who is at one point described as the real hero of the novel (Penguin p. 115, Pléiade edition, I, p. 1329), loses his wife Jeanne because she cannot bear the life of poverty which he has to lead. In the first version of the novel this fragment was written by Stephan, a rather sentimental classics master, who was intended as the principal narrator.

Page 225. 'The liberating plague'. This series of entries was made in April 1941. The most insignificant character becomes Grand. The priest who loses his faith may be a first sketch for the character of Paneloux.

Page 226. The notes for the 'second version' of *The Plague* were made late in 1942. In each of these Biblical references God is described – as he is by Paneloux in the first sermon in *The Plague* – as sending an outbreak of plague either to punish the wicked or to serve the interests of the Israelites.

Roger Quilliot points out that the manuscript of the *Notebooks* does not contain the next paragraph, which has been restored from Camus's notes for *The Plague*. In the Pléiade edition M. Quilliot explains that Camus completed a first version of the novel as early as

January 1943. This explains the number of entries in the *Notebooks* referring to the second version of *The Plague*, and enables us to see how Camus elaborated on his original version. This was made up of notes, sermons, letters and diaries, which were rather clumsily linked together by an impersonal narrator. According to M. Quilliot (Pléiade edition, I, p. 1931), it did not contain the long descriptions of the feeling of separation which take up so large a place in the book as we now have it. The first of these descriptions was nevertheless written fairly soon after the first version had been completed, since it was printed under the title of 'Les Exilés dans la Peste' in *Domaine Français* in Geneva in 1943. It was only after he had completed the first version that Camus made Rieux into the narrator, eliminated the character of Stephan, who had originally been the husband of the fugitive Jeanne, and introduced Grand and Rambert. Similarly, it was in 1945 or 1946 that he introduced the death of Madame Rieux, and also had the idea of extending the duration of the plague to almost a year (from April to February) so that he could link its development with that of seasons (cf. *Carnets II*, Gallimard 1964, p. 82). However, as the Pléiade edition also makes clear, there are a number of other notes that are not printed here and which show how Camus developed his ideas and technique in *The Plague*, so that the *Notebooks* give only a part of his preoccupations and experiments. In addition to revising the general plan of *The Plague* over a period of five years, Camus subjected the final manuscript to the minutest revision: it contains some 1,500 variant readings.

The man who tries to leave Oran on the pretext that it is not his home is Rambert, a journalist, who eventually chooses to stay.

NOTES TO PART FOUR

All these extracts are taken from the two volumes of *Carnets* published by Gallimard in 1962 and 1964 respectively. The title *Carnets* was, as Roger Quilliot explained, given to them in order to avoid confusion with a series of critical studies published under the title *Les Cahiers Albert Camus*.[18] Camus himself, however, always referred to these notebooks as his *cahiers*, and I have thought it better to use the

18. See *Carnets I*, Gallimard, 1962, p. 7. (The first volume of the *Cahiers Albert Camus*, edited by Brian T. Fitch, appeared in September 1968.)

nearest English equivalent. Notebooks, in the headings for the extracts reprinted here. Six *cahiers* have been published, the three that Camus filled between May 1935 and February 1942 in *Carnets I*, the three that he filled between January 1942 and March 1951 in *Carnets II*. The division into two volumes is to some extent arbitrary, and I have not observed it in the main body of the text.

From Notebook I

Page 235. May 1935. There is an obvious link beween this entry, the first which Camus made in his notebooks, and the ideas developed in *Betwixt and Between*. The mother–son relationship recurs in *The Outsider*, *The Plague*, and in the play *Cross Purpose* (*Le Malentendu*), first performed in 1944. In 1952 Camus wrote in a later notebook, so far unpublished, 'When my mother's eyes were not resting on me, I have never been able to look at her without tears springing to my eyes.'

Page 236. January 1936. This description, later incorporated with minor modifications into *Betwixt and Between* (see this translation pp. 63) was written straight out into the notebook with very few alterations or corrections.

From Notebook II

Page 242. 4 October. Camus had just been offered a teaching post at the *collège* of Sidi-bel-Abbès, and this entry analyses his reasons for turning it down.

Page 244. February 1938. These notes already foreshadow the main theme of *The Rebel*, published in 1951.

Page 246. Gignoux. This is probably Claude Gignoux, who was Président de la Confédération Nationale du Patronat Français from 1936 to 1939, and who used to be editor of the *Revue des Deux Mondes*.

From Notebook III

Page 250. 'The war has broken out', etc. Roger Quilliot notes that this passage was intended to be used in *The Plague*.

Page 253. This letter to a man in despair is similar in style but very different in tone and content from the *Lettres à un ami allemand*, written in 1943–4 (see the translation *Resistance, Rebellion and Death*, Hamish Hamilton, 1961). The ideas which it puts forward have a number of parallels in the articles which Camus wrote for *Alger Républicain* and *Soir Républicain* in 1938–40. On April 1939, for example, he wrote in an account of a lecture by M. R. E. Charlier that 'the Versailles treaty is the spiritual father of the Munich agreements', and, in a signed editorial in *Soir Républicain* for 6 November 1939, that: 'We think, in fact, that there is only one fatality in history, and it is the one we put there ourselves. We believe that this conflict could have been avoided, and that it could still be ended to everybody's satisfaction.' Similarly on 18 December 1939 Camus wrote of his 'conviction that war was not inevitable, since it would have been avoided with better luck'. This should not, however, be seen as a sign of any Communist sympathies on Camus's part, for he wrote in *Soir Républicain* on 19 December 1939 that: 'The U.S.S.R. is, today, one of the nations of prey. Revolutionary imperialism is still imperialism.' Nevertheless, he was still fairly optimistic about the possibiliy of an early end to the war when he wrote in the same article that 'a reconciliation of imperialisms can bring about their disarmament'.

Page 255. Paris, March 1940. At the outbreak of war, *Alger Républicain* ceased to appear as a morning paper, and became *Soir Républicain*, under the editorship of Camus himself. There followed a series of disagreements between Camus and the military authorities responsible for newspaper censorship in wartime Algeria, and which reached its climax when Camus and Pascal Pia tried to publish an article entitled 'Profession de foi', which was written partly as a reply to some violent attacks on them by a publication called *L'Émancipation nationale*. What seems to have caused the censors most annoyance was the statement that 'all political parties have betrayed' (see p. 25 of the present volume), and that 'politics have corrupted everything', which were described as 'anarchist principles'. Camus was officially reprimanded by the military authorities, and *Soir Républicain* closed down. According to the criticism of Camus made by the actual owners of the paper, its circulation had been seriously affected by the doubts which Camus seemed to be casting on the necessity for the war, and by what he described in his 'Profession de foi' as his 'profound pacifism'.[19] Camus was unable to find another job in Algeria,

19. See Pléiade edition, II, pp. 1386.

and moved to Paris where Pascal Pia found him work as a secretary on *Paris-Soir*. As will be seen from the entries, Camus did not like Paris.

From Notebook IV

Page 263. Panelier. For health reasons Camus spent several months in winter 1942 and spring 1943 at Panelier, near Chambon-sur-Lignon. He went every week from Panelier to Clermond-Ferrand for medical treatment, and probably travelled on the 'little local train', described in the next entry.

Page 265. *Wuthering Heights*. At the beginning of *The Rebel* Camus contrasts Heathcliff's 'readiness to kill the whole world in order to possess Catherine', which he takes as the prime example of the crime of passion, with the 'logical crime' that in his view is justified by contemporary political philosophers.

Page 267. Kafka. Camus published a study of Kafka in the review *L'Arbalète* in 1943, after having worked on it since 1938. In his notes to the Pléiade edition Louis Faucon suggests that 'L'Espoir et l'absurde dans l'œuvre de Franz Kafka' was not included in the first edition of *The Myth of Sisyphus* in December 1942 because of the difficulties involved in obtaining a censorship visa for a book that dealt not unfavourably with a writer of Czech and Jewish origin. The essay on Kafka, which opens with the remarks noted down in this extract from *Carnets II*, did not therefore appear in *The Myth of Sisyphus* until 1948.

Page 268. This is probably the rich uncle mentioned in the essay on André Gide (of p. 173).

Page 269. Imagination. Camus seems to have varied in his attitude towards his own imagination, for in 1947 he wrote in his preface to the *Poésies Posthumes* of René Leynaud, 'then, as now I had no imagination'. He also stated in an interview in *Le Monde* on 31 August 1956 that it was his 'lack of imagination' which prevented him from doing more than admire the way Christ lived and died. Meursault, who resembles Camus in a number of ways, also states 'imagination has never been one of my strongest points' (Penguin edition, p. 111; Pléiade edition, I, p. 1203, 'Je n'ai jamais eu de véritable imagination').

Page 271. 'Creation against God', etc. Camus repeats the ideas, and the first two of these quotations, on p. 313 of *L'Homme révolté*.

From Notebook V

Page 276. Camus's reply to the charge of pessimism recurs in the text of *L'Incroyant et les Chrétiens* (*Actuelles I*, pp. 212–19, *Resistance, Rebellion and Death*, pp. 49–53).

Page 277. Émile Herriott (1872–1957) was leader of the Radical Socialist Party and, from 1947 to 1954, President of the National Assembly. He was also president of the Université des Annales, an organization founded in 1911 to arrange public lectures on literature and politics, lectures that were then published in the review *Conférencia*. On 27 June 1945 Camus had singled out Emile Herriot, in an article in *Combat* reprinted in *Actuelles I*, as the representative of a moral and political attitude which 'had nothing more to teach us'. Herriot bore Camus no grudge for this remark, however, and published an extremely enthusiastic review of *L'Homme révolté* in *Le Monde* on 26 December 1951.

Page 284. Maurice Merleau-Ponty's article 'Apprendre à lire', defending himself against the criticisms of his book *Humanisme et Terreur* (Gallimard, 1947), was published in *Les Temps modernes* in July 1947 (pp. 1–27). In the fourth volume of *Situations* Sartre describes a quarrel between Merleau-Ponty and Camus in 1947 in which Camus accused Merleau-Ponty of justifying the Moscow trials (pp. 215–16).

From Notebook VI

Page 286. *The Rope* (*La Corde*) was the original title for *Les Justes*.

Page 287. The description of the womanizer recurs, though this time from the other side, when Clamence describes in *La Chute* how, standing on the pavement, in the midst of a passionate discussion he had suddenly 'lost the thread of the argument being developed because a devastating creature was crossing the street at that very moment'. (Penguin, p. 45; Pléiade edition, I, p. 1504).

Page 289. On 29 April 1949 Paul Claudel was received by Pius XII and was present while a number of his poems were recited to the Pope.

FOR THE BEST IN PAPERBACKS, LOOK FOR THE

In every corner of the world, on every subject under the sun, Penguin represents quality and variety – the very best in publishing today.

For complete information about books available from Penguin – including Pelicans, Puffins, Peregrines and Penguin Classics – and how to order them, write to us at the appropriate address below. Please note that for copyright reasons the selection of books varies from country to country.

In the United Kingdom: Please write to *Dept E.P., Penguin Books Ltd, Harmondsworth, Middlesex, UB7 0DA*

If you have any difficulty in obtaining a title, please send your order with the correct money, plus ten per cent for postage and packaging, to *PO Box No 11, West Drayton, Middlesex*

In the United States: Please write to *Dept BA, Penguin, 299 Murray Hill Parkway, East Rutherford, New Jersey 07073*

In Canada: Please write to *Penguin Books Canada Ltd, 2801 John Street, Markham, Ontario L3R 1B4*

In Australia: Please write to the *Marketing Department, Penguin Books Australia Ltd, P.O. Box 257, Ringwood, Victoria 3134*

In New Zealand: Please write to the *Marketing Department, Penguin Books (NZ) Ltd, Private Bag, Takapuna, Auckland 9*

In India: Please write to *Penguin Overseas Ltd, 706 Eros Apartments, 56 Nehru Place, New Delhi, 110019*

In Holland: Please write to *Penguin Books Nederland B.V., Postbus 195, NL–1380AD Weesp, Netherlands*

In Germany: Please write to *Penguin Books Ltd, Friedrichstrasse 10–12, D–6000 Frankfurt Main 1, Federal Republic of Germany*

In Spain: Please write to *Longman Penguin España, Calle San Nicolas 15, E–28013 Madrid, Spain*

In France: Please write to *Penguin Books Ltd, 39 Rue de Montmorency, F-75003, Paris, France*

In Japan: Please write to *Longman Penguin Japan Co Ltd, Yamaguchi Building, 2–12–9 Kanda Jimbocho, Chiyoda-Ku, Tokyo 101, Japan*

FOR THE BEST IN PAPERBACKS, LOOK FOR THE

CLASSICS OF THE TWENTIETH CENTURY

The Collected Stories of Elizabeth Bowen

Seventy-nine stories – love stories, ghost stories, stories of childhood and of London during the Blitz – which all prove that 'the instinctive artist is there at the very heart of her work' – Angus Wilson

Look Homeward, Angel   Thomas Wolfe

A lonely idealist in pursuit of 'the great forgotten language, the lost lane-end into heaven', Eugene Gant, the central figure in Wolfe's account of a young boy growing to manhood, scours literature and the world for fresh wonders, until confronted by the intransigent reality of death and disease.

Chéri and The Last of Chéri   Colette

Two novels that 'form the classic analysis of a love-affair between a very young man and a middle-aged woman' – Raymond Mortimer

Selected Poems 1923–1967   Jorge Luis Borges

A magnificent bilingual edition of the poetry of one of the greatest writers of today, conjuring up a unique world of invisible roses, uncaught tigers . . .

Beware of Pity   Stefan Zweig

A cavalry officer becomes involved in the suffering of a young girl; when he attempts to avoid the consequences of his behaviour, the results prove fatal . . .

Valmouth and Other Novels   Ronald Firbank

The world of Ronald Firbank – vibrant, colourful and fantastic – is to be found beneath soft deeps of velvet sky dotted with cognac clouds.

FOR THE BEST IN PAPERBACKS, LOOK FOR THE

CLASSICS OF THE TWENTIETH CENTURY

Death of a Salesman Arthur Miller

One of the great American plays of the century, this classic study of failure brings to life an unforgettable character: Willy Loman, the shifting and inarticulate hero who is nonetheless a unique individual.

The Echoing Grove Rosamund Lehmann

'No English writer has told of the pains of women in love more truly or more movingly than Rosamund Lehmann' – Marghenita Laski. 'This novel is one of the most absorbing I have read for years' – Simon Raven, in the *Listener*

Pale Fire Vladimir Nabokov

This book contains the last poem by John Shade, together with a Preface, notes and Index by his posthumous editor. But is the eccentric editor more than just haughty and intolerant – mad, bad, perhaps even dangerous . . . ?

The Man Who Was Thursday G. K. Chesterton

This hilarious extravaganza concerns a secret society of revolutionaries sworn to destroy the world. But when Thursday turns out to be not a poet but a Scotland Yard detective, one starts to wonder about the identity of the others . . .

The Rebel Albert Camus

Camus's attempt to understand 'the time I live in' tries to justify innocence in an age of atrocity. 'One of the vital works of our time, compassionate and disillusioned, intelligent but instructed by deeply felt experience' – *Observer*

Letters to Milena Franz Kafka

Perhaps the greatest collection of love letters written in the twentieth century, they are an orgy of bliss and despair, of ecstasy and desperation poured out by Kafka in his brief two-year relationship with Milena Jesenska.

FOR THE BEST IN PAPERBACKS, LOOK FOR THE

CLASSICS OF THE TWENTIETH CENTURY

The Age of Reason Jean-Paul Sartre

The first part of Sartre's classic trilogy, set in the volatile Paris summer of 1938, is itself 'a dynamic, deeply disturbing novel' (Elizabeth Bowen) which tackles 'some of the major issues of our time.'

Three Lives Gertrude Stein

A turning point in American literature, these portraits of three women – thin, worn Anna, patient, gentle Lena and the complicated, intelligent Melanctha – represented in 1909 one of the pioneering examples of modernist writing.

Doctor Faustus Thomas Mann

Perhaps the most convincing description of an artistic genius ever written, this portrait of the composer Leverkuhn is a classic statement of one of Mann's obsessive themes: the discord between genius and sanity.

The New Machiavelli H. G. Wells

This autobiography of a man who has thrown up a glittering political career and marriage to go into exile with the woman he loves also contains an illuminating Introduction by Melvyn Bragg.

The Collected Poems of Stevie Smith

Amused, amusing and deliciously barbed, this volume includes many poems which dwell on death; as a whole, though, as this first complete edition in paperback makes clear, Smith's poetry affirms an irrepressible love of life.

Rhinoceros / The Chairs / The Lesson Eugène Ionesco

Three great plays by the man who was one of the founders of what has come to be known as the Theatre of the Absurd.

FOR THE BEST IN PAPERBACKS, LOOK FOR THE

CLASSICS OF THE TWENTIETH CENTURY

The Second Sex   Simone de Beauvoir

This great study of Woman is a landmark in feminist history, drawing together insights from biology, history and sociology as well as literature, psychoanalysis and mythology to produce one of the supreme classics of the twentieth century.

The Bridge of San Luis Rey   Thornton Wilder

On 20 July 1714 the finest bridge in all Peru collapsed, killing 5 people. Why? Did it reveal a latent pattern in human life? In this beautiful, vivid and compassionate investigation, Wilder asks some searching questions in telling the story of the survivors.

Parents and Children   Ivy Compton-Burnett

This richly entertaining introduction to the world of a unique novelist brings to light the deadly claustrophobia within a late-Victorian upper-middle-class family . . .

We   Yevgeny Zamyatin

Zamyatin's nightmarish vision of the future is both a masterpiece in its own right and the forerunner of Huxley's *Brave New World* and Orwell's *1984*. The story of D-503, who is aroused from acceptance of the totalitarian state by a strange woman, E-330. His revolution is vividly chronicled here in his diary.

Confessions of Zeno   Italo Svevo

Zeno, an innocent in a corrupt world, triumphs in the end through his stoic acceptance of his own failings in this extraordinary, experimental novel that fuses memory, obsession and desire.

Southern Mail/Night Flight   Antoine de Saint-Exupéry

Both novels in this volume are concerned with the pilot's solitary struggle with the elements, his sensation of insignificance amidst the stars' timelessness and the sky's immensity. Flying and writing were inextricably linked in the author's life and he brought a unique sense of dedication to both.

FOR THE BEST IN PAPERBACKS, LOOK FOR THE

CLASSICS OF THE TWENTIETH CENTURY

Gertrude Hermann Hesse

A sensitive young composer, the narrator is drawn to Gertrude through their mutual love of music. Gradually, he is engulfed by an enduring and hopeless passion for her. 'It would be a pity to miss this book – it has such a rare flavour of truth and simplicity' – Stevie Smith in the *Observer*

If It Die André Gide

A masterpiece of French prose, *If It Die* is Gide's record of his childhood, his friendships, his travels, his sexual awakening and, above all, the search for truth which characterizes his whole life and all his writing.

Dark as the Grave wherein my Friend is Laid Malcolm Lowry

A Dantean descent into hell, into the infernal landscape of Mexico, the same Mexico as Lowry's *Under the Volcano*, a country of mental terrors and spiritual chasms.

The Collected Short Stories Katherine Mansfield

'She could discern in a trivial event or an insignificant person some moving revelation or motive or destiny . . . There is an abundance of that tender and delicate art which penetrates the appearances of life to discover the elusive causes of happiness and grief' – W. E. Williams in his Introduction to *The Garden Party and Other Stories*

Sanctuary William Faulkner

Faulkner draws America's Deep South exactly as he saw it: seething with life and corruption; and *Sanctuary* asserts itself as a compulsive and unsparing vision of human nature.

The Expelled and Other Novellas Samuel Beckett

Rich in verbal and situational humour, the four stories in this volume offer the reader a fascinating insight into Beckett's preoccupation with the helpless individual consciousness, a preoccupation which has remained constant throughout Beckett's work.

BY THE SAME AUTHOR

'Probably no European writer of his time left so deep a mark on the imagination, and at the same time on the moral and political consciousness of his own generation, and of the next' – Conor Cruise O'Brien

'Few French writers of this century have been more versatile or more influential than Camus . . . No one in his lifetime wrote better prose than he, no one better blended conviction and grace of style' – *The Times*

'Of all available modern prophets, M. Camus seems to be the most enlightened, the most perceptive, the most helpful' – Philip Toynbee

Novels

The Fall
A Happy Death
The Outsider
The Plague
The Rebel

Short Stories

Exile and the Kingdom

and

Caligula and Other Plays
(Caligula/Cross Purpose/The Just/The Possessed)
The Myth of Sisyphus